CLINICAL SOCIAL WORK
IN HEALTH CARE

CLINICAL SOCIAL WORK IN HEALTH CARE

New Biopsychosocial Approaches

Stephen R. Wallace, MSW, ACSW

Director, Psychiatric Social Work
Associate Director/Outpatient Psychiatry
Rhode Island Hospital
Providence, Rhode Island

Richard J. Goldberg, M.D.

Associate Director
Department of Psychiatry
Rhode Island Hospital
And
Women and Infants Hospital of Rhode Island
Assistant Professor
Psychiatry & Human Behavior
Brown University

Andrew E. Slaby, MD., Ph.D., M.P.H

Psychiatrist-In-Chief
Department of Psychiatry
Rhode Island Hospital
And
Women and Infants Hospital of Rhode Island
Professor
Psychiatry & Human Behavior
Brown University

PRAEGER

PRAEGER SPECIAL STUDIES • PRAEGER SCIENTIFIC

New York • Philadelphia • Eastbourne, UK
Toronto • Hong Kong • Tokyo • Sydney

Library of Congress Cataloging in Publication Data

Wallace, Stephen R.
    Guide for clinical social work in health care.

    Includes bibliographies and index.
    1. Medical social work. 2. Psychiatric social work.
I. Goldberg, Richard J. II. Slaby, Andrew Edmund.
III. Title. [DNLM: 1. Social work. W 322 W194g]
HV687.W34 1983   362.1'0425   83-13744
ISBN 0-03-064183-7

Published in 1984 by Praeger Publishers
CBS Educational and Professional Publishing
a Division of CBS Inc.
521 Fifth Avenue, New York, NY 10175 USA

© 1984 Praeger Publishers

456789 052 9876545321

Printed in the United States of America
on acid-free paper

Acknowledgments

The authors wish to recognize and express appreciation to all of our interdisciplinary collaborators of Rhode Island Hospital whose work with us generated the fertile ideas from which this volume was conceived. We are also truly grateful for the professional commitment continuously demonstrated by our secretarial staff in support of this project. In remembering the group effort, in particular we thank Camille Angeli for her attentive investment and Elaine Haigh for her significant secretarial contribution. Above all, we express our gratitude and respect for the dedication of Marcia Toczko whose limitless and painstaking commitment to the preparation of the manuscript, often at great inconvenience to her personal and family time, made the completion of this work a reality. We recognize with appreciation, as well, the thoughtful and meaningful attention of our editor, Maggie Murray. Finally, we acknowledge the clinical and conceptual contributions of Jackie Wallace whose mastery of clinical skills stands as a model for professionals across the disciplines, and whose rich career experience stimulated many of the ideas that pervade this book.

Contents

Acknowledgments   v
Introduction   1

Chapter 1 Medicine–Social Work Collaboration   3
  Health Care in America: Colonial Period to 1900   3
  The Entrance of Social Work into Health Care   5
  The Early Struggle of Social Work in Medicine   6
  The Predominance of Nurses among the First Medical
    Social Workers   6
  The Professionalization of Medical Social Work   7
  The Impact of World War I on Social Work in Health Care   9
  Conflict with the Medical Profession   10
  Conflict within the Social Work Profession   10
  The Disappearance of Social Diagnosis in Health Care   11
  The Challenge of Social Work in Health Care Today   12
  The Biopsychosocial Model of Health Care   13
  The Social Work Contribution to the Biopsychosocial Model   14
  Return to Early Social Work Principles   15
  Territorial Issues Left To Be Resolved   17
  The Continuing Struggle for Professional Autonomy   18
  Funding and Staffing Problems in Social Work   19
  Summary   21
  Notes   23
  Additional References   24

Chapter 2 The Team Approach of Primary Care   27
  The Background of the Primary Care Movement   27
  Toward a Definition of Primary Care   29
  Difficulties Facing Medicine in the Transition
    to Primary Care   33
  The Potential Role of Social Work in Primary Care   36
  Defining Interdisciplinary Roles   38
  The Impact of Clinical Skills on Team Development   40

Practical Clinical Interventions   48
Social Network/Short-Term Treatment   51
Risk/Benefit Ratios in Information Gathering   53
Enhancing the Team Approach   55
A Case Illustration of the Team Approach in Primary Care   55
Summary   64
Notes   67

Chapter 3   Crisis Intervention Reevaluated   71
The Origins of Crisis Intervention   72
Medical Illness as a Crisis   74
The Contribution of Social Work to Crisis Work   74
The Crisis-Ridden Character   76
Cases That Challenge Present Concepts of Crisis   77
Treating the Crisis Character   80
Legal vs Clinical Conflict in Crisis Intervention   82
When the Crisis-Ridden Character Is in Crisis   85
Summary   87
Notes   88
Additional References   89

Chapter 4   On the Art of Engaging the Patient   93
The Concept of Engagement   95
Techniques of Engagement   95
Usefulness of Engagement Strategies:
   Social Worker as Consultant   98
The Fundamental Principle of Engagement   99
Attention Getting and the Recognition of Ambivalence   100
Professional Ethics   101
Recent History   103
Further Contributions to Engagement   103
Dynamic Concepts and Engagement   106
Further Techniques of Engagement   119
Engagement and the Mental Status Exam   122
Termination and Engagement   124
Summary   126
Notes   128
Additional References   129

Chapter 5   The Biopsychosocial Data Base   131
The Data Base   133
Notes   148

Chapter 6 Medicine for Social Workers   151
   Common Medical and Surgical Illnesses   156
   Laboratory Studies   167
   Doses of Commonly Used Psychotropic Drugs   172
   Summary   174
   Notes   175

Chapter 7 Implications for Training, Research,
          and Role Definition   179
   The Biomedical Dimension
     in Social Work Training   179
   The Psychological Dimension
     in Social Work Training   188
   The Social Context/Environmental Dimension   192
     in Social Work Training
   Primary Psychosocial Concepts Needed in the Curriculum   195
     of the Clinical Social Worker
   The Core Issue for Clinical Social Work   200
   Social Work Research   201
   The Rhode Island Hospital Study   201
   The Role of the Psychiatrist   209
   Health Curricula in Social Work Education   211
   Notes   212

Afterword   217
   Psychiatry/Social Work Relationship   217
   Notes   223
   Additional References   224

Appendixes   225

Index   234

CLINICAL SOCIAL WORK
IN HEALTH CARE

Introduction

It has been estimated that the number of social workers employed in the health setting has increased to 40,000 in the past 15 years[1]. This increase has come about in response to a number of factors, including federal Medicare regulations requiring the establishment of hospital social services and the growing awareness that health care involves attention to psychosocial as well as biomedical issues. Up to 40 percent of all primary practice contacts are now seen as nonmedical services, and nearly half of physicians' time is estimated to be consumed by nonmedical problems[2]. The problems with which patients present have become recognized as so complex that more comprehensive clinical skills are required for effective assessment and intervention in the health setting. Undiagnosed major medical illness can masquerade as psychiatric disorder;[3] primary psychiatric illness can go unrecognized among a majority of medical patients[4] and the apparent need for concrete services can camouflage treatable psychiatric illnesses.[5]

The clinical model required for effective comprehensive care in the health setting is biopsychosocial in content and multidisciplinary in practice. The team approach and philosophy of primary care medicine provides the apparatus and conceptual framework for these interrelated dimensions of patients' needs. Each discipline can focus on a special expertise essential to total patient care complemented by an awareness of the needed contributions of the other participating professions. No one health care provider can fulfill the challenge of primary care without expecting skillful involvement from collaborating health care practitioners.

Primary care represents an approach to health care practice rather than a specialty within the helping professions. Primary care can be practiced throughout the health setting as long as comprehensive and coordinated interdisciplinary practice is in evidence. The basis of primary care can provide the framework from which core clinical skills can be generalized for all health practice. For the physician, nurse, psychiatrist, and clinical social

1

worker the primary care approach is the foundation from which the practice of specialty areas can be pursued.

This book is primarily directed at providing the framework for clinical social work practice in health care. The clinical model that will be described provides the common base of theory and practice needed to consolidate both the generic and specialty perspectives currently being debated for social work in the health setting. Its content in fact is generalizable to many clinical settings and provides a helpful guide for health providers across the disciplines.

The past and present collaborative efforts among physicians, nurses, social workers, and psychiatrists in health care will be reviewed, followed by a look at the primary care approach itself, and an examination of the spectrum of clinical presentations and the skills required in addressing them. A reappraisal of crisis intervention is provided, leading to a guide for engaging patients in the challenging atmosphere of the health care setting.

The usefulness of the biopsychosocial data base is described next, complemented by a chapter focusing on specific medical issues of significance to clinical social work practice. While the medical review is not meant to be exhaustive or highly detailed, it does present many medical problems, which, though commonly encountered by social workers, are generally not addressed in their education. The final chapter addresses the implications of each dimension of the biopsychosocial diagnostic continuum for social work training and interdisciplinary role definition. Included is the review of a research study on medical referrals to social work, emphasizing the biopsychosocial clinical findings involved with concrete services. An afterword focuses on defining the unique and overlapping roles of clinical social work and psychiatry in health care.

NOTES

1. Berkman, Barbara Gordon, "Knowledge Base and Program Needs for Effective Social Work Practice in Health: A Review of the Literature," Society for Hospital Social Work Directors, American Hospital Association, 1978.
2. Slepian, Florence, W., "Medical Social Work in Primary Care," *Primary Care,* 6, 3, (September, 1979): 621-32.
3. Koranyi, E.K., "Morbidity and Rate of Undiagnosed Physical Illness in a Psychiatric Clinic Population, *Archives of General Psychiatry*, (1979): 414-19.
4. Glass, Richard, Andrew Allan, E. Uhlenhuth, Chase Kimball and Dennis Borenstein, "Psychiatric Screening in a Medical Clinic," *Archives of General Psychiatry,* 35, (October, 1978): 1189-95.
5. Goldberg, Richard, Stephen Wallace, Joan Rothney, and Steven Wartman, "Medical Referrals to Social Work: A Review of 100 Cases," *General Hospital Psychiatry*, in press.

Chapter One

Medicine–Social Work Collaboration

The involvement of social work with medicine was an inevitable outgrowth of the attempt to improve the quality of medical care. The widespread recruitment of social workers into medical care began in the early twentieth century. Recognition of the need for social workers coincided with the realization that a patient's disease could not be treated without taking into account the social circumstances of the patient's life.

The call for better medical care did not come from physicians alone; in fact, in most cases it did not come from physicians at all. Though doctors were required to be licensed and more uniformly trained following the American Revolution, the requirements were not enforced until after the nineteenth century. Medical education was soundly criticized as inadequate by the Secretary of the New York Board of Education even in 1910. The same voices of social reform in nineteenth century social work that demanded reforms in labor, housing, relief, and sanitation also worked for changes in health care.

HEALTH CARE IN AMERICA: COLONIAL PERIOD TO 1900

Virtually no organized health care existed in the United States before 1800. Hospitals did not exist as we know them today. As the almshouses had served colonial America to incarcerate its poor, so had they seconded as hospitals. The almshouses, which were usually supported by local government, made poor hospitals since medical care amounted to only one function among many. They were also used to confine criminals, orphans, and the mentally ill. Prior to the establishment of the first almshouse in Philadelphia by William Penn in 1713, the only hospitals in America were temporary structures erected in seaport towns to contain the spread of contagious diseases. In 1736, Bellevue Hospital in New York City became

3

colonial America's second multipurpose almshouse, including medical care as one of its functions.

As urban centers grew, voluntary hospitals emerged with support from gifts, contributions, and patients' fees. The almshouses gradually were relegated to only the sick poor. New York Hospital, founded in 1775, became the first of these voluntary hospitals to offer systematized instruction to medical students. In 1826, New Haven Hospital originated the concept of the primary teaching facility, where serving the community only as its secondary purpose. By 1840, 11 voluntary hospitals had been founded. Quality care was yet to come.

The mortality rate in U.S. hospitals remained high until well after the Civil War. Poor quality nursing care and unsanitary conditions were common. With the exception of the few Catholic hospitals, admission to a hospital remained a terrifying experience through the first three-quarters of the nineteenth century. Contagious diseases spread easily and no nursing care was provided at night except in emergencies. The nuns of the religious hospitals gave the best care and provided the only nursing training in the United States until 1872. In that year, the New England Hospital for Women and Children in Boston initiated the first one-year training program in nursing. The following year, Massachusetts General, Bellevue, and New Haven hospitals started their own nursing schools. These nursing programs did not have the blessings of the medical profession or the hospitals, and commonly had to overcome the opposition of both. The nursing programs were often established by separate organizations in the early years and not incorporated with the hospitals until later. An investigative report of the New York State Charities Association, for instance, citing deplorable conditions at Bellevue, led to the development of that hospital's nursing school. The improvement in nursing care was recognizable. Within a decade, the number of training schools for nurses grew to 22, with about 600 graduates. By 1898, nursing schools mushroomed to over 400 with more than 10,000 graduates.[1]

While scientific advances in anesthesia, antiseptics and sepsis, immunization, and the use of the microscope had greatly changed and improved the technology of medicine by the final quarter of the nineteenth century, major aspects of the delivery of medical care were still lacking. Moreover, some of the advances called for physicians and hospitals to engage in new areas of medical care. Preventive medicine, for instance, largely made no sense before immunization. While improved nursing helped improve patient care, the teaching and practice of nursing remained closely associated with the physical, bodily aspects of medical care. Nursing identified itself as the "art of laying on of hands."

THE ENTRANCE OF SOCIAL WORK INTO HEALTH CARE

As early as the 1860s it was recognized that someone was needed to check patients' homes to make sure that there were not conditions there which might cause or exacerbate illness. A temporary position of "sanitary visitor" at the New York Infirmary for Women and Children eventually led to a full-time home visitor by 1890. Though a few home visitor positions had been developed at outpatient clinics and hospitals by 1890, the last decade of the nineteenth century was a major turning point in recognizing the psychosocial aspects of physical illness. As the charity movement affected the dispensing of relief so did it affect the delivery of medical care. In 1889, Johns Hopkins Hospital and Johns Hopkins University were opened in Baltimore to provide free services to all, regardless of race or religion. The hospital and university were closely, though informally, linked with the Baltimore Charity Organization Society (COS). Dr. Charles P. Emerson of Johns Hopkins served also as a resident physician of the charity society. He was impressed with the idea of "friendly visiting" and decided it had applicability to medical education. Emerson decided the medical students could better understand their patients' medical problems if they became familiar with the patients' home environments. Though Emerson was primarily thinking about improving medical education and had put little thought into the developing notion of medical-social diagnosis, his use of medical students in this way made history. Emerson's students found that to get the patient to follow even the most practical hygienic advice, such as keeping the home ventilated, they had to get to know the patient well and win his confidence. Five years after the program started, the medical student participation grew to over 60, amounting to one-quarter of the enrollment of Johns Hopkins Medical School. Seven years after the program began, Emerson identified the purpose as "training doctors in social service" and said that social service "is, we believe, a very important department of the hospital."[2]

The Contribution of Dr. Richard Cabot

Dr. Richard Cabot visited Johns Hopkins in 1903, five years after his appointment as Director of the Outpatient Clinic at Massachusetts General Hospital (MGH) in Boston. Cabot had an extensive background in charity work and was equally interested in improving medical care. Having served as a director of the Boston Children's Aid Society for a decade, he had become impressed with the careful studies done by caseworkers into the character and social environment of the children as well as the caseworkers' investigative consultations with teachers, doctors, and others involved with each child. When Cabot witnessed the work of the medical students at

Hopkins, he decided to hire a social worker for the outpatient program at Massachusetts General Hospital. Though he put forward the idea in 1905, the hospital was not to embrace and fund social service until 1919. When it did, the MGH program became the first hospital-funded social service department in the United States.[3] In the meantime, Cabot acquired funds from private donors and charities to fund the service within his clinic. The first social worker hired left within the year and Ida Cannon took over in 1906. Although not technically accurate historically, Miss Cannon is often looked upon as the first medical social worker since she served at MGH for decades and was so influential to the development of social work in medicine.

Cabot, himself, became so convinced of the value of employing social workers in the delivery of health care that over the first three decades of the twentieth century, he wrote about the idea extensively and lectured about it nationally and internationally. In one of his books, *Social Work: Essays on the Meeting Ground of Doctor and Social Worker*, Cabot refers to the importance of the social work role:

> in other words, one must take account of the totality of influences in the patient's environment, the physical influences of nutrition, ventilation, clothing, but also the psychological influences exerted upon him by his family and friends, by his own half-conscious thoughts, by his worries, his remorse, his fears. . . . Nothing can be excluded here. It is utterly unscientific to close our eyes to any human interest, no matter how little we may sympathize with it personally. It is one of the facts of the case, and must be understood and allowed for in our treatment.[4]

THE EARLY STRUGGLE OF SOCIAL WORK IN MEDICINE

Despite Cabot's and Cannon's enthusiasm and influence, change and new ideas did not come easily. Massachusetts General Hospital referred to the social work program as an "unofficial department" in its annual report of 1906. A common obstacle for early medical social work programs was the unwelcome reception by nurses, whose own professional respect and control of the wards had been only recently gained. Initially, social workers were restricted from the wards. Johns Hopkins started its own social work program in 1907, and its first social worker resigned after only eight months on the job. Social work was not officially recognized on the wards at MGH until 1914.

THE PREDOMINANCE OF NURSES AMONG THE FIRST MEDICAL SOCIAL WORKERS

Some of the tension between nurses and social workers was eased by employing nurses who had had experience in the charity organizations in social work positions. Such a nurse was Helen Athey; she got the social work program at Johns Hopkins going again in August, 1908 after it had been dormant for four months. Athey was a graduate of the Johns Hopkins Training School for Nurses and had worked at the Baltimore Charity Organization Society as well as at a settlement house in New York City. It may also have helped that she was the daughter of one of the hospital trustees. When Athey left, she was succeeded by another graduate of the Hopkins nursing program.

It was not uncommon for the social worker to have been nurses in the early days of medical social work. A survey in 1920 by the American Hospital Association of 61 social service departments found that 193 out of 350 paid workers had had nursing experience; of the 61 social work directors, 36 were nurses.

These nurses did not identify themselves as nurses; they were vocal in their insistence that casework was not an extension of nursing, but rather a distinct profession, with different and even more constructive goals. Ida Cannon had herself formerly been a nurse. While she felt nursing training was useful, it was judged not to be sufficient for successful social work. There was another reason why social workers did not want to be identified with nursing. Though improved nursing training had led to improved patient care, the training had not cultivated the recognition of nursing as a true profession. The nurse was felt to be a handmaiden to the doctor in an area in which the physician's expertise was considered primary. Social workers believed they represented another, equally important, dimension in patient care. They were willing to concede the physician's superiority in medical diagnosis, but they hoped to gain equal recognition for their expert ability to provide social diagnosis. Though social work was conceived to augment the physician's role, the goal of social work practitioners was to eventually rise to the professional status and respect of law, medicine, and the ministry.

THE PROFESSIONALIZATION OF MEDICAL SOCIAL WORK

As the early charity and relief workers had abandoned the volunteer approach as unprofessional, so did the medical social workers insist on paid employment and began to work for eductional requirements and professional recognition. Only seven years after Cabot hired Ida Cannon, she arranged with Jeffrey Brackett at the Boston School of Social Work (then

Harvard-Simmons, later Simmons) to begin a one-year training program for medical social workers. The program began in 1912. It required 10 months of practical supervision at Massachusetts General Hospital; academic lectures and conferences reflecting what was known of psychology, mental hygiene, sociology, dietetics, biology, and basic medicine; and a review of the community resources of the day. Cannon began to require graduation from this course as a prerequisite for full-time employment as a social worker at the hospital. By 1920, the New York and Philadelphia Schools of Social Work had identified minimum criteria for students entering medical social work including the social elements of disease, chief groups of diseases which were dealt with by hospital social workers, and the related problems of hygiene and public health. The courses emphasized interviewing techniques, history taking, record keeping, how to ask difficult personal questions, and how to overcome personal prejudices and idiosyncrasies which could interfere with patient care and staff relationships. The training of hospital social workers had come a long way and had become far more systematized than the trial and error freindly visiting of the Johns Hopkins medical students. Just as the training hospitals had been established primarily to improve medical education, the social work programs were developed as much to establish a profession as to add to the dimensions of patient care.

Despite the efforts of the early training programs to establish uniform professional competence, uniformity in practice and education came slowly. It was not until 1932 that the American Association of Schools of Social Work adopted a specific social work curriculum policy. Medical social workers were the first social workers to organize professionally and they set the highest standards for membership and practice as well. Their professional organization, the American Association of Hospital Social Workers (AAHSW) was formed in 1918. Membership in the AAHSW in 1925 required graduation from a school of social work, specifically mandating a full course in either medical or psychiatric social work, and a year's practical experience. Nurses were allowed membership if they had 18 month's experience in medical or psychiatric social work. Nevertheless, a 1921 canvass of 1,248 social workers (1,020 women, 228 men) who were not members of the AAHSW, revealed that only 60 percent of the men and 40 percent of the women were college graduates. A 1925 study of 204 agencies in Ohio revealed that 23 of 66 agencies responding to the study admitted to having workers with only a grammar school education.[5] Leaders in social work were aware that without uniform standards of practice and education their goals of widespread credibility, and respect for the profession could not be gained. The standards set for medical social work at least guaranteed growing prestige for that segment of the developing profession.

THE IMPACT OF WORLD WAR I ON SOCIAL WORK IN HEALTH CARE

Medical social work increased its visibility during and after World War I. The war years led to masses of medical social workers being recruited to work with families and returning veterans in the armed services, Red Cross, and Veterans Administration. A training program for psychiatric social workers was established at Smith College in 1919 in cooperation with the Boston Psychopathic Hospital to deal with the mental problems of war veterans and the impact of the war's effects on their families. Skilled medical social workers had to be drawn from the hospitals to do the teaching. This led to an expansion of medical social work programs throughout the country.

A shortage of schools of social work developed in proportion to the demand. The war needs were not the only cause of the increased demand. The influenza epidemic of 1918 created an urgent need for more medical social workers to care for the sick in hospitals and homes, arrange for child care, make burial arrangements, provide charity in the absence of lost wages, and so on. Epidemiological studies of the disease also relied on medical social workers to trace the sick, canvass social centers, give basic medical instruction, and encourage compliance with medical routine.

In addition to influenza, tuberculosis and venereal disease were also highly communicable diseases presenting public health hazards at that time. Aside from helping the tubercular patient and family adjust emotionally and socially to the often lengthy disablement, the medical social worker also took on the task of convincing the former employer to accept the patient back to work after recovery. There was much public fright about the disease.

During and after World War I, venereal disease reached epidemic proportions. Medical social workers were extensively involved with the treatment of VD. A 1916 survey by the Committee on Hospital Social Service of the National Organization for Public Health Nursing found that out of 126 social service departments, 50 were giving special attention to syphilitic patients and 70 others were involved in service to either children or adults with gonorrhea.[5] Social workers were not necessarily any more comfortable with these patients than other clinic and hospital staff; their attitudes reflected the morality of the day. The job was one of responsibility, not choice, and the social worker was considered essential to any venereal disease program. Their job was to trace the illness, and to establish the kind of helping relationship with the patient that would get the patient to inform contacts as well as comply with the 18-month-long, unpleasant treatment.

CONFLICT WITH THE MEDICAL PROFESSION

The role of the social worker in treating syphilitics was unpleasant not only because of the moral taboos of the day; despite the view that the social worker was essential to any venereal disease program, the relationship between the social worker and the doctor was not the one of equal professional respect to which the leaders of medical social work aspired. One article published in *Hospital Social Service* in 1924 advised: "The private physician is often entitled to more consideration than he gets from the social worker and will prove an invaluable ally if properly approached . . .The physician is quick to suspect indiscretion if the social worker is too great a talker . . . Confine yourself to pertinent facts only and respect his time . . . The physician doesn't like to be told. He does like to be asked."[6] The social worker's expectations are not addressed. It is noteworthy that the advice did not come from a professional social work publication. *Hospital Social Service* was published by the Hospital Social Service Association of New York City and was always edited by a physician.

Medical social work was getting widespread recognition of its need but not a high professional status; this may have been because the demand for social work far outstripped its ability to produce enough trained workers through its educational programs. The professional social worker, that Ida Cannon had in mind and the social diagnostician, of which Mary Richmond conceived were not being differentiated from the masses of untrained workers who had been recruited following World War I. The historical accidents of the war and the 1918 epidemics rushed the development of social work beyond its capacity to consolidate a professional identity. In the interim, there was no lack of vocational opportunities, but not of the status of professional careers. Other than by restricting membership in the AAHSW, professionally trained medical social workers had no authority to sanction or prohibit the hiring of workers who were below AAHSW standards. Many states lack licensing requirements even in the 1980s. This remains a problem in the social work profession, though most hiring institutions now recognize the Master of Social Work degree as a minimum requirement for identification as a social worker.

CONFLICT WITHIN THE SOCIAL WORK PROFESSION

Throughout the 1920s there was movement within the field to no longer permit the training of social workers through agency or hospital apprenticeships and to require at least a one-year program at a school of social work coupled with a practical field internship. The one-year educational requirement was accepted by the American Association of Schools of Social Work in 1933 and was expanded to a two-year Master of Social Work degree requirement in 1939. What seemed to be lost, however, was the notion of providing specialized training for practicing in certain settings, such as hospitals. By 1944, "medical information" was only one of eight core curricula uniformly available in schools of social work. In the 1920s and 1930s the field was pervaded with debate as to what was "generic" and what was "specific" to the practice of social work.

Though social workers did practice in a number of settings and at times appeared to be doing vastly different jobs, the push to find something common or generic to all social workers was spurred as much by the splitting-off of psychiatric social workers. Originally, they had been a branch of the medical social workers' organization (AAHSW) but formed their own group in 1926. All social workers were affected by the rapid rise in prestige among psychiatric social workers and their focus on the mind of the patient as the primary intervention. Psychiatric social workers boasted of their claim to superiority and did not camouflage their contempt for social workers who concerned themselves with the social dimensions of patient care. To share in the prestige and to avoid a label of inferiority, medical social workers also claimed to have expertise with mental or psychological dimensions of patients.

THE DISAPPEARANCE OF SOCIAL DIAGNOSIS IN HEALTH CARE

In the 30 years following 1920, little was said about medical-social diagnosis in comparison to the mass of lectures, conferences, and publications on the psychological realm of patient care. It was during this period that the community psychiatry of Adolf Meyer, which had promoted the relevance of the social environment, was largely forgotten in favor of the intrapsychic emphasis of Sigmund Freud. The ideas of Ida Cannon and others who prospered between 1912-1920, advocating specialized training to equip social workers to work in the health field, went virtually unmentioned for the next half century. By the mid-1970s, the Boston School of Social Work, Simmons, which had originated the idea of training medical social workers in 1912, offered one elective course on "the psychologcial aspects of medical illness." Training in basic medicine, pharmacology, and the like is still largely available only in field placements, if at all, in virtually all 87 schools of social work in the United States. (In 1982, the Boston University School of Social Work initiated a promising health care curriculum with a focus on social/health policy and some attention to direct clinical practice, though it apparently does not yet include a systematic training component in biomedicine.)

With the intention of consolidating the profession and emphasizing the generic elements of social work practice, the specialized organizations such as the American Association of Hospital Social Workers were absorbed into the National Association of Social Workers in 1955. Though medical social work was retained as a division at the outset, the divisions were later disbanded. A reemergence of organizations for medical/health social work began in 1965, however, with the founding of the Society of Hospital Social Work Directors, which by its nature involves mostly department directors. Small speciality groups such as the Social Work Oncology Group (SWOG) in Boston have developed in the past few years and today there exists a proliferation of over 40 such groups across the country.

THE CHALLENGE OF SOCIAL WORK IN HEALTH CARE TODAY

The disappearance of specialized training for medical social workers and the lack of a single national organization to represent their specific needs pose problems for social workers in health care in the 1980s in determining curriculum and practice directions. Some of these needs may be addressed by the planned reorganization of the National Association of Social Workers into membership divisions including Health Care Settings and Clinical Social Work/Mental Health.[7] Two helpful forums for dialogue among educators and clinicians did develop in the 1970s with the creation of the professional journals, *Health and Social Work* and *Social Work in Health Care*. The connection between past and present in shaping the most effective and viable role of social work in the health field is gaining increasing exposure.[8,9]

The need for social workers to rediscover their early historical inclination to require some training in basic medicine is prompted by two related historical repetitions: primary care medicine and consultation-liaison psychiatry. The emergence of primary care medicine's emphasis on the care of the whole patient can find its heritage in Richard Cabot. Meanwhile, psychiatry's rediscovery of the relatedness and importance of biology and the social environment recaptures much of what motivated Adolf Meyer's attempts to conceptualize mental hygiene and community psychiatry in the first two decades of the twentieth century. That the psychological dimension dominated differential diagnosis in the half century following 1920, largely serves to explain why both social work and psychiatry are at an early stage of conceptualizing and articulating the equally important interdependence of the biologic and social dimensions of patient care. The community mental health movement of the 1960s and 1970s was virtually left to social work, but since the late 1970s psychiatry has taken an expanded interest in differential diagnosis and employed this more thorough approach in the general hospital. The biopsychosocial diagnosis comprises three dimensions that are conceptually equal and essential components of any consultation in liaison psychiatry. Just as the early medical social worker sought professional recognition for expertise with the psychosocial aspects of the diagnosis and treatment of medical illness, now the consultation-liaison psychiatrist in the general hospital seeks recognition for expertise in sorting out all three dimensions of differential diagnosis. That psychiatry is not fully equipped by training and exposure to claim superiority in all three dimensions leaves open a challenging contribution for social workers in health settings. While professionally trained social workers should have expertise with psychological assessment, the social worker traditionally has even more familiarity with the patient's social context than does the psychiatrist.[10]

When experience with the social environment is contributed to the diagnostic process, a more thorough conceptualization of the interplay among biomedical, psychological and social factors can be realized. In this sense, the social context completes the diagnosis horizontally, that is, across the biopsychosocial gestalt. The tutored skills and exposure to social/environmental issues possessed by some social workers can help to identify the spectrum of nuances and vulnerabilities within this single dimension of the diagnostic picture, thereby enhancing diagnostic comprehensiveness vertically on the grid of assessible pertinent factors.[11]

DIAGNOSTIC SPECTRUM

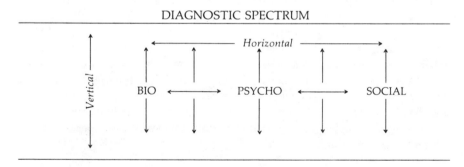

THE BIOPSYCHOSOCIAL MODEL OF HEALTH CARE

Though the use of the terms "horizontal" and "vertical" are new to the nomenclature of differential diagnosis, the embodiment of the practice of carrying out assessments and interventions along these lines has been a matter of ideal clinical work. Skillful clinicians often extract concepts from proven practice experience. Less than ideal practice can be distinguished by a lack of appreciation for one dimension of the biopsychosocial diagnosis at the expense of the other; for example, failing to assess and treat hypertension in a spouse who complains of headaches, irritability, and dissatisfaction with the marital partner. The exclusive use of couple's therapy in such a case would be incomplete diagnosis, and poor practice, and could result in unnecessary conflict for the marriage. The spouse's dissatisfaction with the partner could be more tolerable or even nonexistent once the blood pressure is lowered. The fact that vital signs are not taken in many helping settings is perhaps the best argument for stress to be assessed and treated in a setting in which all three aspects of the horizontal (biopsychosocial) differential diagnosis are available to the patient.

An appreciation for the vertical differential diagnosis is a complex but equally important conceptualization of diagnosis and treatment. Psychiatrists, social workers, and other helping professionals who have had training in personality development, psychodynamic theory, ego psychology, and family theory, among others things, should be able to rely on these conceptual frameworks when the psychological dimension of the biopsychosocial differential diagnosis is the area of attention. Vertical diagnosis in this case means a perspective in which the diagnostician recognizes that people are different psychologically and can have very different personality types and that assessing this has critical implications for how the helper can and should intervene with the patient. An example of this is the type of patient who tends to idealize the helper at the outset and then becomes very difficult to handle in later contacts. Specific strategies can be relied upon if the patient is assessed correctly along the vertical continuum of psychological possibilities at the outset. The conceptualizations do not have to be rigidly fixed or positivistic, but appreciation for different types of patients leads to an appreciation for developing more helpful intervention strategies. Vertical differential diagnosis within each of the three dimensions of the biopsychosocial schema demands a thoughtful, creative, and responsible approach. While it will require training, further research, and test the wits of the helper, it will also provide less stress and conflict for the patient and helper alike.

THE SOCIAL WORK CONTRIBUTION TO THE BIOPSYCHOSOCIAL MODEL

When vertical assessment of the social component of the biopsychosocial approach is the area of attention, social workers have been consulted since at least the time of Richard Cabot. The ability to diagnose the social dimension differentially should be taken as seriously as the biologic and the psychologic dimensions of patient care. Often the social element can be either directly or indirectly as life threatening as the physical and/or psychologic illness. Recalling the earlier example, the patient with significant hypertension may ignore medical advice that life is threatened because of an underlying nonmedical problem—job dissatisfaction for example. Readily helping the patient change jobs could be equally harmful unless the problem is assessed with professional sophistication. Initially, the patient may be no more aware than the health provider that there is a latent issue. If closely observed, only a look of mild dissatisfaction may be apparent in the patient's expression. A question to the patient such as "By the way, how are things for you in general?" may bring the answer "Fine." Yet the next thing that the patient says often identifies the hidden issue; this is the phenomenon of the mental association. It is often at this point that the patient may speak of the job problem, without even recognizing that this is the issue behind the dissatisfaction and the key social problem which could be expressed indirectly as a subtle defiance in not following recommended medical treatment. If, on the other hand, no pertinent mental association is forthcoming from the patient, additional explorative techniques can be used. For example, the question can be posed, "Any changes you'd like to make in your life?" or "What is your biggest worry at the moment?"

Diagnosing the hypertension (biologic), identifying the feeling of dissatisfaction (psychologic), and discovering that the job (social) is the cause of this discontent is only the beginning of the intervention. One way to determine which dimension is the most needed point of engagement with the patient is to notice how much an issue, such as a job, is invested with emotion once the patient does start talking about it.

Should it be determined that the social dimension is the most pressing from the patient's point of view, deciding what to do about, for example, the job dissatisfaction is a complicated endeavor in itself. While sorting out feelings psychologically is important, it may turn out that an actual modification of the social environment may be the remedy to prescribe. A change to a different part of the factory may be needed. A supportive call to the employer may be required, but not before it is assessed whether such a call may feed into dependency feelings which again could eventually result in the patient being noncompliant with the prescribed antihypertensive medication. For one patient, the call may be indicated; for another, it is better left to the patient. Such seemingly trivial details require astute clinical acumen, and though at first seemingly distant from the problem of hypertension, could actually be so intimately involved as to affect the life and death of the patient. Such examples will be amplified and used continuously throughout this book.

RETURN TO EARLY SOCIAL WORK PRINCIPLES

While the primary care physician and the consultation-liaison psychiatrist need the contributions of the social worker for the psychosocial dimensions of patient care—particularly with a differential assessment and intervention with the social environment—social work in health settings also experiences an interdependence with medicine and psychiatry. The biologic dimension of patient care and the effects of this dimension on the mental and social functioning of the patient are not areas of primary expertise for social work. Moreover, social workers in health care today possess less knowledge and training in the biologic dimensions than did their counterparts in the era of Ida Cannon.

The emergence of primary care medicine and the investment of psychiatry in consultation-liaison work in general hospitals, presents both opportunities and challenges for professional social work and its collaboration with medicine over the next decade. In order to participate in consultation-liaison teams, to better communicate with primary care providers, and to perform adequately within the biopsychosocial model, social work in health and even mental health must recover and reestablish the specialized training in biomedical issues that the field was beginning to develop up to 1920. Psychiatry and medicine are rediscovering the importance of the social environment in patient care and this presents a challenging opportunity for social work to contribute services and conceptualizations reflecting that dimension. Similarly, social work must rediscover the significance of understanding at least a minimal level of biology and the related sciences. As collaborators in health care, medicine and general hospital psychiatry should be engaged to help with such training.

The linking of social work and psychiatry must be a careful enterprise. The last time that social work closely associated with psychiatry, the result was the birth of a psychoanalytically oriented psychiatric social work. This branch of social work gained in prestige through its thorough and systematic emphasis on the psyche, but lost its interest in the social environment and lost as well the original goal of medical social work to be equal in social diagnosis to the medical doctor's prestige in medical diagnosis. It is sometimes overlooked by social workers and others that psychiatry too lost its appreciation not only for the social environment but also abandoned for several decades the dawning interest in organicity and neurology that had preceded Adolf Meyer at the turn of the twentieth century. Like social work, psychiatry in the United States was both beneficiary and victim of the psychoanalytic influence in the decades following 1920.

While the status of psychiatric social work prospered in child guidance centers throughout the 1930s and 1940s, medical social workers continued to be employed in health settings with less prestige but in ever-increasing numbers. In addition to hospitals, social workers expanded to public health, visiting nurse associations, and by 1970, to community health centers. Hospital social workers have remained in the majority among social workers involved in health settings. The reemphasis of the general hospital together with the increasing development of health maintenance organizations (HMOs) as the centers of medical care in the 1980s will tend to make these two groups the core of social workers in health care. Though it has been widely recognized that social workers in general hospitals have existed in a feudal system in which their roles have been defined to a significant extent by the medical hierarchy, an unusual opportunity for more equal partnership presents itself in the primary care atmosphere both within hospitals and HMOs as well as within smaller community practices. Primary care medicine is a natural environment for social workers to develop conceptualizations and practice models which can recognizably contribute to the emerging biopsychosocial model of health care. Social workers have the opening to pursue this new avenue to enhance patient care and to develop creative career opportunities.

TERRITORIAL ISSUES LEFT TO BE RESOLVED

Despite Ida Cannon's efforts to have professional medical social workers be considered equal but different to the physician in patient care, social workers in hospitals have continued to be viewed—and to have preceived themselves—as working in a "host" setting; that is, a setting dominated, defined, and controlled by physicians. Psychiatrists have been barely more accepted in the general hospital, and in some cases, less accepted. When psychiatrists have been accepted, it may have been because they are physicians or perhaps because there have been far fewer psychiatrists than social workers employed in general hospitals, involved in patient care, and visible on the wards and in the ambulatory clinics. Notwithstanding the ideas of primary care, total patient care, the whole patient, and so on, many physicians have remained skeptical, distrustful, and uncomfortable with psychiatrists and other providers of the psychosocial dimensions of patient care. Many medical doctors equate psychiatry with severe psychopathology, and the idea of involving a psychiatrist or even a social worker has remained a course of last resort. The recognition of stress in otherwise "normal" patients, or in patients reacting to health problems or hopitalization, for whom referral to a helping professional might be beneficial, has remained a foreign and unwelcome idea to many physicians. Even more obvious psychiatric illnesses, that is, disorders of mood, thought, and/or behavior receive insufficient attention from medical providers; for instance, while psychiatric morbidity has been found in 30 to 60 percent of general hospital inpatients, only 1 to 13 percent are referred for psychiatric evaluation[12, 13]

THE CONTINUING STRUGGLE FOR PROFESSIONAL AUTONOMY

Social workers in the health setting have long recognized and experienced not only the challenge of engaging patients in helping relationships but also in engaging physicians to refer patients for help at the earliest possible time. A study at Mount Sinai Hospital in New York found that when social workers picked up their own cases without waiting for a physician's referral, they were able to help significantly more patients earlier in the hospitalization.[14] The problem of getting referrals before unfortunate or unnecessary circumstances set in for the patient is part of a larger problem for social workers in hospitals. The issue is having the profession of social work defined by other than social workers. It turns out not only to be a disservice to social work, and to the patients served or unserved, but to the associated hospital professions, chiefly medicine, which have been allowed to define social work. Though the majority of hospitals now commonly hire master's degree-level (MSW) social workers, the problem of role definition and quality care has at times been exacerbated by the hiring of social workers by non–social workers. To correct these practices, a joint committee of the American Hospital Association (AHA) and the National Association of Social Workers (NASW) met in 1976 and published 11 standards for hospital social service. The standards were presented for adoption to the Joint Commission for Accreditation of Hospitals (JCAH). Ten of the standards were accepted and included in their 1979 publication *Manual for Accreditation of Hospitals*.[15] The standard which was not accepted required that the social service program in every hospital should be directed by an MSW or at least a BSW (baccalaureate degree specifically in social work) with an MSW as a consultant.

The ruling of the JCAH is characteristic of the continuing struggle of the profession of social work to set uniform standards of practice and be in a position to regulate itself. The JCAH wanted the standard to include the wording "MSW or documented equivalent," stating that to require an MSW would amount to "restraint of trade." However, the JCAH did not see the requirement of an MD degree for doctors as an unfair labor practice, nor the recognized nursing degrees as "restraint of trade." The dispute remained in the hands of the NASW and JCAH lawyers through the summer of 1983.

Realistic Collaboration with Medicine

The lack of recognized uniform standards and licensing requirements has continued to place social work in a dependent position to medicine which poses a new challenge for the collaborative effort of medicine and social work over the next decade. In many states, social workers are not yet eligible for third party reimbursement of outpatient fees for services without supervision from a physician. Some Blue Cross contracts list supervision from a physician without requiring the physician to be a psychiatrist. Such supervision is ironic since the physician is not considered by the helping professions in general to have any training in psychosocial interventions. When the physician is at least a psychiatrist, many social workers have been faced with obtaining supervision from psychiatrists who may be less experienced than the social workers, just to be eligible for third party payment.[16] This situation has made a mockery of the collaborative concept and the interdisciplinary idea. The physician's dominant position on the team is decided not by his expertise or by his ideally unique contribution in biomedicine but by his roots to the funding base. This has caused many ill feelings among social workers and has reinforced their determination to seek recognition in every state for third party payment directly. It has also put some physicians in the unfortunate position of having to direct sometimes more experienced clinicians from other disciplines; this leaves the physician in an often impractical role to learn from other staff. The authors have suggested elsewhere[17] a "captain of the team" concept in which the functional director of the health care team would be determined by leadership ability and not by profession. In this alternative to the medical hierarchical model, when the physician is not team leader, the physician's authoritative expertise is restricted to biomedical issues only.

FUNDING AND STAFFING PROBLEMS IN SOCIAL WORK

Though the arrangement is not likely to change until social workers achieve uniform standards for practice and licensing, social work cannot afford to wait for direct payment in order to produce revenue. Currently, most social work positions in hospitals nationally are supported by the per diem bed rate, that is, the inpatient bed fee. This funding source makes the availability of social workers to patients and staff dependent upon the commitment of the hospital and its general budget to the psychosocial needs of patients. This commitment and recognition of the value of meeting such needs greatly vary from hospital to hospital. In a 1978 study of 21 hospitals conducted by the Henry Ford Hospital, it was learned that the number of social workers per patient beds varied drastically. In two similar hospitals, for instance, Massachusetts General Hospital had 1,084 beds and 99 social workers while Houston Memorial had 1,000 beds and only 4 social workers (see Appendix I).[18] An even more elaborate nationwide survey of hospital social work published by Coulton in 1979 corroborated the dimensions of the problem.[19]

While the employment of social workers is uneven for inpatients, it is far worse for social workers in ambulatory care. In most hospitals, no funding is provided for social work services to outpatients. Inpatient social workers spend time in the ambulatory clinics only as their inpatient demands permit. While federal funding in the 1960s, such as the comprehensive Health Planning and Public Health Service Amendments (P.L. 89-749) provided for the expansion of health care to ambulatory services, no major additional funding for social work services was included.

If social work is to provide services in the ambulatory area, and especially if a primary care approach is to be realized, funding sources must be found. Other than grant funding, in most cases this will mean seeking third party payments for outpatient services on a fee for service basis.[20] At present, this calls for a continued collaborative effort between social work and medicine to bill for social work services under the technical supervision of medicine, as is required by most of the insurance programs. While many social workers shudder at the thought of being "supervised" by physicians, and reliving a secondhand professional role, medicine too must recognize that to provide adequate staff and effective quality patient care, respect for social work is long overdue. Social workers are, for instance, the largest provider group of trained mental health professionals in the country.

The time may be ripe for optimal respect and collaboration between medicine and social work. Medicine seems to be gaining a security and maturity that requires a shedding of the need to profess expertise in all areas. Consumer scrutiny has caused some of this loss of false omnipotence. Medicine also may be gaining adequate distance from the relatively recent trauma of gaining its own professional respect. Only a century ago, the average physician could not earn a living, and attracted little respect from the public. Just before the turn of the twentieth century a survey of 100 recently graduated doctors was conducted; of that number, 75 left medicine within five years of graduation because they could not earn a living. Medical education itself was judged to be so inferior only seven decades ago that a Carnegie Foundation study led to the closing of nearly 100 medical schools between 1908 and 1929.[21] As social workers become more familiar with the history of medicine, as well as their own professional history, the potential for joint efforts with medicine will increase. Such awareness would provide perspective on the course of development of the two professions. The prestige of medicine as a profession is extremely recent and more fragile than is often appreciated. In the great challenge of providing effective health care and funding it needs all the public respect that can be gained. The efforts of social work to improve and contribute to health care can be enhanced by the mutual engagement of medical providers and social workers as renewed collaborators in the cultivation of primary care. The original spirit of Cabot and Cannon has the opportunity to be recaptured within the primary care approach, for the good of patients as well as for achieving the effective complementary contributions of both medicine and social work.

There has been stress in the professional growth of both medicine and social work. But despite evidence of frequent territorial strain, each has continued to work together in ever-increasing areas of health care. Training programs for residents in family medicine and primary care are testimony to a renewed interest and commitment to a model of patient care that is more than disease-oriented. Medicine needs to share its knowledge of human biology; social work must contribute its expertise with the psychological and social dimensions of patient care; psychiatry can add its own specialized training involving the interaction of biology and the patient's mental functioning. Effective and efficient health care is an interdisciplinary effort. It is also the present endeavor in the 75-year chronicle of medical-social work collaboration.

SUMMARY

Social work first became involved in the delivery of medical care because the social and environmental components of some diseases (e.g. tuberculosis and venereal disease) could not go unaddressed. The recognition of these unavoidable social factors enjoyed advocacy and leadership from within medicine,[22] and many of the actual social work practitioners in the health care setting emerged from the ranks of nursing.[23] Since many of the early medical social workers were nurses, they saw the importance of including training in basic medicine in the development of educational programs for medical social work and they influenced the curricula of some of the newly developing schools of social work. However, pressured to produce practitioners for the needs of returning veterans from both world wars, the new schools and early apprenticeship programs could not keep pace with demand. Hospitals and other health programs came to employ social service workers who lacked both the medical training and the tutored social diagnostic skills envisioned by the original medical social workers. The hierarchical medical setting itself also restricted the development of medical-social diagnostic skills by functioning as a feudal system in which the social work role became defined by those outside of the emerging social work profession, chiefly by physicians.

The psychoanalytic influence, although beneficial in developing psychological sophistication, provided another detour to the direct cultivation of the interface of the environmental context and physical health or illness. While some social workers and psychiatrists still focus on the psyche and many medical providers remain restricted to a germ theory of illness, today it is being increasingly recognized that one dimension of the biopsychosocial continuum cannot be seen in isolation from the others. The biomedical, psychological, and social-environmental components of health and illness are interrelated. While one dimension may require a priority intervention, such a clinical decision cannot be effectively made without assessment of all three.

The renewed interest in the primary care approach to medical care appears to present an opportunity for psychosocial practitioners and medical providers to collaborate as an effective team in a comprehensive model of health care. For social work, this sets a natural stage for continuing the training in biomedicine envisioned by the early medical social workers, while reaping the benefits of combining this potential training with established social work sophistication in psychotherapeutic skills and the profession's long experience with the social-environmental context. With the primary care approach, a forum for further conceptual development and the testing of imaginative intervention strategies presents itself.

Manpower shortages in the health setting, however, remain as obstacles to pursuing this clinical development. New ways of funding social work in health care in an era of economic contraction will be a challenge to create. Not all services may be possible to provide and social workers are faced with having to select priorities and measure interventions that will render the most effective outcomes. While social workers are understandably seeking independent insurance reimbursement for their services, the present structure of health reimbursement need not be sidestepped as a funding base in the interim. The atmosphere of the primary care model includes a climate of collaboration with more equal partnership so that the requirements for medical supervision to satisfy insurance reimbursement need not carry the tone of the social work role being defined by medicine. Each has a significant role to play and each contribution is unique and essential to the delivery of comprehensive health care. While the language of health insurance reimbursement appears to lag behind the potential collaborative nature of primary care, social work and medicine have the opportunity to negotiate their complementary roles among themselves and still seek reimbursement on a fee for service basis—particularly in ambulatory services—from the insurance industry as it currently exists. Comprehensive health care cannot be provided without the adequate staffing of both medical providers and psychosocial practitioners. Collaboration over the funding of positions will likely be the crucial test as to whether a comprehensive model of health care can be realized.

NOTES

1. O'Connor, Robin, "American Hospitals: The First Two Hundred Years," Bicentennial Report, *Hospitals: Journal of the American Hospital Association*, 50 (January 1, 1976): 62-72.
2. Emerson, Charles P. "The Social Service Department of a General Hospital," *National Hospital Record*, March 15, 1909.
3. Cannon, Ida M., *On The Social Frontier of Medicine*, (Cambridge, Mass.: Harvard University Press, 1952).
4. Cabot, Richard C., *Social Work: Essays on the Meeting Ground of Doctor and Social Worker*, (New York: Houghton Mifflin, 1919).
5. Lubove, Roy, *The Professional Altruist: The Emergence of Social Work as a Career, 1880-1930*, (New York: Atheneum Press, 1977).
6. Cumming, H., "The Part the Social Worker Plays in the Work of Combating Venereal Disease", *Hospital Social Service*, 10 (1924).
7. *NASW News* (Board Adopts Concept of Reorganization: Membership Divisions Centerpiece), 28, 4 (April, 1983):1.
8. Nacman, Martin, "Social Work in Health Settings: A Historical Review," *Social Work in Health Care* 2, 4 (Summer 1977): 407-18.
9. Caputi, Marie A., "Social Work in Health Care: Past and Future," *Health and Social Work*, 3, 1 (February 1978): 9-21.
10. Slaby, Andrew E., Richard J. Goldberg, and Stephen R. Wallace, "Interdisciplinary Team Approach in Emergency Psychiatric Care," *Psychosomatics*, 24, 7, (July 1983): 627-37.
11. Leigh, Hoyle, Alvan Feinstein, and Morton Reiser, "The Patient Evaluation Grid: A Systematic Approach to Comprehensive Care," *General Hospital Psychiatry*, 2, (1980): 3-9.
12. Lipowski, Z.J., "Review of Consultation Psychiatry and Psychosomatic Medicine: II Clinical Aspects, *Psychosomatic Medicine*, 29, (1967): 201-24.
13. Kligerman, M.J., S.P. McKegney, "Patterns of Psychiatric Consultation in Two General Hospitals," *International Journal of Psychiatry Medicine*, 2, (1971): 126-32.
14. Berkman, Barbara Gordon, and Helen Rehr, "Early Social Service Case Finding for Hospitalized Patients: An Experiment," *Social Service Review*, 47, (1973).
15. Joint Commission for Accreditation of Hospitals, *Manual for Accreditation of Hospitals*, 1979 Edition.
16. Knoll, Donald, "Psychiatric Supervision for Social Work?" *Clinical Social Work Journal*, 7, (1979). 214-17.
17. Slaby, Andrew E., Richard J. Goldberg, and Stephen R. Wallace, "Interdisciplinary Team Approach in Emergency Psychiatric Care," *Psychosomatics*, 24, 7, (July 1983): 627-37.
18. *Social Work Manpower Survey*, Henry Ford Hospital, Detroit, 1978.
19. Coulton, Claudia, *Nationwide Survey of Hospital Social Work Practice* (Cleveland Human Science Design Laboratory, Case Western Reserve University, August 1979).
20. Society for Hospital Social Work Directors, "Social Work Reimbursement: Direct Patient Services," Memo to Members, American Hospital Association, Chicago, Illinois, June 1982.

21. Shyrock, Richard Harrison, *The Development of Modern Medicine: An Interpretation of the Social and Scientific Factors Involved* (New York: Knopf, 1947).
22. Cabot, Richard C., Social Work: Essays.
23. Cannon, Ida M., *Social Work in Hospitals: A Contribution to Progressive Medicine* (Beverly Hills, Calif.: Russell Sage Foundation, 1925).

ADDITIONAL REFERENCES

American Hospital Association, *Hospital Statistics: 1978 Annual Survey,* 1979 edition.

Bartlett, Harriet M., *Analyzing Social Work Practice by Fields* (New York: National Association of Social Workers, 1961).

Bartlett, Harriet M., *Social Work Practice in the Health Field* (New York: National Association of Social Workers, 1961).

Black, Bertram, "Social Work in Health and Mental Health Services," *Social Casework* (April 1971): 211-19.

Bracht, Neil F., "Health Care: The Largest Human Service System," *Social Work* 19 (September 1974).

Cabot, Richard C., ed., *The Goal of Social Work,* (New York: Houghton Mifflin, 1927).

Cabot, Richard C., *Social Service and the Art of Healing,* NASW Classics Series (1915; reprint, Washington, D.C.: National Association of Social Workers, 1973).

Commission on Hospital Care, New York, *Hospital Care in the United States,* The Commonwealth Fund, 1947.

Dana, Bess, H. David Banta, and Kurt W. Deuschle, "Agenda for the Future of Interprofessionalism," in Helen Rehr, ed., *Medicine and Social Work: An Exploration in Interprofessionalism* (New York: 1974).

Goldstine, Dora, *Readings in the Theory and Practice of Medical Social Work,* (Chicago: University of Chicago Press, 1954).

Hallowitz, Emmanuel, "Innovations in Hospital Social Work," *Social Work* 17 (July 1972): 89-97.

Hirsch, Sidney, and Abraham Laurie, "Social Work Dimensions in Shaping Medical Care Philosophy and Practice," *Social Work* 14, 2 (April 1969): 75-79.

Kerson, Toba Schwaber, "Sixty Years Ago: Hospital Social Work in 1918," *Social Work in Health Care* 4, 3 (Spring, 1979): 331-43.

Massachusetts General Hospital, *Selected Papers and Report: Fiftieth Anniversary Celebration Social Service Department,* October 1955.

Meyer, Adolf, *The Commonsense Psychiatry,* McGraw-Hill Book Co., Inc., New York, 1948.

Meyer, Henry J., "Profession of Social Work: Contemporary Characteristics," in *Encyclopedia of Social Work* (New York: National Association of Social Workers, 1971): 959-72.

National Association of Social Workers, *Standards for Hospital Social Services,* NASW Policy Statement, No. 6 (Washington, D.C., 1977).

Olsen, Katherine M., and Marvin E. Olsen, "Role Expectations and Perceptions for Social Workers in Medical Settings," *Social Work,* 12, 3 (July 1967): 70-78.

Packard, Francis R., *History of Medicine in the United States,* Vol. I and II, (New York: Hafner Publishing Co., Inc., 1963).

Phillips, Beatrice, "Social Workers in Health Services," in *Encyclopedia of Social Work* (New York: National Association of Social Workers, 1971), 567-75.

Rice, Elizabeth, "Social Work Practice in Medical Health Service," in *Enclyclopedia of Social Work* (New York: National Association of Social Workers, 1965), pp. 470-76.

Segal, Brian, "Planning and Power in Hospital Social Service," *Social Casework* 52 (July 1970): 399-405.

Shyrock, Richard Harrison, *Medicine and Society in America: 1660-1880,* (New York University Press, 1960).

Teague, Doran, "Social Service Enterprise: A New Health Care Model," *Social Work* 16, 3 (July 1971): 67-74.

Thornton, Janet, and Marjorie Strauss Knauth, *The Social Component in Medical Care* (New York: Columbia University Press, 1937).

Ullman, Alice, Mary E. W. Goss, Milton S. Davis, and Margaret Mushinski, "Activities, Satisfaction, and Problems of Social Workers in Hospital Settings: A Comparative Study," *Social Service Review* 45 (March 1971): 17-29.

Chapter Two

The Team Approach of Primary Care

This chapter will provide an overview of the primary care approach to medicine and describe the potentially unique and complementary clinical roles of the contributing disciplines, particularly medicine, social work, and psychiatry. The issues facing professionals in each of these three disciplines in making the transition to this comprehensive model of health care will be addressed. The biopsychosocial clinical skills required in primary care will be conceptualized as generalizable to all health care practice, and potentially serving in particular as the fundamental skills base for all clinical social workers in health and mental health practice.

A brief review of the early history of primary care, and a look at some recent events that have stimulated renewed interest in the primary care approach will serve as an introduction to a consideration of its promises and parameters.

THE BACKGROUND OF THE PRIMARY CARE MOVEMENT

The notion of primary care first surfaced in 1921 with the Sheppard-Towner Act, part of which was directed at the early identification of health hazards in maternal and child health. The social context of medical care was appreciated in funding the federal Children's Bureau to administer and develop programs with state agencies to make home visits for the purpose of "promoting the welfare and hygiene of maternity and infancy".[1] By today's standards, the Act was limited by its emphasis on parental as opposed to children's rights; its efficacy and social prominence soon paled as the economic and social programs of the 1930s drew the attention of the government and citizenry. The developing field of Social Work experienced the 1930s and 1940s, with attention divided between depression era social reform and the increasingly popular intrapsychically focused psychoanalytic casework. Even the community-oriented mental hygiene movement virtually disappeared in the face of the mushrooming, nonsocial, Freudian influence.

Medicine, meanwhile, having survived both the societal distrust engendered by nineteenth century quackery, and the closing by 1929, of over 100 incompetent medical schools, began to consolidate an identity of public approval and increasingly unquestioned scientific expertise. Unlike the situation at the turn of the century, when substantial numbers of qualified doctors had to resort to other careers to earn a living,[2] physicians by the 1930s began to be able to count on their medical practices for respectable financial security. Gradually, however, medicine began to gravitate toward specialization and away from family practice. By the 1950s, this shift toward specialization (associated with the impressive triumphs of technological medicine), combined with the move of the family practitioner away from the urban population centers,[3] to lead to an overwhelming increase in the use of general hospital outpatient clinics for routine and ongoing medical care. This was a state of affairs for which the clinics had not previously existed and had not been equipped to absorb. Since 1954, the number of visits to general hospital outpatient clinics has tripled, far exceeding the rate of growth in population and the general increase in visits to physicians. In 1970, there were 180 visits to these clinics; two years later it was estimated that there were 200 million visits—which was, at that time, the equivalent of one visit for every citizen. In 1954, one hospital outpatient visit was listed for every nine visits to a physician's private office; by 1970, hospital visits rose to one for every four to the private office.[4]

The emergency rooms of general hospitals have also experienced tremendous increases in use for routine medical care and a variety of social and psychological problems. The increase in use of one urban hospital emergency room climbed from approximately 800 visits in 1970 to 1,500 in 1980. This is consistent with a national pattern of increased use, estimated to vary between 120 percent and 600 percent in the years between 1965 and 1980. It is estimated that if the generally expected rate of increase of total emergency room visits continues at the present 11 percent per year, the patient volume in general hospital emergency rooms alone will double every seven years.[5]

The move toward specialization and the migration of existing family practitioners to the suburbs has led both to a reappraisal of general hospital ambulatory care as well as to governmental planning and support for a reemergence of primary care programs. Despite public and governmental demands for some portion of medicine to become less specialized and more available, it has not been easy for consumers or health care professionals to achieve a consensus as to what this model of health care—primary care—should actually entail.

When asked by the National Academy of Sciences to contribute to a conceptualization of primary care, various organizations and individuals put forward no less than 83 definitions at an open meeting in Washington, D.C. in January 1976. From this array, and after the input of a multitude of position papers by appointed subcommittees, the academy published a report listing five attributes that it concluded were essential to the practice of good primary care: accessibility, comprehensiveness, coordination, continuity, and accountability.[6]

TOWARD A DEFINITION OF PRIMARY CARE

The report of the National Academy of Sciences concluded that primary care is distinguished from other levels of personal health services by the scope, character, and integration of the services provided. It was decided that primary care could not be sufficiently defined by the location of care, by the provider's disciplinary training, or by the provision of a particular set of services. It was also decided that because services rather than disciplines define primary care, good practitioners could be trained in a variety of specialities. Although it was recognized that primary care medical providers graduate from family practice programs more often than from, for example, surgery, it was emphasized that graduates from either program could provide exemplary primary care.

The academy put forward that primary care could be furnished by a solo practitioner, a group practice clinic, or a health maintenance organization. It was further concluded that excellent primary care services could be delivered by a nonphysician, such as a family nurse practitioner with suitable backup. A fundamental point recognized by the academy was that, in most cases, the complete array of services could not be offered by a single individual and should be provided by a team that might include physicians, nurses, physicians' assistants, social workers, technicians, administrators, secretaries, and others. This realization will be amplified and explained later in this chapter.

The definition of primary care as embodied in the five attributes of accessibility, comprehensiveness, coordination, continuity, and accountability will be repeated with the same degree of comprehensiveness as was reported by the academy. Though the detail may at first seem too elaborate, it is very important for social workers and other health care providers to have a real understanding of the dimensions of primary care in order to appreciate its potential promise as well as its potential limitations.

Accessibility of Services

Accessibility refers to the responsibility of the health provider team to assist the patient or the potential patient to overcome temporal, spatial, economic, and psychologic barriers to health care.

Ideally, patients should be able to reach the practitioner or a member of the team at all times. The physical location and internal facilities of the primary care unit should be such that the patient can reach and use the provided services. The provider should be concerned that the cost of services and the way in which they are provided are acceptable to patients so that those who need care are not deterred from seeking it.

Secondary to accessibility are availability, attainability, and acceptability. Availability refers to the temporal aspects of accesss; for example, the maintenance, if possible, of 24-hour coverage and reasonably fast response to requests for service. Attainability covers physical and economic aspects of access. Acceptability refers to psychologic and social aspects of access.

The academy recognized that primary care programs must support themselves financially to stay in existence, so that some provision for payment must be expected. Nevertheless, it was emphasized that the primary care provider should be concerned about the economic status of the patients, and should assist them whenever and however possible to overcome financial barriers. More will be said later in the chapter about how many of the critical dimensions involving accessibility fall outside the routine capacities of the primary physician and generally require the expertise of other contributing primary care providers, particularly the social worker. It is, in fact, an emphatic limitation of the academy report that accessibility was not recognized as needing to be specifically assigned to other disciplines in order to realize the objective of primary care.

Comprehensiveness of Services

The academy report defined comprehensiveness as the willingness and ability of the primary care team to handle the great majority of health problems arising in the population it serves.

It was recognized that a primary care practitioner may limit practice to a single age group (for example, pediatrics, or internal medicine) or sex (for example, obstetrics and gynecology). Nevertheless, it was emphasized that any primary care practitioner should handle most of the problems arising in the chosen served population. For example, it was concluded that an obstetrician/gynecologist who refers patients to other doctors for general physical examinations, headaches, febrile illnesses, and similar problems is not practicing primary care. Further, primary care in this case would include the provision of such preventive services as blood pressure and weight measurement, in addition to pap smears and breast examinations.

Comprehensiveness of services was viewed as the distinguishing characteristic of the primary care practitioner from the secondary care practitioner or referral specialist. It was noted that the primary care practitioner could have an area of special medical interest, such as heart disease or diabetes mellitus, but would not limit services to concentrate on this interest.

Nurse practitioners, physician's assistants, social workers, and others were viewed as valuable members of the primary care team; not only because of their ability to increase the number of patients seen, but also because their unique professional skills can add to the physician's usual range of services. A central part of this chapter will be devoted to clarifying and demonstrating the unique contributions of social work and psychiatry to the primary care team.

Coordination of Services

The third attribute to primary care decided upon by the academy was that of coordination. The primary care provider coordinates the patient's care, including any care provided by other specialists. Though it was not mentioned in the academy report, the role of patient care coordinator at times calls for the contribution of the team social worker, particularly when environmental/network/systems issues both within and without the health care establishment appear to threaten, disrupt, or preclude the process of diagnosis and treatment. (See the case illustration later in this chapter.) The primary care physician was seen by the academy as the ombudsman for patient contact for other providers, sensitive to the need for referring patients to appropriate specialists, providing pertinent information and seeking opinions from these specialists, and explaining diagnosis and treatment to patients.

In addition, the primary care practitioner was seen as the coordinator, or of the patient's plan of care by also taking into consideration the patients financial capability and personal desires. It was recognized that such coordination requires an understanding of the patient's family and occupational environment, financial circumstances, preferences, and way of life. It will be contended later in the chapter that this is a central contribution of social work and that the academy went too far here in expecting medical providers of any kind to be able to extract from any of their training or experience this significant part of the primary care service.

Continuity of Services

Continuity was seen as an essential attribute of primary care and one that could not exist without the first three factors mentioned above. The academy report pointed out that the inaccessibility of practitioners encourages patients to use emergency rooms or other providers of services, thereby destroying continuity. Referral of patients to others for services that should be within the scope of the primary care approach promotes discontinuous and fragmented care. The failure of the primary care practitioners to seek pertinent data from referral sources and to incorporate this information into the patient's record or the failure to accommodate and adapt to the patient's preferences also destroys continuity. The question of adapting to the patient's preferences, however, is a complex issue which the academy did not adequately treat in its report. This issue will be examined later in this chapter. The contribution of social work to primary care is essential when it comes to insuring continuity of care with poor, uneducated, perpetually crisis-prone, or barely functioning patients. Intervention with these cases often requires experience with a particular set of values and with a lifestyle which is distant from middle class proprieties and preoccupations.

The academy report considered other issues regarding continuity, for example, that the primary care provider should be more aggressive in seeking continuity than has commonly been the case. It was pointed out that an instruction to return in one year for an examination should be followed by a reminder card or telephone call before the scheduled visit, and a missed appointment should evoke an effort to determine the reason and to reschedule for a later time.

Another issue involving continuity is the medical record itself. The academy report recognized that in today's health care practice the patient's record is of increasing importance in achieving continuity of services. The solo practitioner of the past may have been able to recall the relevant facts about patients. In modern practice, however, with extensive quantitative data from tests and where coverage is shared among partners, more importance needs to be placed on a readily accessible record in which significant problems are highlighted and the treatment plan is outlined clearly.

Accountability

The academy report saw accountability as an attribute not unique to primary care but essential to it. It was recommended that the primary care practice should regularly review the process and outcomes of its care. These reviews should lead to educational activities to correct deficiencies and expand skills and services. All members of the staff should be included.

In addition, the report recommended that the professional staff of the primary care practice should establish a policy of providing appropriate information to the patient about risks and possible undesirable effects of treatment and about unexpected or undesirable outcomes, so that the patient can make informed decisions about proposed care.

Finally, the academy report concluded that the physician had an obligation to maintain appropriate financial accountability, including adequate professional liability coverage. Though the report did not say so, this certainly should be said for other primary care staff members as well.

DIFFICULTIES FACING MEDICINE IN THE TRANSITION TO PRIMARY CARE

Even a cursory review of the attributes of primary care as delineated by the National Academy of Sciences would lead many to conclude that at present because of costs, staff shortages, and the current structure of most health care programs—including general hospital outpatient clinics—the possibility of most programs achieving the full definition of primary care in the near future is unlikely. Monetary concerns, availability of staff, and present program structure are not the only barriers to realizing some of the objectives of primary care. Despite significant growth of family practice and general internal medicine programs and some shift in the training philosophy of certain medical schools, the promise of a medical care system that extends beyond a strict biomedical model is yet to be fulfilled. Despite at least two decades of research demonstrating a multitude of factors in the etiology of medical illness, much of the training and practice of medical providers has remained firmly ingrained in the germ theory, that is, deductive medical diagnosis from the perspective of singular and specific etiology. In contrast, Cassel among others, has contributed research in the epidemiologic perspective of psychosocial factors in disease etiology.[7] Various indicators of social or familial disorganization have been related to increased rates of tuberculosis,[8] mental disorders,[9] fatal stroke,[10] hypertension,[11] and coronary heart disease.[12, 13] Other writers have pointed out the importance of social supports or the lack of them in the etiology, exacerbation, or alleviation of biologic illness.[14] Cassel also studied the important role of low social status and subsequent low self-esteem as a contributing factor in biologic illness as well as the importance of generalized stress as enhancing the susceptibility to disease in general.[15] The biomedical model, in itself, fails to take into account a comprehensive systems view of illness and has, of course, been widely criticized for its narrow focus[16, 17, 18] in which sociodemographic or psychological variables are ignored.

So far, the background provided by the psychosomatic studies of Alexander and French[19] or Dunbar[20] or the personality perspectives of Kahana and Bebring[21] or more recently by Leigh et al.[22] or Kimball[23] have not had much of an impact on the education or training or practice of medical providers. Equally significant, the sociologic and epidemiologic studies and conceptualizations of health behavior, illness behavior, and sick role behavior by, for instance, Kasl and Cobb[24], Mechanic[25],

Parsons[26] or Locke and Slaby[27] have only been remotely incorporated into the education and practice of medicine.

The "medical model" when used to refer solely to a biomedical perspective is a necessary but not sufficient component of health care. Biomedical diagnosis and treatment is specific, technical, and firmly rooted in the biological paradigm. However, such a model of medicine will never encompass the multiple dimensions involved in overall health care.

The false hope that physicians could actually treat illness from a biomedical perspective alone has apparently been cultivated from societal forces both within and without the field of medicine. To separate itself from the widespread public distrust and scorn of the nineteenth century, modern medicine, until recently, colluded in accepting social expectations to cure every ill and provide some answer to any and all complaints of patient distress. Modern society contributed an inevitable part in its quest for the omnipotent shaman and healer. Equally inevitable is the eventual disillusionment which our culture expresses in the form of litigation, noncompliance, and the erosion of unquestioned respect for the authority and wisdom of the physician[28, 29, 30] Many medical providers are themselves increasingly resentful of having to serve as a societal gatekeeper and dispenser of public funds every time a disability determination requires a physician's signature to authorize entry or rejection for unending eligibility programs. (Other than those for financial assistance to dependent children, eligibility for even temporary income maintenance [welfare] programs for adults in most states now requires evidence of psychiatric or medical disability signed to by a physician. The doctor is today routinely confronted with the dilemma of deciding whether to medicalize social destitution when actual disability is not apparent and the need for food or shelter is the real albeit camouflaged presentation.)

One of the major risks of adopting a primary care model is that it is a double-edged sword that responds to the clamor for less specialization and more availability by moving the medical provider into a role of responsibility for more than the patient's biomedical problems. It does this while at the same time deemphasizing the technical diagnostic role which provides medicine with the claim to unquestioned expertise, autonomy from public regulation, and its raison d'etre for exulted prestige and attendant financial reward.[31] Primary care, as put forth by the report of the National Academy of Sciences, recognizes the input of other health care disciplines such as nursing and social work as valuable, but appears to omit a delineation of the specific contributions of these disciplines while seeming to actually make even these contributions and roles the ultimate responsibility of the medical provider. For instance, the primary care practitioner is expected to coordinate the patient's plan of care with a knowledge of the patient's financial capabilities and personal desires. This implies an understanding of the patient's family and occupational environment, financial circumstances, preferences, and way of life.[32] Not only does this task take medical practitioners away from a specialized technical field where requirements are already voluminous and exceedingly demanding, but it moves them into areas of social and psychological sciences with their own extensive training requirements. The physician is expected to span the biomedical, social, and psychological dimensions of care without the benefit of recognizing that mastering all dimensions is likely to be an unrealistic task.[33] The physician who does recognize this unrealistic task may understandably fear that such a broadened scope will result in dilution of biomedical skills, which if extreme, might cost the medical practitioner what prestige the field of medicine has worked long and hard to achieve.

Howe[34] has pointed out that medicine, in fact, enjoys its autonomy, prestige, and financial rewards predominantly because of its very specialized, technologic attributes. This aspect has kept medicine distant from public review. In addition, Howe points out that the medical profession's sense of obligation to the individual fee for service client and its distance from more collective social or public concerns has contributed to its achievement of self-regulation as opposed to direct public accountability. Those professions which have been identified as serving the public needs, as servants to collective concerns, have in turn, suffered from obscure professional identities and have not achieved independence, autonomy, self-regulation, and the attendant prestige and financial reward.

Social work has experienced mixed public and private status, providing one-to-one services but at other times initiating social changes for the collective good. This is a part of the profession which social work would choose not to abandon, but it has cost the profession in terms of status and financial reward.

The lesson for medicine is that while it cannot ignore the demand for a more thorough health care model such as primary care, it does not need to jeopardize its status by abandoning the phenomenon of specialization altogether, even within primary care. In essence, the primary care physician can remain the biomedical specialist as part of the primary care team, appreciative of the psychological and social dimensions but not inexpertly attempting to provide them in every case. This is why collaboration with other health care disciplines such as psychiatry and social work is essential as team contributors to the health care process involved in the provision of primary care.

The report of the academy on primary care by its implications seems to have set up some unforeseen pitfalls to the status of medicine. If primary care is interpreted as implying that the physician address the social and psychological needs of the patient, the medical provider is threatened with loss of the specialist role in becoming much more of a generalist. The true foundation of primary care lies instead in the realization that operationalizing this comprehensive model of health care requires a collaborative effort which often will go beyond the scope of the physician as sole provider. The foremost responsibility of medicine and its actual area of expertise is the biologic dimension of health care. This is the case whether the physician be cardiologist, endocrinologist, or internist. The primary care physician should be more sensitive to the psychological and social dimensions of health care, but genuine expertise in these is unrealistic and, in fact, such an expectation is naive to their complexities and attendant training requirements.

THE POTENTIAL ROLE OF SOCIAL WORK IN PRIMARY CARE

The challenge of the primary care model for social work is at the same time an opportunity for the profession. The wide scope of primary care requires the social work role to be that of a broadly based clinician, with superior interventive skills in some areas and at least basic screening and assessment skills with nearly any patient presentation conceivable. Often the social worker could be asked to handle problems beyond his or her capacities[35] yet the primary medical practitioner may trust that the clinical social worker in primary care will know as well when to seek further specialized consultation. For instance, considering the reported high prevalence (43.3%) of psychiatric disorders among patients in ambulatory medical care settings[36, 37] and with estimates of psychiatric morbidity among general hospital inpatients ranging from 30 to 60 percent,[38, 39] there is a definite need for clinical social workers in health care to have both a psychiatric background and a clear understanding about when to seek consultation from the team psychiatrist. This interface with psychiatry is best achieved through the development of interdisciplinary teams[40] which will be described as the chapter proceeds.

Since primary care represents an approach to health care rather than a branch of medicine, the skills required of the clinical social worker in this comprehensive model can serve as a basis for clinical social work throughout health care. Social workers focused in specialized areas of health care such as oncology, rehabilitation medicine, or burn units can adopt the comprehensive clinical approach of the primary care social work model while continuing to develop complementary specialty skills unique to their area.[41]

The need for the comprehensive primary care approach for clinical social work in health is supported by estimates that between 20 and 70 percent of all medical visits involve biopsychosocial problems such as complaints of the worried well, substance abuse, domestic violence, sexual dysfunction, stress reactions, educational problems, and grief as well as more classical psychiatric disorders such as anxiety and depression.[42] Many of these presentations require the clinical social worker to have a basic understanding of biomedical and psychiatric issues; for example, the social worker must appreciate that sexual dysfunction can be secondary to (that is, caused by) diabetes mellitus and does not always represent a "psychological" problem. Working with patients who have substance abuse problems requires a knowledge of the appropriate use of toxicology screens, symptoms indicative of withdrawal states, behavioral manifestations of different toxicotives, and so on. Other problems on the list of presentations mentioned above require the clinical social worker to have a sophisticated psychotherapeutic understanding of grief and of the dynamics of depression, in addition to an appreciation for the fact that such symptoms may have medical and psychiatric aspects. Further, the clinical social worker would need to know what temporary community shelters are available in domestic violence situations, and equally important, when to offer these alternatives and when to help reconcile the parties in conflict.

The complexities of real patients, including an interaction of biomedical and psychological factors, must be faced within the medical system. While it might be tempting to consider simply referring these patients immediately to other facilities, studies of the health system indicate that such solutions fail to grasp what health care is all about. Medical sociologist David Mechanic doubts that these patients actually could be successfully rerouted to other sources of assistance. "Since such patients appear with problems at medical settings, and since such problems are intertwined in a complex fashion with bodily symptoms and feelings, the responsible course is to develop a strategy for patient management at the point at which help is sought."[43]

A central role of the clinical social worker involved in a primary care approach would be evaluating these cases as referred by other primary care disciplines, treating some, arranging for treatment with others, seeking consultation as needed, and utilizing intrafacility, social network, and community resources as determined by the comprehensive evaluative process. It has been suggested that screening mechanisms be developed to identify patients at high risk using epidemiologic data rather than relying on physician referral[44] but it appears at present that social work staff shortages could limit the ability to meet identified needs no matter how specific the screening instrument. Another idea is the development of a screening mechanism designed to preserve the use of a scarce resource—social work—by setting priorities as to which patients need the services most and by offering services only when social work intervention has some likelihood of solving the problem.[45] Experience in the practice setting already indicates that there is a vast population for which social work intervention may at least be more appropriate and less costly than medical intervention. One recent estimate is that from 10 to 40 percent of all primary practice contacts are for nonmedical reasons, and that the time physicians allot to nonmedical problems is as high as 50 percent.[46]

While there is evidence in the United States that the use of social workers is a major cost effective component in primary medical care,[47] studies in Great Britain indicate that the involvement of social workers led to more physician time being spent on cases.[48] Nevertheless, the majority of the physicians felt that the time was well spent because it also led to the provision of more comprehensive care.

DEFINING INTERDISCIPLINARY ROLES

There is a great difference of opinion as to what services physicians see social workers being capable of delivering and as to which cases physicians are willing to refer to social workers. In the United States, some observers maintain that most physicians accept social workers as resource finders and enablers, but reject social work's potential with the psychosocial aspects, let alone biopsychosocial.[49] One study of private physicians in Washington, D.C. revealed that these providers reported referring problems related to money and resource access to social workers but tended to refer couples in conflict, child or spouse abuse, suicide attempts, substance abuse, and abortion counseling mainly to psychiatrists or other physicians.[50] However, another survey of U.S. family practice residents in the mid-1970s demonstrated that when physicians are trained with social workers, they tend to identify the psychotherapeutic capacities of social work more highly. The latter group of residents ranked the functions of social work as (1) financial aid, (2) patient evaluation, and (3) service coordination, in that order.[51] Many of the British studies represent the other extreme. Semistructured interviews of physicians whose practice involved intervention of social work services in one South London study revealed that the social work referral was to some extent replacing the use of psychotropic drugs and that patients previously referred to psychiatrists were now being referred to social workers employed in their own general practice.[52] Another study found that the social worker was thought by physicians not to have been helpful in only 5 or 6 percent of the cases referred.[53] Generally, British research indicates that the physicians are more likely to understand and value the different capacities of the social worker when the latter is on-site and in regular person-to-person contact with the physician.[54]

While physicians' views may greatly affect referral patterns, identifying medical providers' perceptions of the potential contributions of social work and psychiatry does not answer what services and skills each discipline actually has to offer. In a review of several studies of social work in primary care in the United States, the role of the clinical social worker has been described as helpful with:

- economic problems: income, housing, food
- health: mental health, adjustment to physical illness, arranging for health care
- family issues: separation and divorce, adolescent adjustments, abortion, adoption, child abuse and neglect, education, and the law.[55]

In England, where the contribution of social work to primary care has been studied most extensively, four social work roles have been identified:

- assessors of social difficulties,
- links and coordinators with social services
- psychotherapists,
- helping to secure the patient's cooperation in medical care.[56]

A clear role distinction between the social worker and the psychiatrist in these studies is not to be found, however. This lack of clarity among the disciplines only further confuses the referring physicians. The Caversham Project, which looked at 9,000 patients served in a primary care group practice, 1,000 of which were referred to the social worker over a four-year period, mentioned the need for a psychiatrist only with the chronically mentally ill. Even then, the contribution of the psychiatrist is implied to be one of greater depth than the social worker, rather than a distinct and different role. "The team felt in need of regular consultative sessions with a psychiatrist, not only to define the problems and diagnoses more sharply, but also to establish more appropriate ways of helping these patients and their families."[57]

For the primary care approach to be effectively comprehensive, the contributing professions need to have a basic understanding of the unique skills and limitations of each discipline.[58] The medical provider needs to be able to rely on the clinical social worker to provide a core evaluation covering the biopsychosocial continuum and to expect the social worker to call upon the psychiatrist when the skills of the psychiatrist are required. To accomplish this task, the clinical social worker needs to be able to recognize the signs and symptoms which would indicate a psychiatrist's intervention and, concomitantly, to appreciate the likely outcomes of various psychiatric interventions. In making such assessments and in understanding the appropriate role of the psychiatrist, the clinical social worker is actually functioning as a "front line" component of a multidisciplinary psychiatric service. Such assessment services can be within the capacities of clinical social work to provide and need not be misunderstood as replacing the unique and specialized role of the psychiatrist. It is likely at this time that social workers could provide this service if they were working daily within a comprehensive team approach in which both social workers and psychiatrists were routine collaborators.[59]

For instance, the clinical social worker needs to be able to recognize and list the symptoms of a major depression[60] to question whether the depression is primary or could be secondary to a known or potentially undiagnosed medical condition, and to be aware of the likely treatments and their outcomes. The social worker who knows that the symptoms of a major depression (disturbed sleep and appetite, dysphoric mood, decreased energy, and thoughts of doom or suicide) can be alleviated 70 percent of the time in just a few weeks with antidepressant medication, would not be likely to provide an exclusive "talking" therapy and delay seeking the consultation of the psychiatrist. In fact, seeing psychotherapy as an alternative to chemotherapy in the treatment of major depression, rather than as essential complementary treatments as the research has demonstrated[61] would not only unnecessarily prolong a patient's suffering, but could also diminish the social worker's credibility as a clinician with other team members. Similarly, if a medical provider refers to the team social worker an elderly patient with recent onset of depression, reportedly over a rent increase and consequent need to relocate, the social worker needs to be aware of the importance of possible medication-induced changes in mood as could happen with a patient's use of steroids for her arthritis. The identified housing problem may need direct resolution but the case also would need to be presented to the psychiatrist since the steroids could account for the depressive symptoms. It may turn out that the steroid regimen is changed and the patient feels she could manage the rent increase after all. Or it might turn out that even though an antidepressant was prescribed, the patient still needed help solving financial and housing problems. In one case, an elderly gentleman had not been aware that his rent increase made him eligible for a nearly proportionate increase in food stamps which offset the rent increase. Moreover, the social worker spent four sessions over six weeks engaging the patient in a plan to eat his lunches at a senior citizens' meal site, resulting in his saving a small but significant amount in his monthly food budget and reducing his social isolation which was another factor known to contribute to his depressive symptons.

THE IMPACT OF CLINICAL SKILLS ON TEAM DEVELOPMENT

The psychological and social contributions of the clinical social worker in primary care are indispensable to comprehensive health practice. The impact of these clinical social work skills can be strengthened when the social worker is able to cultivate a basic knowledge of the biobehavioral dimension of patients as well. For example, the social worker who contends that a patient is psychogenically depressed but has failed to notice potential indicators of underlying organicity such as disinhibited affect (unprovoked tearfulness which abruptly starts and stops unrelated to apparent stimuli) demonstrates unfamiliarity with an important clinical dimension and therefore deprives the patient of consideration and consultation of a more complete spectrum of differential diagnostic possibilities. It is unlikely that any clinical social worker at this point could become aware of the significance of such signs unless there is ongoing integration with a well-trained psychiatrist. Nevertheless, the social worker who repeatedly excludes or minimizes the biomedical dimension may not enjoy respect as a clinician in the medical setting even though he or she has not had medical training beyond the team experience. To be accepted and optimally useful as a clinician in the health setting, the clinical social work role requires the skill to enable the social worker to pursue a complete biopsychosocial assessment even when the patient's problem seems to have a facile psychosocial explanation. For example: in one such case in which the social worker identified financial and marital problems as a cause of depression, the patient's CT scan was subsequently read as positive for a subdural hematoma. The blood clot was subsequently drained in a surgical proce-dure and the patient's depressive symptoms, bizarre crying, and attentional deficits were alleviated. Not only was the patient's life saved, but his marital and financial difficulties were reversed with proper brain functioning restored. Ironically, presurgery evaluative sessions with the family had proved to be diagnostically misleading because the wife and two adult daughters were vague historians who were unsure as to whether they had ever witnessed similar behavior on the part of the patient in the past nor could they help chart a course of the present symptoms. Nevertheless, the evaluating social worker etched out enough history on family genograms and life line scales to account for the symptoms along the lines of functional psychiatric illness. Exclusive focus on the psychosocial diagnostic dimensions, in the absence of appropriate attention to the biomedical sphere can tend to make these former contributions less credible in later cases when the psychosocial factors may in fact be critical.

The more the social worker grasps issues involving the biomedical dimensions of behavior, the easier it becomes for the social worker to recognize when the more medically trained disciplines are ignoring critical psychosocial elements. It is only when the social worker increases knowledge in the biomedical area that he or she can fulfill the responsibility to contribute a psychosocial diagnostic formulation without being intimidated or misled by the technical language of medicine. While this unique social work contribution may not be popular or easily penetrable, it could be essential to completing an accurate diagnosis and a workable treatment plan. For example, it can happen that a psychiatrist with a medical rather than biopsychosocial orientation might identify a symptoms cluster indicating the need for psychopharmacologic intervention. However, the personality structure and social context of the patient might be overlooked even though including this would provide a more comprehensive perspective crucial to an effective and realistic treatment plan.

Example: A 27-year-old woman was admitted to the general hospital after a suicide attempt. She was described as an ex-heroin addict, married to an ex-heroin addict, both with chaotic histories of abusing their two children, criminal convictions, unemployment, welfare, and a documented record of noncompliance with past psychiatric providers. The psychiatrist identified a symptom picture of affective disorder (depression) and concluded that this had been untreated and was the key to improving the patient's functioning. However, the treatment plan did not take into account the personality and social systems dimensions of treating this psychiatric disorder.

First, the husband was relied upon as a treatment ally despite his drug history and record of antisocial behavior.

Second, the state hospital was expected to admit the patient and monitor the trial on antidepressants after discharge from the general hospital even though expecting the state facility to provide this service was unprecedented and, therefore, unlikely to succeed from a systems perspective.

Finally, little data and focus was provided at the disposition conference on the social circumstances of the patient's life that could be useful in understanding if these might shed some light on the suicide attempt.

Such data to consider include change in income level or source of income, eviction notices, utility shut-offs, petitions for child custody, welfare fraud investigation, factory closings, food stamp adjustments, disability reviews, and probation violation hearings. Any one of these can prove to be the significant event in individuals regressing below their normal functioning. Even those accustomed to a lifestyle of disruption and turmoil can experience one added circumstance as a final intolerable burden. Carefully seeking out such data can be essential in making sociotherapeutic interventions which might help the patient reestablish a chaotic but nonsuicidal baseline level of functioning.

In the case described, the main focus was too narrowly drawn around the identification of a "treatable" major depression. A week later, the case was re-presented at the same disposition conference. The patient had attempted suicide again, this time more lethally by stabbing herself five times with a pair of scissors. The patient had signed herself out of the state hospital after two days. The psychiatrist described his intentions of repeating the earlier plan, but adding to the earlier plan the strategy of committing the patient to the state hospital and initiating antidepressant drug treatment while the patient was recovering in the general hospital from the stab wounds. Social work staff pointed out that the state hospital would be unlikely to accept such a commitment even with the "pressure" promised by the psychiatrist and would probably let the patient go within the first 48 hours (the time required to have two physicians attest to continuing the certification for the full ten day commitment). The state facility would do this because it had been reorganized for chronic care for several years and would provide acute care only for psychotic patients. These psychotics were usually schizophrenics, predominantly readmitted deinstitutionalized patients and rarely if ever "borderline" or chaotic characters even during the psychotic phase of a borderline's turmoil.

One of the social workers at the earlier conference had recommended engaging the patient's child welfare worker as leverage to establish her on antidepressants at her local mental health center. When the social worker inquired about this at the later conference, the psychiatrist merely said that "child welfare wasn't helpful." Social work staff had to push to get the social dimension explored and the social work challenge that commitment would not work was termed "cynical" by one of the other team psychiatrists. The conference concluded with the plan focused on the antidepressant treatment.

This case illustrates several points. First, the clinical social worker must be prepared to function at times in a setting in which the biomedical dimensions are solely addressed at the expense of the psycho-social/environmental perspective. The social worker may function as the voice for the appropriate consideration of the psychosocial dimensions of a case. The team could therefore benefit from the fact that the social worker had a knowledgeable grasp of the psychiatric disorder under discussion and the biomedical (i.e., antidepresent) intervention being recommended. The social worker in this case was aware of this regimen and knew under which conditions it could be effective. Further, the social worker was able to make a valuable team contribution because of a solid understanding of chaotic patients, the welfare system, child welfare, the state hospital, the capacities of the local mental health center, experience with criminal offenders, and experience with addictive personalities. Without knowing the diagnostic issues involved with the psychiatric disorder and its treatment, however, the social worker would not have been able to articulate recommendations for a clinical reformulation of the intervention strategies and treatment priorities in the case.

This case also illustrates a cardinal principle of primary care mentioned earlier: patients who present in the health setting cannot be easily transferred to outside providers. The elaborate treatment plan proposed by the psychiatrist in this case was established with the expectation that it would and could be carried out by professionals and institutions outside of the setting in which the patient presented. When the health setting cannot offer the service, the plan must be modified to conform to what services are available. This is not a cynical but a clinical perspective. To be comprehensive, the clinical service must be biopsychosocial in establishing the treatment plan as well as the diagnosis. Discharge planning and community referral requires that the clinician take into account what kind of care is realistically available. Cases such as the one described require a full-time primary clinician to be therapeutically available and on-site to coordinate care. A less perfect but often effective alternative is a full-time community advocate with some clinical skill to adopt the case and relentlessly pursue the patient and the treatment. Sometimes a public welfare caseworker, a child welfare worker, or a parole officer can be engaged to champion the patient's needs. These professionals can be effective when they have basic therapeutic skills, some financial or legal leverage over the patient to augment client motivation, and when they have community mental health services (CMHCs) available to them. This latter element is increasingly missing because the CMHCs are focusing almost exclusively on chronic care. Considering this, the primary care clinicians in health settings are faced with becoming truly comprehensive with on-site 24-hour service or by developing treatment plans tailored to realistic resources. Since this era of economic contraction affects all health and mental health facilities, it is likely that clinicians will need to cultivate more skill than ever with social-environmental community resource considerations. It is also not helpful to community relations or to staff morale to downgrade what resources are available or to try to dictate to agencies what services they should provide for cases being referred to them. The referring clinician performs most effectively as a community consultant when patient care plans are formulated as closely as possible to what the provider resource can deliver. Disposition plans beyond the usual run the risk of failure when a provider agency does not possess the skill or system to meet the services requested. At present, many CMHCs, for instance, are so overwhelmed with cases and so short staffed from cutbacks, that time-consuming plans for chaotic patients may be even less possible at the CMHC than at the referring health care facility itself.

Even when optimal resources are available, comprehensive clinical care requires the matching of intervention strategies with the patient's personality style. With the noncompliant patient, treatment plans must take into consideration mechanisms of leverage or payoffs which could be tapped to reward the patient for complying. Involvement with a patient's eviction problems, for instance, can develop a bond and suggest possible contingencies for taking medication or modifying behavior in return for concrete problem solving.

Example: A 61-year-old widow and factory worker presented often in walk-in clinic requesting help for numerous social problems and medication for her headaches. She had significant hypertension but seldom followed medical advice including taking her medication. A repeated complaint was her dissatisfaction with her rooming house, particularly her leaky refrigerator which was ruining the linoleum she had laid down herself. She was not an effective negotiator with her landlord despite her verbal aggressiveness around the clinic. She resisted regular follow-up in medical clinic and remained an unpredictable visitor to unscheduled walk-in clinic morning sessions. Referral to the clinic's social worker led to productive interest in the patient's refrigerator and deteriorating linoleum.

The social worker volunteered to engage the landlord into fixing the leak and replacing the linoleum if the patient enrolled in medical clinic and took her antihypertensive medication. The social worker won the assistance of the landlord by expressing concern about code violations inadvertently mentioned by the patient. He agreed to fix the refrigerator and floor if the violations were overlooked. This was easy to accommodate since the patient was most interested in other issues. Moreover, the social worker realized that the legal process involved in correcting housing code violations would take months, and the gutter and plaster problems in this case were relatively minor anyway. Through this process with the social worker and beyond, the patient complied with her medication regimen, eventually felt better, and found a better apartment as well.

Social work expertise of combining social context and concrete services with an understanding of personality and network dynamics may not always alter what at times is clearly an inappropriate team focus on biomedical issues. But this need not discourage contributing clinical social workers. Repeated formulations of the social work perspective provide other team members with an opportunity to understand and integrate this dimension into their clinical thinking. Just as social workers do not easily absorb biomedical diagnosis and the medical aspects of psychiatric intervention into their practice, it similarly requires daily collaborative practice for the other medically trained disciplines to recognize the interrelatedness of the social environment with physical and mental functioning. A common finding, in fact, throughout the vast British research social work in primary care was that medical staff tended to recognize the valuable role of the social work practitioner and in so doing provided more comprehensive care proportionate to increasingly daily contact with social workers.[62, 63, 64] In time, the effective team integrates these divergent yet complementary contributions, and the process requires a healthy tolerance for conflict at every stage of development.

The interdisciplinary health care team approach is as susceptible to group dynamics as any constituted group of human beings. In this process, a basic grasp of biomedical issues can also help the clinical social worker recognize when medical staff might rely on the technical concepts of their training to navigate the direction of a case discussion or to minimize the formulations of the nonmedical group members. It is human nature at times of personal uncertainty or group rivalry for one member to use any leverage such as a knowledge base to increase power or control over other group members.

Example: A 23-year-old single woman seen sporadically in ambulatory medical clinic over a two-year period presented with complaints of stomach distress and auditory hallucinations. Medical examination including the toxicology screen were negative, after which she was asked to be evaluated by the team clinical social worker. She had no significant medical history and no psychiatric history though the social worker gathered from the patient's family that she had been slowly withdrawing from social relationships for the past 18 months. The patient had continued to work as a clerk in a bookstore but conveyed that in recent months a number of customers had been "studying her." The patient admitted hearing a voice she thought might be God's and she expressed a tentative belief that she might have to die soon. The patient did not have adequate health insurance for private care but did live within the catchment area of a good community mental health center (CMHC). After discussion with the referring physician, the social worker arranged for referral by ambulance to the local CMHC. At the team conference later, the social worker presented the case as a first psychotic break, probably schizophrenic with a positive family psychiatric history of a schizophrenic aunt reported by the patient's mother. The social worker explained the disposition of transferring the patient to the emergency service of the CMHC rather than wait for a routine appointment because of the quasisuicidal ideation obtained. Though the referring physician had not yet joined the team meeting, the psychiatrist expressed alarm that he had not been consulted and emphasized possible diagnosis of organic psychosis, secondary to the name of a stomach condition with which the social worker was totally unfamiliar. The social worker expressed surprise that the psychiatrist wanted to be consulted on every psychiatric case, especially one in which the disposition seemed safe and appropriate. The psychiatrist voiced disagreement that the disposition was safe, considering the organic hypothesis for the psychosis. The social worker became disturbed pointing out she had discussed the case medically with the referring physician. At this point, the primary medical provider entered and thought the psychiatrist was advocating referral of the patient to a local private psychiatric hospital, rather than the the CMHC. The medical provider had debated this point with the social worker earlier and thought he was now hearing support for this argument from the team psychiatrist. The social worker repeated the substance of her earlier response to the physician, that the patient had to be examined by the local CMHC before outside hospitalization could be arranged and the decision would be, by statute, the province of the CMHC. When the physician realized that the dispute between the psychiatrist and the social worker had been over the organic issues, he minimized this diagnostic consideration, citing literature with which the psychiatrist seemed familiar to support his point. Later, the psychiatrist told the social worker that he agreed with her diagnosis; and each agreed on a procedural change—he would be called on all psychotic patients and any patients with any more than mild suicidal ideation.

No matter how much familiarity clinical social workers develop with biomedical and psychiatric information, there will be times when they will not be able to distinguish legitimate issues raised by medical staff from those more reflective of professional rivalry or other dynamics. As team members become more comfortable with each other, a useful question for the social worker to ask is "How likely would it be that this biomedical issue could explain the patient's symptoms?

Interdisciplinary Role Blurring

Based on the wide scope of services within health care, especially within the primary care approach, the team concept optimally enhances comprehensive care, even though role confusion and overlap can occur among the contributing disciplines. Not only should duplication of services be avoided, but role blurring can create confusion for the referring physicians, patients, and providers themselves. While overlapping of certain skills such as psychotherapy may occur, clinicians of each profession should be clear about their unique disciplinary contribution to the team.

It is true that individual clinicians may bring to the team some prior experience that cuts across disciplines. The nurse may have done some community social service type work, the social worker may have been an attendant or orderly, while the primary care physician may have spent some time in a psychiatric residency before choosing medicine. Moreover, daily exposure to the thinking of the other professions in the context of diagnostic and dispositional conferences does in fact cultivate some basic interchangeable skills. Cross-fertilization can be a helpful and healthy asset to comprehensive care and team cohesion as long as clinicians do not pursue the domain of another discipline at the expense of abandoning the duties and ongoing cultivation of needed skills in their own profession. The psychiatrist, for instance, might enjoy community work to the degree that he becomes so immersed in contact with welfare workers, disability review teams, and family therapy sessions that he also becomes unavailable for psychopharmacologic evaluations or primary psychiatric consultations. The social worker might develop such an interest in the dimensions of medical diagnosis or psychiatric evaluation that he begins to accept more responsibility in this area than is in his or the patient's interest. The social worker might then lose touch with an awareness of community resources or cease to as fully explore the social/environmental issues in case evaluations. It is not uncommon in a busy hospital clinic or emergency room in fact for a social worker to be handed a patient in turmoil without a medical workup and for the social worker to have to struggle to obtain medical or psychiatric consultation. It is understandable that the social worker may feel resigned to ruling out medical issues without benefit of consultation, but this role should never be accepted. Frequently, social workers in health and mental health do find themselves asked by physicians to assess a disability determination; they then often experience a struggle obtaining the physician's necessary signature on the form or gaining the medical provider's cooperation not to sign the disability form as part of a rehabilitative treatment plan. The pressures of utilization review in the inpatient discharge planning process also find social workers being expected to make quasimedical decisions when asked to estimate discharge dates without the benefit of a team conference. These issues need to be addressed in interdisciplinary team meetings; one service is not adequate without the other.

As discussed in the previous section, the social worker does need to know a basic level of biomedical information in order to organize a biopsychosocial core evaluation and to know when and why to seek medical or psychiatric consultation, but should never be expected to assume medical duties or responsibilities. Extending social work skills from psychosocial to biopsychosocial is not intended to make the social worker a physician. Similarly, the need for medical staff to develop a sensitivity to psychosocial issues is not aimed at expecting expertise with these issues. It would be rare for even the psychiatrist to master the domain of social work without jeopardizing the cultivation of expertise with the medical aspects of diagnosing disorders of mood, thought, and/or behavior.

While the psychiatrist and the social worker on the health care team will undoubtedly experience the most pointed overlap with psychotherapy skills, too much focus on this debate misses the point in understanding the unique disciplinary contribution of each.

PRACTICAL CLINICAL INTERVENTIONS

Social context issues and concrete services are integral components of comprehensive clinical care in the health setting. The needs and coping style of the patient population, in fact, often require very practical interventions. While patient presentations in a medical clinic setting may initially focus on bodily symptoms, as much as 50 percent of the help required turns out to be nonmedical.[65] One study of 1,000 referrals to social work in medical practice found that the physicians most often (41 percent) sought consultation when patients presented with vague psychosomatic complaints.[66] Some clinical social workers may be inclined to treat such patients using an intrapsychic therapy model. However, Mechanic[67] recommends a nonintrapsychic approach in the practice of primary care: helping to define issues, exploring alternative coping strategies for patients, and if necessary instructing patients in different coping behaviors. In the large scale British Caversham Project, the social worker "learned to try simple solutions first, realizing for instance that progress at work or in a leisure pursuit can have considerable repercussions on difficult personal problems and relationships. This implied that she paid more time than she or other social workers have done in the past to patients' versions of their most vexing problems, giving up the quest for 'underlying problems' when they were not directly relevant."[68]

Often social workers in the health setting are faced with patients who have numerous complaints but have difficulty defining problems or solutions. A useful way to sharpen the cognitive focus is to ask the patient "What is the worst problem for you right now?" Frequently, the patient who had rattled off ten unmanageable issues will choose one. Next, the social worker or other clinician can find out a possible solution as well as what the patient expects to happen by then asking "What do you think will happen with that?" In gaining some closure or in developing a mutual contract with the patient the question "What do you think makes sense to do now?" tends to elicit both the patient's perspective and expectations.

Example: The social worker was called by a primary care medical resident to see a patient in what was described as "desperate circumstances." The patient, Mrs. Connors, was a 46-year-old divorced woman, employed as an attendant at the state hospital, being examined in medical clinic on her day off. Though emergency situations were normally referred to the emergency room crisis team, the social worker agreed to see the case when his present patient interview ended because he knew the resident was newly adjusting to the clinic and he felt the description of the situation lent itself to brief intervention. The resident, Dr. Horn, said the patient had no heat in her house and her water pipes had burst. It was a bitter, cold New England February afternoon. The social worker met with the patient for about ten minutes from which the following dialogue is an excerpt:

Social Worker: How long has the heat been off?

Mrs. Connors: Since September. My oldest daughter had the gas in her name and she moved out owing a $760 bill.

Social Worker: You owe a back bill also?

Mrs. Connors: Yes, it was turned off in my name two years ago. Now they've combined the accounts but I've got it down to $500. (The patient shows the legal agreement on which she has been making $100 per month payments).

Social Worker: How have you been managing for heat?

Mrs. Connors: I have a quartz heater so I've kept the electric bill up to date.

Social Worker: I understand you have no running water?

Mrs. Connors: Three weeks ago the main line froze and burst. My cousin next door says he can fix it cheaper than a plumber when spring comes.

Social Worker: You use his facilities 'til then?

Mrs. Connors: Not every day. I go to my daughter's around the corner or my eldest girl a block away when the young one gets moody.

Social Worker: What needs to be done today?

Mrs. Connors: I have to get a note to get back to work.

Social Worker: I see from your chart that Dr. Horn is trying to help you cut back on your drinking.

Mrs. Connors: I have to have a note or I'll get suspended. I've used all my sick time.

Social Worker: I'll talk to Dr. Horn about the note if you'll agree to meet with me on your day off next week to get a better picture of what's happening with you.

Mrs. Connors: What time?

The social worker assumed that the heat had not been turned off that very day because the resident appeared more worried than the patient. Moreover, patients often have other interim alternatives and the task is to elicit these; sometimes even the patient has forgotten his or her options. The social worker knew the patient had a back bill since it would not have been in her daughter's name in the first place.

The mention of the daughter's name in context rendered a beginning outline of social supports. The fact that the patient had a civil service job demonstrated a level of intelligence to pass an exam and was evidence of a steady, higher than welfare income. The social worker reacted to the heat and water shutoffs as matters needing only explanation from the patient. If the answers did not reveal self-management, the social worker would have pursued problem solving on these issues. With the original presenting problems temporarily in hand, the social worker focused on asking the patient what the actual current problem was ("What needs to be done today?") Even after patient lists ten problems, it is useful to ask the focused question "What brings you to the clinic today?" Surprisingly, a patient will sometimes list a problem not even mentioned among the original ten. Many patients have learned to obtain the emotional interest of professionals by listing all their daily problems of survival even though they have most of these in order or expect little change in these areas. Finally, the social worker recognized an area of dysfunction, alcohol abuse, which suggested a priority of intervention and engaged the patient in a preliminary contract contingent upon having a note signed to get back into work. The entire intervention was made with a knowledge of personality dynamics, coping styles, and community experience but translated in practice onto the terrain of tangible, real life problems. It is on this level that the medical staff and the patients in the health setting are effectively engaged.

SOCIAL NETWORK/SHORT-TERM TREATMENT

A number of studies which have examined the nature of referrals to social work in the context of health practice have found that between 47 and 52 percent have been for concrete services.[69, 70] Yet even when both hospital inpatient and outpatient referrals have been included, social workers tend to deliver a higher percentage of counseling and mental health services rather than concrete services.[71] Interviews with pediatric and adult social workers in medical clinic settings reveal that they do prefer to provide psychotherapeutic over concrete services.[72] However, other research evidence demonstrates that counseling and some psychiatric service such as psychobiologic assessment or medication recommendation is in fact required in nearly 20 percent of the concrete service referrals themselves despite the original perception of the referring medical provider.[73] It was also found that social work assessment in medical practice most frequently led to crisis-oriented or short-term intervention with both concrete and psychotherapeutic services.[74] While some research has not provided a conceptual focus on the virtually inseparable relationship between concrete services and mental health needs, other studies have emphasized this connection[75] and recognized the challenge to use this combination to engage patients and achieve comprehensive care.[76]

The interwoven quality of tangible social deficits and emotional disturbance presenting so commonly in the health setting often creates a sense of urgency in the tenor of the referrals. The need for food, shelter, or transportation to obtain medical care are so tied to issues of survival that they generate an atmoshpere of crisis for the referring medical providers even when the patients in need have already made some manageable adjustment to these conditions. This is partly because the patient's self-management is not always immediately visible or easily identified. Insofar as such situations initially define themselves as emergencies, social workers regularly intervene on a crisis basis. In most busy settings some alternate coverage systems for emergencies (e.g. crisis teams) may need to be developed in order to respond to this need.[77] Similar to the example cited earlier of the patient without heat or water in the cold of winter, crisis contacts tend to result in immediate problem solving, drawing upon the self-management and existent resources within the command of the patient, and concluding with a helping contract focused on specific short-term follow-up interventions. The follow-up with Mrs. Connors provides an illustration of short-term intervention utilizing social network resources.

Example: Mrs. Connors did come for a few sessions, reduced but did not terminate her alcohol abuse, and improved her work attendance before fading out of contact with the social worker. A year later, she recontacted the clinic when her employer threatened suspension again. This time, she allowed the involvement of her family in the helping process, though contact with those around her revealed that her boyfriend provided a more therapeutic alliance. Although he had a drinking problem as well, the only income of both the patient and her boyfriend was her civil service job. The boyfriend proved quite successful in the short term, helping her cut back on drinking and he took it upon himself to get her up for work each day to safeguard their one good financial resource. His added attention improved the patient's mood and attitude and in return for working, she got him to spend more time with her and less time playing cards with his friends.

Outpatient social work interventions in the health setting commonly occur in some sporadic fashion over a long duration. Medical patients seldom seek ongoing psychotherapy but do see the health facility as available when needed for a multitude of complaints. When the immediate stress or concrete agenda is addressed, the patient often ceases contact until the next problem arises. In one review of 70 patients involved with social service in a general hospital outpatient clinic, staff was found to have experienced some contact with 22 of these patients even six years later.[78] Further, because of the sociodemographic characteristics of patients presenting in the health setting (e.g., poor, living alone), these brief, sporadic interventions more regularly involve collaborative or linking relationships with patient's companions or landlords than with family. In the study mentioned above, only nine percent of the 70 cases reviewed involved school-age children.[79] In another study, 50 percent were unemployed in an area with a 9 percent unemployment rate; 43 percent lived alone.[80] Accordingly, the skills required involve less of a traditional family therapy orientation and more facility engaging other social network contacts over issues such as rent, housing, and financial assistance combined with a capacity to identify, treat, and/or arrange treatment for exacerbating or interwoven psychiatric disorders.

RISK/BENEFIT RATIOS IN INFORMATION GATHERING

While comprehensiveness is an essential attribute of primary care its achievement cannot be approached without some calculated caution on the part of the clinician. The practitioner needs to be aware of the risk/benefit ratio always present in the very process of gathering information from any patient. For instance, it is important to take a sexual history but completeness and accuracy are often not obtainable in the initial interview. The historical discomfort among physicians, social workers, nurses, and others in approaching the task of assessing sexual functioning has been transformed into a sense of determination by many contemporary clinicians to gather "all the facts" at the outset. Despite an easing of societal mores, the potential desensitization of the clinician on the subject of sex can lead to a misperception of the patient's affect with the issue. If the patient's feelings are not estimated and effectively attended to, the benefit of assertively acquiring the information can be jeopardized by the risk of causing undue stress, influencing a distortion of the data, frightening the patient away from returning again, or all three. The enthusiastic practitioner can be left with the "facts" but not the "true facts" and possibly with no chance to correct the misperceptions forever detailed in the patient's record.

The goal of comprehensive care is achieved by the clinician knowing both the data to be obtained and an effective method of obtaining it. It takes time to get to know any patient and some take more time than others. The personality style and areas of sensitivity must be noted and matched with different interviewing strategies. The patient who seems to enjoy listing the details of sexual experiences requires benevolent focus on only the issues pertinent to an understanding of the patient's functioning. Entertainment of the clinician demands careful avoidance to insure that the patient is not embellishing the narrative to please the interviewer. Similarly, the patient who minimizes or denies sexual content can be supported away from guilt or embarrassment by the clinician commenting "These things are hard to talk about with someone you don't know . . . maybe we can get back to it at another time." The permission to leave the subject often allows the patient the feeling of control that frees him or her to commence exploration of it with greater comfort even at that moment. In either case, it is of value to ask the original evaluation questions in later interviews should contact be maintained. Sometimes it is profitable to ask the identical questions even later in the same interview. More accurate and less colored details can become more accessible to the patients' consciousness once they feel safe with the clinician. The old maxim that a therapeutic alliance must be established is true for any helping relationship in the health setting and is not restricted to the psychotherapy context alone. Sometimes patients will consciously lie in early interviews to avoid self-criticism, to sidestep imagined disapproval from the clinician, or to report what they think might please the practitioner. Asking the basic questions again at a later time can provide more accuracy. The discrepancy need not be pointed out by the clinician unless some therapeutic work is intended. Should the clinician suspect memory deficits or other cognitive impairments, they can be assessed by mental status tests using content other than the affect-laden material.

The area of sexuality is by no means the only issue on which distortion or withholding of data pose risk/benefit ratios in the initial evaluation process. Money and strategies for financial problem solving commonly present obstacles to a comprehensive understanding of the patient's history and current status. Clinicians can sometimes be misled, for instance, by their apparent success in obtaining the amount of income on which welfare or disability patients live. It is a much different task to get a clear picture of how the money is spent. It is only when the patient feels he or she can trust the health care provider that information on these matters can be accurately gathered. When time is at a premium, as in the cases of social crises over shelter or food, the interviewer needs efficient interventive strategies to arrive at a sensible assessment and disposition. In these instances, the social worker on the team can be potentially the most effective. For example, in one case of a 57-year-old man on SSI for arthritis who routinely gambled a portion of his monthly disability income, the social worker stimulated a solution from this patient (who this time was without food one week short of a check day) by venturing "Do you think you'll have to wind up relying on the church soup kitchen?" The patient responded," If it comes to that, I'd rather borrow 15 bucks from my landlady again. She's always after me anyhow." In less urgent circumstances, the clinician can influence the patient's openness on the dispersal of income by demonstrating an absence of surprise on how people close to survival try to enjoy life. For instance, when helping a patient figure out a better budget, and when the social worker suspects the patient enjoys alcohol, it should be the social worker who volunteers a suggested sum for liquor.

The ability to gather comprehensive and accurate information from patients requires an appreciation for pace and an understanding of the impact of evaluation questions on patients. The goal of comprehensiveness cannot be achieved without recognition of the helping process as an inseparably mutual endeavor matching the skills of the practitioner with the differential needs of the presenting patients.

ENHANCING THE TEAM APPROACH

Different professionals working well together is proportionate to the recognition by any one discipline of the capacities of another. Such recognition is enhanced when the various disciplines are actually trained together in the same setting. While interdisciplinary training is more common in hospitals at present, health maintenance organizations (HMOs) and group practice settings are likely to provide similar team training opportunities in the years ahead. Some advances have been reported in establishing the meaning and spirit of primary care at the entry level of all the involved disciplines. The Houston Consortium Program[81] appears to be the most comprehensive example in integrating the efforts of the University of Houston Graduate School of Social Work, the University of Texas School of Nursing at Houston, and the Baylor College of Medicine (Departments of Psychiatry, Community Medicine, Internal Medicine, and Pediatrics), among others. In the Houston program, social workers train psychiatrists, primary care physicians, and nurses to develop sensitivity and expertise with the interface of psychological and social issues of patient care and are in turn trained by these disciplines in the neurologic, psychiatric, and generally biomedical dimensions of patient care. Others have reported that it is actually cost-effective to combine training and service delivery in the primary care approach to health care.[82]

A CASE ILLUSTRATION OF THE TEAM APPROACH IN PRIMARY CARE

The value of the intregration of disciplines is best realized in the practice of primary care. The following is typical of cases seen at Rhode Island Hospital's Primary Care Medical Unit, a general hospital outpatient program:

A 42-year-old, married man, recently unemployed, presented with headache, fatigue, increased irritability, and general malaise. He was worked up by a second-year medical resident whose primary diagnosis was essential hypertension, which had been previously undiagnosed. The patient had not been to a doctor in years and when he tried to get an appointment with the physician he last contacted, the patient learned that the practitioner had relocated to a distant suburb. The patient next considered the local hospital's outpatient department because, without a job, he was also without health insurance and he remembered the long established reputation of hospital outpatient clinics providing care for the indigent. The patient was prescribed a regimen of HydroDiuril and Inderal, two antihypertensive medications that were recommended by the resident's medical preceptor. At the day's end conference, the medical resident raised the issue of what to do about the patient's lack of money for medication. The resident had consulted with the social worker earlier in the afternoon while seeing the patient, and the social worker had been able to provide a short-term solution by utilizing an established hospital procedure of stamping the back of the patient's bill for later payment. It was agreed at the team conference that the patient would be interviewed by the social worker to see whether the patient might be eligible for governmental assistance or what other avenues could be possible.

The resident had been systematic in obtaining not only that the patient had a positive family history of hypertension, but of depression as well. Though the resident did not have enough data to make any conclusions about the extent or quality of the patient's present affective state, the social worker accepted this task as part of his routine biopsychosocial evaluative process, since he would be assessing the patient's financial predicament anyway.

The social worker interviewed the patient within a week. The social worker learned that the patient would have a two-week waiting period for unemployment compensation benefits since he had been laid off, and in the meantime would be eligible for temporary welfare, but the patient was too proud to apply for it. While application for medical assistance could have been made separately, the expected level of compensation from the unemployment benefits would have made the patient ineligible for medical assistance. The social worker actively involved this rather independently minded patient in the problem-solving process until a workable solution was mutually achieved. The patient accepted the social worker's help in mediating with the business office for the hospital to accept small but regular monthly payments from the patient until his financial circumstances were improved.

The social worker learned in the first interview that the patient's mother had been treated throughout her life for episodic depression and indeed the patient had some signs of clinical depression. However, the patient was not suicidal and it was agreed with the resident to pursue the treatment for the hypertension first. In this light, the social worker got the impression from the patient that the patient's spouse was his closest advisor. Accordingly, the social worker managed to have the patient also bring in his wife for the next few interviews. The wife was, initially, adamantly against her husband taking any medication. This seemed to be tied to unresolved feelings toward the death of her own father and resentment toward the medical establishment.

Over a couple of interviews, the social worker devoted specific focus on the wife's feelings towards the loss of her father. The social worker also arranged for the resident to come in for a brief time for each of the sessions and provide some conjoint education about hypertension and its treatment. The couple was successfully engaged in the treatment plan for the hypertension, but this was set back after a couple of interviews when the patient's depressive symptomatology seemed to increase.

The increase in the patient's depressive symptoms resulted in the social worker obtaining further consultation from the team psychiatrist. The psychiatrist evaluated the patient, prescribed a trial dose of an antidepressant medication and suggested an adjustment in the level of the antihypertensive. The resident implemented the recommendation, but the patient and spouse were reluctant to add further medication. The task of the social worker was to spend the next interview or so exploring the couple's concerns while drawing upon the resident's input for any further education on the medical regimen.

By the middle of the first interview following the consultation from the team psychiatrist, the patient and his wife were willing to go along with both the antihypertensive and the antidepressant medication. With compliance reinitiated, the patient's sleep improved in the first few days and by the end of the week, the patient was less irritable and had some newfound energy to begin a job hunt.

After about seven weeks, both the patient and spouse were feeling reasonably healthy and hopeful, and the social worker began to withdraw his services over the next two to three weeks. By the eleventh week, involvement with the Primary Care Medical Unit staff was down to a once-per-month contact with the primary care resident with as-needed consultation from the social worker and team psychiatrist. At this point, the patient had found a job but was continuing on the antihypertensive and antidepressant medication.

Case Discussion

In addition to the traditional medical preceptor, the Rhode Island Hospital Primary Care Medical Unit also functions with a daily behavioral sciences preceptor, a role which, on two afternoons, is filled by one of the team's clinical social workers. In the case just described, routine contributions from team consultants and the involvement of the primary care medical resident in the psychosocial aspects of patient's care is part of the program design of the Primary Care Medical Unit. The nature of the training program for primary care residents is such that gathering psychosocial data on the patient is encouraged to be part of each workup. It is still too soon to tell, however, whether these trainees are in fact obtaining substantially different patient data than the other residents in the regular program. In 1981-1982, there were four primary care residents among a total of about 40 residents all together rotating through the medical clinic. In 1982-1983, the primary care contingent increased to eight with proportionate increases expected in the years ahead, while the total number of residents will remain approximately the same. As the number of primary care residents continues to make up a greater proportion of the whole and if funds become proportinately available for the contributions of clinical social workers and psychiatrists, it is hoped that a thorough biopsychosocial approach will become uniformly established.

While the case described above provides a common scenario, if the clinician serving in the role of the behavioral sciences preceptor were not specifically scheduled to see the patient, the resident would have been coached by the team social worker or psychiatrist to more thoroughly evaluate the patient's mental status, including sleep, appetite, mood, thought content and process, hopes and aspirations, discouragement and disappointment, change in problem solving or coping abilities, possible mood cycles, as well as any medication history for depression and nature of response. While the team psychiatrist would be the primary expert in providing this kind of diagnostic consultation to the residents, social workers in the context of the primary care team have enough exposure to the elements of such evaluation that they too can contribute this teaching dimension to the training of residents. The presence of the psychiatrist on the team provides this added cross-fertilization to the social worker's capacity for consultation. With the benefit of the psychiatrist's influence, the social worker can develop the ability to help guide the medical resident in the identification of biomedical and psychiatric issues pertinent to presenting disorders of mood, thought, and/or behavior.

In the case example, the social worker's training in personality and family systems also emerged as critical to an effective and efficient treatment plan. First, this unemployed, hypertensive man was not easily engaged without an appreciation for his personality style. The patient turned out to be an extremely independent fellow who was not, by nature, demonstrative of his needs or distress. It required skill to recognize the patient's disguised sense of shame over his job loss, a circumstance well understood by a clinician whose training included psychodynamics, despite the nonexistence of a reality-based etiology. In actuality, the patient had been one of many permanently laid off by production cutbacks and a relocation of part of the firm's assembly. Though the patient possessed a quality of ingenuity and adaptive intelligence through which he had cognitively assessed the hospital outpatient service as an affordable resource, it was nevertheless incongruent with the patient's personality to easily seek any kind of help at all. A professionally sophisticated assessment of this individual trait was pointedly relevant to sizing up not only the parameters of the patient's need for a substitute health insurance, but was also central to engaging the patient in any solution to obtain such a subsidy as well as to cultivate an emotional atmosphere which would not be regressive to the patient's already assaulted self-esteem. In brief, one does not engage a self-reliant character by doing everything for the person.

Clients of all kinds need information, but the seasoned clinician *who also has long experience with concrete needs*, knows that those in need of these services often need far less information and certainly vastly less custodial service than is commonly imagined.

Whether the consumer of the concrete service be in crisis or just in need of a resource, the predominant strategy for enhancing self-esteem and thereby reestablishing baseline psychosocial functioning (and probably biologic as well), is that intervention that helps the patient mobilize the coping and problem-solving abilities which he or she already possesses. Sometimes these abilities are, in fact, forgotten by a person in stress and the service needed is one of taking an inventory of problem-solving alternatives reflective of the person's own history of handling similar problems, a history which should be obtained by the clinician. This type of clinical strategy is a creative adaption of crisis intervention practice. It is also a seasoned clinical understanding of what ego support really means. Providing concrete services directly for clients whether they be patients in health care or consumers of any helping process, can be an ego regressive rather than an ego supportive intervention. Doing things for patients rather than helping them utilize their own skills can actually make patients worse. This is especially true for individuals or systems that are already vulnerable due to a loss of health, a psychological distress, or the onset of some social or environmental hardship. A psychodynamic understanding of the independent, perhaps even stoical character teaches one that this personality type is a life stance against the fear of dependency (though almost universally unconsciously so) and so to do something for the independent character at a time of stress can make him or her feel even more dependent, less in control, and therefore even more dysfunctional. (Contrarily, to do something for dependent personalities as opposed to helping them rely on their usual network allies, can threaten to add the helper to the patient's repertoire of network resources, thereby setting in motion a series of inevitable testing patterns whose process will unnecessarily cause the person anxiety. Doing for the dependent personality style creates a reemergence of the unresolved wish that maybe this new person, that is, the clinician, will finally be the one to meet all needs. The skillful and seasoned clinician recognizes this potential scenario well and knows that no such omnipotent satisfier of needs can so exist because the wish is but the embodiment of a characterologic fantasy.)

Further conceptualization of the clinical dimensions of providing concrete services is greatly needed throughout the helping professions. So often the inexperienced and untrained helper providing concrete services unknowingly takes the path of what appears to be the least resistance. If the patient needs medical assistance, the form is filled out for him as a matter of routine. If the patient is not eligible for medical assistance, a phone call is reflexively made to a local church or civic group in an attempt to get the funds. Only later does this worker learn that the patient did not return for follow-up visits, or if he returned is not complying with the treatment plan. At this point, such a social service worker often loses interest in the case, blames the patient, gives further cognitive instruction on proceeding with the established plan, and so on. Sophisticated clinical strategies are not easily learned and are seldom learned at all without close supervision and formal education and training in one of the applied behavioral sciences programs. The MSW degree is one such program.

To return more specifically to the details of the case illustration, this patient did have a good deal of self-blame over his job loss, and a therapeutic atmosphere was created by the social worker so that the patient could express some of his feeling of being displaced, but this ventilation was purposely limited to keep within reasonable bounds of the patient's customary style of playing his cards close to the chest. A sure way to lose a patient and lead him to later experience undue remorse is to let the person share too much in the initial contact.

Some emotional and cognitive restoration appeared to be effected when the social worker secured the patient's attention and made the identification for the patient that he seemed to be blaming himself for the job loss when, in fact, he and many others had been laid off. Providers or laymen without clinical training in the applied behavioral sciences commonly state that making such clarifications are pointless, thinking that if this patient is blaming himself he must be aware of it. This observation is almost universally false. First, it takes training and cultivated talent to recognize a not so obvious dynamic process, such as self-blame; secondly, clinical experience bears out that the patient is seldom aware of the process, though the self-blame can be brought to a conscious level with a well-timed and properly conveyed interpretation. The value of providing such a psychologically oriented service to the patient or his or her social network is that cognitive and potentially affective awareness of an underlying psychodynamic process provides a renewed sense of control and regained mastery over one's mental state and consequently over one's state of affairs. The strategy is not to focus all interventions on underlying processes but to know how to combine the skill with the patient's practical problems. If the patient can separate, for instance, a personal feeling of self-blame from an actual circumstance of unemployment for which the patient is not to blame, then the patient has more energy and a reestablished sense of self-esteem with which to examine and develop alternative solutions. Even if the patient were to blame for the circumstance, often the guilt exceeds the behavior; moreover, the rumination over "spilt milk" unnecessarily absorbs all the person's attention away from picking up and moving in a problem-solving direction.

Employing skill with community resources and a tutored understanding of the patient's personality style, the social worker involved the patient in doing as much for himself as possible. The patient was not eligible for medical assistance because his unemployment benefits would become effective in less than a week, which was the end of a two-week waiting period. Though the unemployment benefits did not provide medical coverage, the weekly payment of $104 equaled an annual income level of $5,408 which, while below the poverty level for a family of three, was above the allowable medical assistance income eligibility level of $4,400. It should be the business of any well-trained clinical social worker to know the scope and eligibility criteria for human service programs. While one needs to help a patient in congruence with the style of the patient's personality and social network, it is neither kind, efficient, nor facilitative of engagement to send the patient in pursuit of resources for which he will not be eligible. The social worker can know the outcome of the referral ahead of time if aware of relevant eligibility criteria. This patient would have been eligible for general assistance (welfare) while waiting for his unemployment benefits (which would last 26 weeks) but the patient had never been on welfare and was against applying. Since the unemployment benefits would be coming through relatively soon, the social worker sided with the patient's inclination on this. Otherwise, referral to welfare would have required skillful strategy. It might be noted that if the patient had accepted referral for temporary welfare, in Rhode Island (as in many states since the mid-1970s) the patient would not have been eligible based on lack of income or assets. Instead, the patient would need a temporary medical or psychiatric disability signed by a physician. Again, this fact must be known to the social worker to be properly facilitative within the health care system. The patient could have been construed to have been temporarily disabled if necessary, based either on his significant, and at this point, only initially treated hypertension. He may as well have been considered temporarily disabled based on the depressive features which were subsequently diagnosed. Such a process also requires of the social worker that consultative skills be drawn upon since the physician's signature is needed for the disability. The medical providers rely heavily on the information and educative input of the social worker since they are not by profession sufficiently aware of these human service programs and often are faced with making medical/social decisions for which they do not feel prepared. The social worker's role here when performed as optimally as described is usually a relief and a support to medical staff who are bewildered by the attendant complications.

The solution to this patient's lack of medical insurance that best fit his available resources and his personality style was to facilitate an arrangement with the hospital billing office. The patient was advised that a call to the business office in his behalf would pave the way for a payment schedule which he could manage with his unemployment benefits until he could secure improved health and another job. Though generally better to let most patients do for themselves, this initial encounter with the cashier, particularly for the independent character, can be quite discouraging. Billing offices are naturally instituted to collect established fees and extraordinary arrangements are not a simple matter. Rather than allow an interchange that might swell the patient's already existent resentment that he was in need of help in the first place, the referral call was made with his permission. Such resentment could otherwise lead the patient to unwittingly sabotage his own health care plan and cause him and his family further undue stress which can tend to snowball into exacerbated illness, emergence of psychiatric disorder, marital discord, child abuse or neglect, problems with alcohol, and so on. All of this can fester into an even greater strain on society as well as the patient and his or her associated social network. Pursuant to the social worker's facilitating intervention with the billing office, the patient was able to avoid the feeling of "going hat in hand." An arrangement was worked out in which the patient could pay $20 per month on the accumulating bill until he secured new employment. The concerns of the billing office were allayed by the reassurance that the social worker would be working with the patient to find a job.

With the issue of aiding the search for new work, it was the social worker's plan to focus on the patient being treated for hypertension, obtaining full evaluation for his depression (as will be described), and drawing out the patient's own ideas and wishes for seeking appropriate employment.

Beyond a knowledge of personality dynamics and a skillful utilization of expansive community resource information, the social worker also had to have training and expertise with family and social network dynamics in order to be comprehensively helpful with this patient. The social worker learned from the patient that his father-in-law had died of a stroke at this very hospital and had been treated there for high blood pressure as well. The social worker subsequently asked if the patient could bring his spouse to the next session so that a thorough history of hypertension could be obtained. This opening, related to gathering information, allowed the inclusion of the spouse in the evaluation without being regressive to the patient or creating an atmosphere of emasculation. The supreme value of getting the wife involved was to make sure she did not have any investments regarding hypertension and its treatment, considering the nature of her own father's death. Sure enough, the patient's spouse assertively detailed her convictions in the follow-up sessions that the medications for high blood pressure only make the sufferer worse. She reported her perception that her own father had a "personality change" on the medication. It sounded as if her father had become very depressed on the antihypertensive medications, stopped taking them, and suffered a stroke a few months later. Apparently, the family in part handled their grief by blaming the medical providers. Accordingly, the wife's feelings became a critical focus for engaging her husband in a successful medical regimen.

Two sessions were devoted to sorting out reality from myth and providing some long overdue grief work as well. The patient and his spouse, in collaboration with the medical resident, were educated that antihypertensives can cause depression but that the medications can be adjusted or changed, and the alternative to no treatment is quite precarious. Even after the first session with the wife involved, the couple agreed to try the HydroDiuril and Inderal. As might be expected, whether by autosuggestion from the family's past experience or from actual side effects, the patient did become seemingly more depressed.

At this point, the social worker asked for a consult from the psychiatrist member of the primary care team. The social worker had followed a systemic data base (as will be described in Chapter 5) to evaluate and monitor the patient's depressive features both before and after the prescription of antihypertensives. The social worker had on record a mental status examination for each of the three visits prior to the patient being seen by the psychiatrist. The patient had been having sleep and appetite problems since his job loss in the past month, did have a markedly decreased energy level, had been having some uncharacteristic crying spells at home, but denied any suicidal ideation. The patient had no personal or family history to indicate suicidal risk, but his mother had apparently been treated for episodic depression and sleep disturbance throughout her life by her family physician. The patient reported having had two other depressive episodes each lasting about six months; one followed high school graduation and another roughly following military discharge after two four-year tours of voluntary air force duty. The patient did not seek treatment for these depressions, partly because his wife felt he would "get over it," which he did. However, since the natural course of a major depression is six to nine months, the fact that he did "get over it" did not argue against the diagnosis.

Subsequently, the psychiatrist was able to utilize the data base as obtained by the social worker and recommended a trial of a tricyclic antidepressant. The family required a great deal of engaging therapy to accept this regimen but with it, the patient did regularly take the prescribed antidepressant, in this case, amitriptyline (Elavil). As is typical with this regimen, the dosage was progressively increased from 50 mg to 150 mg over the initial ten days. Within a week, the patient was out actively looking for work. Meanwhile, the antihypertensives were also adjusted following the recommendation of the team psychiatrist and the patient's blood pressure became stabilized.

This case illustration is one instance of three primary care team members working together to provide complementary and comprehensive, coordinated health services. Within three months, the patient had found work and was able to be seen in the Primary Care Medical Unit once per month exclusively by the primary care resident. The other collaborators gradually withdrew their services as the patient's need for assistance diminished. In some cases, more collaborators are needed, including nutritionists, pharmacists, and nurses. In many cases, the nurse practitioner is able to serve as the medical provider. The combination of collaborators is determined by the needs of the patient. In the end, the effective and complete service of the patient is the realization of the primary care approach to health care.

SUMMARY

The team approach of primary care is a model of comprehensive health care delivery that provides the basis for integrating the clinical contributions of several disciplines, including medicine, social work and psychiatry.

Primary care medicine represents a philosophy of health care delivery which can be used in any medical setting and need not be limited to general medical practice. Primary care is provided even in specialty settings as long as health services are accessible, comprehensive, coordinated, continuous, and accountable. By definition, the primary care provider team assists the patient or potential patient to overcome temporal, spatial, economic, and psychological barriers to health. To be comprehensive, the services need to be biopsychosocial with the providers being willing and able to handle the great majority of health problems arising in the presenting patient population. Should it be necessary to obtain outside specialty services, the primary care approach involves the ombudsman role of coordinating patient contact with other consultants, providing pertinent information and seeking opinions from these specialists, and explaining diagnosis and treatment to patients. Continuity of care could not exist without accessibility, comprehensiveness, and coordination because patients would need to resort to outside services when the primary care team is not available or is not assuming primary responsibility—resulting in fragmented care. The primary care approach is accountable when it regularly reviews the process and outcomes of its care, leading to educational activities for all staff to correct deficiencies and expand skills and services.

While all dimensions of primary care may not be possible in every setting, the conceptual framework provides a basis for expansion beyond a disease model or traditional biomedical model. Medical care, in fact, is not equivalent to health care and alone probably never will be so. The education and practice of medicine is an essential but not a sufficient component in any health care delivery system. Medical diagnosis and treatment is specific, technical, and firmly rooted in the biological paradigm. Medicine will never encompass the concept of health care, let alone primary care. The true foundation of primary care lies in the realization that operationalizing comprehensive models of health care require a collaborative effort beyond the expertise of medicine no matter how less specialized it becomes. The foremost responsibility of medicine and its unique area of expertise will be the biological dimension of health care. In essence, the primary care physician is the biomedical specialist as part of the primary care team, appreciative of the psychosocial and social dimensions but not inexpertly attempting to provide them. *This is why other health care disciplines such as social work and psychiatry are essential as team contributors to the health care process to primary care.*

The need for psychosocial services to complement medical care is demanded by the high prevalence of psychiatric disorders and socioeconomic deficits characteristic of patient presentations in the health setting. The wide scope of assessment and intervention skills required in the primary care approach offers a framework on which to conceptualize the comprehensive clinical role of the social worker and other disciplines throughout health care. A central role for the clinical social worker as a member of a multidisciplinary health care team which includes active participation of a psychiatrist would be that of initially assessing all psychosocial referrals, treating some patients, arranging for the treatment for others, seeking consultation as needed, and utilizing intrafacility, social network, and community resources as determined by the comprehensive evaluative process. The social worker needs some mastery of basic biomedical and psychiatric information in order to identify diagnostic issues and seek appropriate consultation. Interaction with a health care team that includes the disciplinary contribution of psychiatry is one effective model to assure acquisition and development of such skills.

Since medical providers lack expertise with psychosocial issues yet spend as much as half their time with these nonmedical problems, the skills of clinical social workers in collaboration with psychiatrists can be useful. While some studies demonstrate the cost-effectiveness of employing social workers in health care, others have found that even when teamwork with social workers does not save physician time, it does lead to more comprehensive care.

For the primary care approach to be effectively comprehensive, the contributing professions need to have a basic understanding of the unique skills and limitations of each discipline. Research findings indicate that this awareness is enhanced when disciplines train together and when medical staff have daily face-to-face contact with the psychosocial providers. While there is often a role overlap with psychotherapy, for instance, teamwork can help distinguish the social worker's expertise in combining psychotherapeutic and social/environmental skills with the psychiatrist's skill in sorting out medical and psychiatric illness.

A fundamental knowledge of biomedical and psychiatric information assures more comprehensive diagnostic skills and can facilitate the integration of the clinical social worker among medically trained team members. This knowledge can help the social worker recognize when biomedical issues receive inappropriate emphasis, thereby clarifying the importance and responsibility of contributing psychosocial diagnostic formulations.

Role blurring can occur especially when staff shortages are evident. Overlap need not cause concern, however, unless the contributing disciplines pursue extra professional interests at the expense of their unique areas of expertise. While social workers in health care need to master some basic biomedical information, they need not accept the task of medical or psychiatric diagnostician. Should the unavailability of necessary consultation persist, the clinical social worker is wise to have the issue addressed directly. Addressing such procedural issues fulfills the important accountability attribute of the primary care approach.

The needs and coping styles of the patient population in the health setting often require very practical interventions. Social context issues and concrete services are inseparable from counseling or psychotherapy services. Engagement and intervention strategies in the health setting require the conceptual development of combined sociotherapeutic and psychotherapeutic skills. Research on social work in the context of medical practice demonstates that interventions prove more effective and relevant when focused more on patients' perceptions of everyday problems than on pursuing further understanding of underlying psychological issues. Success with this patient population suggests the cultivation of helping strategies geared toward narrowing the field of multiple complaints to one or two major issues selected by the patient combined with a drawing out of the patient's own problem-solving abilities. Other characteristics of the patient population in the health setting such as the prevalance of those living alone and the sporadic nature of their contact with health providers, suggests the need for skill with short-term interventions and less traditional family therapy strategies. A focus on engaging other social network figures such as landlords or neighbors over concrete needs would appear indicated.

NOTES

1. Sheppard-Towner Act, 1921, Chapter 135, 67th Congress.
2. Shyrock, Richard H. *The Development of Modern Medicine: An Interpretation of the Social and Scientific Factors Involved* (New York: Knopf, 1947).
3. Berarducci, A., T. Delbanco, and M. Rabin, "The Teaching Hospital and Primary Care," *New England Journal of Medicine* (March 1975): 615-20.
4. Piore, N., D. Lewis, and J. Seehgir, "A Statistical Profile of Hospital Outpatient Services in the United States: Present Scope and Potential Role," New York Association for the Aid of Crippled Children, 1971.
5. Bassuk, Ellen and Stephen Schoonover, "The Private General Hospital's Emergency Service in a Decade of Transition," *Journal of Hospital and Community Pyschiatry* 32, 3 (March 1981): 181-185.
6. *A Manpower Policy for Primary Health Care*, Insitute of Medicine, National Academy of Sciences, Washington, D.C., May 1978.
7. Cassel, J.C., "An Epidemiological Perspective of Psychosocial Factors in Disease Etiology," *American Journal of Public Health* 64 (1974): 1040-43.
8. Holmes, T., "Multidisciplinary Studies of Tuberculosis" in *Personality Stress and Tuberculosis*, ed. P.J. Sparer, (New York: International Universities Press, 1956).
9. Leighton, D.C., J.S. Harding, D.B. Macklin, A.M. Macmillan, and A.H. Leighton, *The Character of Danger*, (New York: Basic Books, 1963).
10. Neser, W.B., H.A. Tyroler, and J. Cassel, "Stroke Mortality in the Black Populaton of North Carolina in Relation to Social Factors," presented at the American Heart Association Meeting on Cardiovascular Epidemiology, New Orleans, March, 1970.
11. Harburg, E., "Stress and Heredity in Negro-white Blood Pressure Differences," Progress Report to National Heart Institute, 1969.
12. Syme, S.L., M.M. Hyman, and P.E. Enterline, "Some Social and Cultural Factors Associated with the Occurrence of Coronary Heart Disease," *Journal of Chronic Disease* 17 (1964): 277-89.
13. Syme, S.L., M.M. Hyman, and P.E. Enterline, "Culture and the Occurrence of Coronary Heart Disease," *Health and Human Behavior* 6 (1965): 178-89.
14. Cobb, S., "Social Support as a Moderator of Life Stress," *Journal of Psychosomatic Medicine* 38 (1976): 300-14.
15. Cassel, "An Epidemiological Perspective."
16. Brody, Howard, "The Systems View of Man: Implications for Medicine, Science and Ethics," *Perspectives in Biology and Medicine* (Fall 1973): 71-92.
17. Sheldon, Alan, Frank Baker and Curtis McLaughlin, (eds.), *Systems and Medical Care* (Cambridge, Mass.: MIT Press, 1970).
18. Dubos, Rene, *Man Adapting*, (New Haven: Yale University Press, 1965).
19. Alexander, Franz, and Thomas French, *Psychoanalytic Therapy* (New York: Ronald Press, 1946).
20. Dunbar, Flanders, *Mind and Body: Psychosomatic Medicine (New York: Random House, 1947).*

21. Kahana, R.J. and G.L. Bibring, "Personality Types in Medical Management," in *Psychiatry and Medical Practice in a General Hospital*, ed. N. Zinberg, (New York: International Universities Press, 1974): 108-23.
22. Leigh, Hoyle, Alvan Feinstein, and Morton Reiser, "The Patient Evaluation Grid: A Systematic Approach to Comprehensive Care," *General Hospital Psychiatry* 2 (1980): 3-9.
23. Kimball, Chace P., "The Personality Puzzle," *Behavioral Medicine*, April, 1981.
24. Kasl, S., and S. Cobb, "Health Behavior, Illness Behavior and Sick Role Behavior," *Archives of Environmental Health* 12 (February, 1966): 247-66.
25. Mechanic, David, "Response Factors in Illness: The Studies of Illness Behavior," *Patients, Physicians, Illness: A Source Book in Behavioral Science and Health.* ed. G. Jaco (New York: The Free Press, 1979).
26. Parsons, Talcott, *The Social System* (New York: Free Press, 1951).
27. Locke, Ben A., and Andrew E. Slaby (series editors), *Monographs in Psychosocial Epidemiology 3; Symptoms, Illness Behavior, and Help-Seeking*, ed. David Mechanic (New York: Prodist, 1982).
28. Bloom, S., *The Doctor and His Patient* (New York: Russell Sage Foundation, 1963).
29. Entralgo, L., *Doctor and Patient* (World University Library, 1969).
30. Szasz, Thomas S., and Marc H. Hollender, "A Contribution to the Philosophy of Medicine: The Basic Models of the Doctor-Patient Relationship," *Archives of Internal Medicine* (1956): 592-95.
31. Zola, Irving K. and Stephen J. Miller, "The Erosion of Medicine from Within," in *The Professions and Their Prospects*, ed. Eliot Friedson (Beverly Hills, Calif: Sage Publications, 1973).
32. *Manpower Policy*
33. Mechanic, David, "The Management of Psychosocial Problems in Primary Care: A Potential Role for Social Work," *Journal of Human Stress* 6 (1980): 16-21.
34. Howe, E., "Public Professions and the Private Mode of Professionalism," *Social Work* 25 (1980): 179-91.
35. Goldberg, Richard, Stephen Wallace, Joan Rothney, and Steven Wartman, "Medical Referrals to Social Work: A Review of 100 Cases." *General Hospital Psychiatry*, in press.
36. Hankin, J., and J. Oktay, "Mental Disorder and Primary Medical Care: An Analytical Review of the Literature," National Institute of Mental Health, Series D, No. 5, Rockville, Maryland, 1979.
37. Rosen, Beatrice, Ben Locke, Irving Goldberg, and Haroutun Babigian, "Identification of Emotional Disturbance in Patients Seen in General Medical Clinics," *Hospital and Community Psychiatry* 23, 12 (December 1972).
38. Lipowski, Z.J., "Review of Consultation Psychiatry and Psychosomatic Medicine: II Clinical Aspects," *Psychosomatic Medicine* 29 (1967): 201-24.
39. Kligerman, M.J., and F.P. McKegney, "Patterns of Psychiatric Consultation in Two General Hospitals," *International Journal of Psychiatry and Medicine* 2 (1971): 126-32.
40. Goldberg et al., "Medical Referrals."
41. Kane, Rosalie A., "Lessons for Social Work from the Medical Model: A Viewpoint for Practice," *Social Work* 27, 4 (July, 1982).

42. Rosen et al., "Identification of Emotional Disturbance."
43. Mechanic, "Management of Psychosocial Problems."
44. Ell, Katherine, and Diane Morrison, "Primary Care," *Health and Social Work,* Supplement on Specialization and Speciality Interests, 6, 4 (November 1981).
45. Kane, "Lessons."
46. Slepian, Florence W., "Medical Social Work in Primary Care," *Primary Care* 6, no. 3 (September 1979): 621-32.
47. Nason, Frances, and Thomas Delbanco, "Soft Services: A Major Cost Effective Component of Primary Medical Care," *Social Work in Health Care* 1, 3 (Spring, 1976).
48. Williams, Paul, and Anthony Clare, "Social Workers in Primary Health Care: The General Practitioner's Viewpoint," *Journal of the Royal College of General Practitioners* 29 (September 1979): 554-58.
49. Frangos, A., and D. Chase, "Potential Partners: Attitudes of Family Practice Residents Toward Collaboration with Social Workers in Their Future Practice," *Social Work in Health Care* 2, 67 (1976).
50. Slepian, "Medical Social Work."
51. Frangos and Chase, "Potential Partners."
52. Williams and Clare, "Social Workers."
53. Forman, James, and E.M. Fairbairn, *Social Casework in General Practice: A Report on an Experiment Carried Out in a General Practice* (London: Oxford University Press, 1968).
54. Corney, Roslyn H., "Factors Affecting Operation and Success of Social Work Attachment Scheme to General Practice," *Journal of the Royal College of General Practitioners* 30 (March, 1980): 149-58.
55. Slepian, "Medical Social Work."
56. Goldberg, E. Matilda; Neil, June E., *Social Work in General Practice,* (London: George Allen and Unwin, 1972).
57. Goldberg and Neil, *Social Work.*
58. Goldberg et al., "Medical Referrals."
59. Wallace, Stephen R., "The Unique Contribution of Social Work to the Interdisciplinary Consultation Liaison Psychiatric Team," *Psychiatry by Teamwork* (Frontiers in Psychiatry, Roche Report), 12, 4 (March 1982).
60. DSM-III, *Diagnostic and Statistical Manual of the American Psychiatric Association* (DSM-III), 1980.
61. DiMascio, Alberto, Myrna Weissman, Brigitte Prusoff, Carlos Neu, Maggie Zwilling, and Gerald Klerman, "Differential Symptom Reduction by Drugs and Psychotherapy in Acute Depression," *Arch. Gen. Psychiatry* 36 (December 1979).
62. Williams and Clare, "Social Workers."
63. Forman and Fairbairn, *Social Casework.*
64. Corney, "Factors."
65. Slepian, "Medical Social Work."
66. Goldberg and Neil, *Social Work.*
67. Mechanic, "Management of Psychosocial Problems."
68. Goldberg and Neil, *Social Work.*

69. Stoeckle, John, Ruth Sittler, and Gerald Davidson, "Social Work in a Medical Clinic: The Nature and Course of Referrals to the Social Worker, *"American Journal of Public Health* 56, 9 (1966): 1570-79.
70. Goldberg et al., "Medical Referrals."
71. Ullman, Alice, and Gene Cassebaum, "Referrals and Service in a Medical Social Work Department," *Social Service Review* 35 (1961): 258-67.
72. Salvatore, Ellen P., *Social Work in Primary Care: Opportunities and Obstacles,* unpublished doctoral dissertation, Brown University, Providence, Rhode Island, 1981.
73. Goldberg et al., "Medical Referrals."
74. Goldberg and Neil, *Social Work.*
75. Goldberg et al., "Medical Referrals."
76. Goldberg and Neil, *Social Work.*
77. Wallace, "Unique Contribution."
78. Stoeckle et al., "Social Work."
79. Stoeckle et al., "Social Work."
80. Goldberg et al., "Medical Referrals."
81. Brochstein, Joan, George Adams, Michael Tristan, and Charles Cheney, "Social Work and Primary Care: An Integrative Approach," *Social Work in Health Care* 5, 1 (Fall, 1979).
82. Nason and Delbanco, "Soft Services."

Chapter Three

Crisis Intervention Reevaluated

The theory and practice of crisis intervention have become increasingly incorporated into health care in the past decade. This is partly because crisis intervention is socially effective but also because it is a method of intervention which is required to serve a changing consumer population of health services. Poorer, less educated, more disorganized and chaotic individuals and social networks are increasingly resorting to health care providers—particularly in primary care settings and general hospital emergency rooms—to obtain problem-solving help, often for complaints which are only tangentially medical. Even when presenting complaints are emphatically medical, the psychosocial component is commonly so integral that medical attention cannot be provided without immediately addressing the nonmedical issues as well.

The patient population which is increasingly turning to health care settings for emergency service, routine medical care, the settlement of family and neighborhood conflict or its resultant casualties, has long been the clientele of some parts of the profession of social work. Many of the social workers who have worked with poor and often disorganized individuals and groups have had to draw upon the tenets and techniques of crisis intervention and have learned to adapt these concepts to this population. The short-term nature of crisis work and its emphasis on the strengths of the person in crisis are in fact an integral part of the theory and practice of professional social work today.

This chapter will provide an updated appraisal of crisis intervention, the contribution of social work to crisis work, and the relationship of both to health care. Social work's understanding and treatment of the so-called "crisis ridden character," which is not accounted for in crisis theory, will be given special emphasis. The emerging pressure of legal concerns on crisis practitioners will be examined as well.

Though emergency psychiatric services in particular are usually not revenue producing nor inexpensive, the wider use of crisis services in general throughout the health care system can be cost-effective and can decrease morbidity. Costs can be reduced both for the health care industry and the patient in crisis when the incidence of illness is prevented, the exacerbation of illness is avoided, or when hospitalization can be made unnecessary or abbreviated. The general well-being of patients and their social networks are similarly enhanced when patients can be aided to remain in or be restored to their normal environments and regain their previous levels of functioning at the earliest possible time.

With potential crisis in the health care setting or when actual crises do occur, social workers who have had *both* professional training and experience with the population described above can be instrumental in resolving or helping to manage the turmoil. To make clear the intimate relationship between crisis work and social work, a brief review of the concepts in crisis theory and their origin would be helpful.

THE ORIGINS OF CRISIS INTERVENTION

The beginning concepts in crisis intervention were developed from experiences gained in treating casualties in the first and second world wars. When soldiers who required psychiatric help were treated promptly, and near the front lines, more were able to return to combat duty and in a shorter period of time. The effectiveness of this approach, substantiated by later developments, led to the conceptualization that to treat a victim of crisis close to the environment and social group from whence he came results in the quickest recovery.

Further development of crisis concepts was gained from the treatment of patients who lost a family member in the Coconut Grove Fire in Boston. In 1944, Erich Lindemann published his observations of the grief-stricken survivors.[1] Lindemann concluded that a period of mourning following the loss was necessary for full recovery. Those who did not have the opportunity or capacity to express their grief at the time of the crisis, suffered greater distress and impaired functioning at a later date, sometimes months and years after the event. A crisis concept which grew out of this was the importance of getting help for the victim at the time of the crisis. Lydia Rapaport has emphasized that a little help earlier can be more effective than extensive help later.[2]

Another contribution from Lindemann's work was the realization that persons having a severe reaction to a present loss may be experiencing a rekindled unresolved grief of a previous one. As will be explained later, this observation has not been universally appreciated by later crisis theoreticians and practitioners.

The development of crisis concepts and strategies proceeded as writers expanded the notion of crisis beyond the traumas of war, natural accidents, and bereavement. Growth experiences such as puberty or life transitions involving work, school, or family came to be seen as normal life changes which could result in a crisis.

What effect personality development prior to crisis has upon the occurrence of the crisis and its course has remained an unsettled question. Some thinkers postulate that only the nature of the crisis matters while others say that personality determines vulnerability to crisis and reaction to crisis varies with indiviuals. Nevertheless, practitioners tend to focus on the present situation and the specifics of the crisis rather than early life when taking the patient's history. The practitioner who restricts his exploration entirely to the present, however, fails to benefit from Lindemann's contribution that the current crisis may be a trigger for previously unresolved crisis. Obtaining such data could be essential to resolving the present problem and providing an opportunity for improving the quality of the patient's life in the long term. What really needs to be emphasized is that history taking in the crisis situation should be selective and skillfully traced with the starting point being the details of the present crisis itself. A systematic data base of selected biopsychosocial information is the most practical solution. The data base should include: sociodemographic information, the exact specifics of the patient's presenting complaint, past psychiatric history (if any), significant childhood history such as placement in special education or with a child welfare agency, involvement with law enforcement, recent life events, drug and alcohol use, significant medical history, medications, brief family history, and a mental status. (The data base is examined in detail in Chapter 5.) The overall guiding question for the clinician to consider in any crisis evaluation is whether the patient(s) is a danger to self or others.

Other characteristics of the crisis situation which theoreticians have conceptualized can be summarized as follows:

1. There are stages to development of crisis.
2. An identifiable precipitating event is required to be considered a crisis.
3. The patient in crisis must perceive the event as being meaningful and threatening.
4. The patient's normal coping ability has broken down.
5. The patient in crisis is more accessible to intervention.
6. Since the patient is open to influence, positive change could occur. Hence crisis can be seen as an opportunity for growth.
7. The crisis period is time limited, usually four to six weeks.
8. Without help, the crisis may result in a maladaptive adjustment, i.e., a poorer level of functioning.

The notion of stages in crisis was developed by Gerald Caplan.[3] He conceived of the sequence beginning with the hazardous event, normal coping mechanisms failing, disequilibrium developing, and finally overwhelming tension resulting in dysfunction.

MEDICAL ILLNESS AS A CRISIS

The formulation of the idea of stages to crisis suggested that intervention prior to the final stage, or what has been called "active crisis" could prevent the crisis.[4] Reflecting an appreciation of this view, the literature on crisis expanded with preventive plans and recommended strategies. The spectrum included recommendations for rapid access to patient,[5] early case finding,[6] and, in general, the placement of crisis workers near the situations which may be likely to produce crisis. Medical hospitalization and the onset of illness or the incidence of injury came to be recognized as high risk precipitants to crisis. Preoperative and postoperative patients have also been identified as beneficiaries to preventive intervention. The social work literature is vast in its description of present programs and recommendations for others which involve social workers with cancer patients,[7] on coronary units,[8] with the elderly following hip fractures,[9] and so on.

Since reaching all patients preventively who may experience crisis is not always possible, the involvement of social workers in the development of crisis intervention teams (secondary and tertiary prevention) is constantly increasing. This is being accomplished by employing social workers either exclusively or as part of multidisciplinary teams in medical emergency rooms and emergency units of mental health centers.[10, 11]

THE CONTRIBUTION OF SOCIAL WORK TO CRISIS WORK

The contribution of professional social workers to crisis work derives from their knowledge and expertise with social networks and the social environment. An essential part of crisis intervention always includes the assessment and involvement of the social environment. The distinguishing identity of social work in its ideal practice has been its long experience in working with patients' families and other significant relationships. In addition, social workers have traditionally been most familiar with community resources and expert in negotiating these to resolve problems. These skills are crucial in alleviating the turmoil of crisis.

A central tenet of crisis theory is the idea of preventing further regression by keeping a patient in his normal environment or by returning him or her to it as soon as possible, when brief hospitalization is necessary. To accomplish this intervention, a tutored understanding of the environment is indispensable. Resorting to a community resource manual is not a professional skill. Knowing how a community really works and how to make it work in one's behalf is not quickly learned. The sociologist Robert K. Merton has described institutions as having manifest and latent functions, that is, what institutions claim to be designed for and profess to do versus what they actually do and what purposes they actually serve.[12] By repeated exposure to the community and by ingenuity and training, competent professional social workers make it their business to know what agency is worth calling for particular services and who in the agency is a bona fide resource. Timing in a crisis is critical, and the crisis situation is no time to learn what social workers do as a profession. Even when social workers do not have the resource at hand, they usually know the path to find it. The employment of social workers becomes synonymous, therefore, with one aspect of effective crisis intervention.

To understand the antecedents and the parameters of the patient's crisis, contact with the family or other members of the social network is usually vital. This is particularly true when it comes to case disposition. Interviewing significant others can prevent overestimating the patient's apparent recompensation following initial ventilation. Depressed patients sometimes appear less desperate in the context of a supportive interview; psychotic patients sometimes appear more organized in response to the structure and safety provided by the clinician. The members of a patient's social network can contribute observations beyond those available in the clinical interview. Similarly, information gained from family or friends as well as the opportunity for enlisting their help in appropriately caring for the patient can prevent unnecessary hospitalization or overcautious treatment recommendations. The family's knowledge of the patient could alter a crisis therapist's advice, for example, to return to work or rest at home. For some individuals it would be better to be occupied; others can benefit from an idle rest period.

The patient's assessment and his or her own treatment recommendation must also be sought when possible. At times, the patient may disagree with the family or friends' assessments. The social worker's potential experience with families and groups provides a useful instrument to judge the interaction and establish a plan which should not exacerbate individual stress by playing into family or social network conflict.

The particular experience of those social workers who have had both professional training and extensive exposure to chaotic families and groups needs to be drawn upon and further conceptualized for the use of all of social work as well as primary care medicine, psychiatry, and nursing.

THE CRISIS-RIDDEN CHARACTER

One of the shortcomings of crisis theory as presently constituted is its apparent lack of appreciation for patients who are constantly in crisis. This often referred to "crisis ridden character" defies the usual concepts in crisis theory. It is with these patients that the crisis often pervades the network as well. In this case, family and "friends" are often less alleviators of turmoil and more contributors or partners in it. Because these patients and families to some degree require a different set of interventions, it would be useful to distinguish them from the usual conceptualization of being in crisis.

It would be inaccurate to say that these patients are experiencing "an upset of a steady state."[13] Relatively speaking, their turmoil may have increased but the lifestyle itself is generally chaotic and not "steady" (if steady is to mean stable). What at first may appear to be a precipitating hazardous event, such as the breaking with a spouse or lover, turns out to be an occurrence of some frequency. The usual coping mechanisms have not so much broken down as the seeking of help from an emergency facility is part of the regular coping behavior of the chaotic style itself. These patients present in an excited fashion in nonemergency settings as well, commonly in the outpatient medical clinics of any general hospital, as well as during any phase of a medical hospitalization.

Since there is technically no actual crisis period for these patients, one cannot say that "the crisis" is time limited. For the patient or family that is intermittently though regularly in turmoil, the crisis atmosphere tends to be resolved only temporarily. Due to a low tolerance of frustration and a life of perpetual conflict, the crisis personality or social network will present with the appearance of crisis at emergency facilities, medical clinics, and other helping agencies over and over again.

Crisis intervention is usually conceived of as from one to six sessions resulting in problem resolution and termination. Neither such brief intervention nor long-term sustained psychotherapy has seemed to meet the needs of "clients from particularly deprived and low socioeconomic backgrounds, clients whose lives are a series of crises."[14] One writer has suggested a long-term relationship with a helping agent which would at times be intensive and at other times minimal.[15] Since there is no empirical evidence to support previous claims that it is possible for a patient to experience a "transference to the agency," that is, a sustaining relationship with an institution, it would appear advisable for programs to try to maintain staff and encourage assignments of specific personnel to the same patients. Moreover, so-called "burn out" of individual staff could be avoided, in part, if staff did not expect their crisis interventions to result in resolution when dealing with crisis-type personalities and systems. Staff would need to be trained not only in conventional crisis techniques but also aided to identify and intervene with individuals and networks that depart from present crisis concepts.

Resolution does differ with the patients described above. Instead of the crisis temporarily disabling the victim, the crisis atmosphere serves as a medium to seek a desired change or gain in the patient's life and social network. While the patient may not at all be aware of his or her intentions, in this case the patient and/or family is not so much open to influence or help, but instead seeks to influence the helper. The following case examples, common to crisis work, will illustrate this phenomena of underlying, often preconscious, motive. The examples are also atypical to crisis theory.

CASES THAT CHALLENGE PRESENT CONCEPTS OF CRISIS

Case 1: The social worker covering the primary care medical clinic in a general hospital receives a call from a frantic-sounding mother who has been a sporadic patient of the clinic. She demands that her three children be taken away immediately, stating that she is on the verge of abusing them. Although sensitive to the contemporary social and legal pressures regarding child abuse, the social worker is able to ward off the inclination to quickly make arrangements for removal, and attempts to get more information from the mother. Since the mother excitedly continues to seek immediate action, it is not easy for the social worker to obtain data. Being familiar with such behavior, however, the social worker makes mental note of the demanding quality of the mother, and manages to acquire the name, address, phone, and other pertinent demographic data. Next, the social worker tries to understand the context of the mother's call, that is, why is she calling at this point, what has been happening in the family recently, and so on. Two pieces of important information emerge. First, it is learned that an argument occurred between the mother's 13-year-old daughter and the mother's boyfriend. The boyfriend is now refusing to take the mother on a weekend outing. Secondly, the mother feels frustrated by the refusal of the local welfare office to replace her "lost check". Next, the social worker scans the clinic intake cards and notices that this mother has called twice in the past eight months with identical threats to drop off her children. Each time child welfare had been notified and a state worker visited within a day and found that things had calmed down with no evidence of past history of abuse. Given this information, the clinic social worker decides to interpret for the mother that what she hopes to achieve (and of which she might not be aware), that is, reconciliation with the boyfriend and favorable attention from the welfare department, would not be gained by dropping off her children either at the hospital or at child welfare. Moreover, the social worker clarifies that not only might the separation do psychological harm to the younger children but the strategy would not be allowed by the authorities. She is told that just dropping the children off would be considered abandonment under the legal statutes and she could well lose custody of the children. Among other things, by losing custody, she would forfeit her eligibility for welfare. Finally, the social worker asks the mother if she knows any other way to handle her stress. At this, the mother offered the solutions that she would call the boyfriend herself and also borrow money from her uncle who had come through in the past. The clinic social worker arranged for the visit of a child welfare worker within a day. As before, the mother had resolved the crisis on her own with the help of the intake worker's benevolent limit setting.

Case 2: A social worker on an admissions team at a children's psychiatric hospital participates in the review of a request to readmit a 7-year-old boy to the inpatient unit. The request is made on an emergency basis by the child's mother who reports that her son has been saying he wants to die. She said he picked up a knife the previous night and she feared he would use it on himself. The boy had been discharged a month earlier following a year's inpatient stay. He had originally been hospitalized for uncontrolled aggressive behavior alternating with depressive and withdrawn affect. There had been a history of suicidal behavior and ideation, but these had not been witnessed or heard by the staff, only by the boy's mother. The social worker initiated discussion as to how the boy's discharge might have affected the mother. It was learned that the mother had welcomed the discharge but that her life had become filled with the activities of a single life in the year without the child. In fact, following her divorce four years earlier, the mother had freely expressed ambivalence about assuming custody. The social worker asked the specific team member involved with the mother what the mother expected of his hospitalization. At first, answers seemed to be protective of the mother, that is, "She wants to save her son's life, naturally!" Soon it was realized that what the mother might hope for had not been fully explored. Another preadmission interview was recommended and conducted. It became clear from the ensuing interview that the mother experienced the son's presence as cramping her style. Moreover, she falsely assumed the hospital would take the child for brief periods to spell her. When she was supported that parenting was difficult but also warmly confronted that the hospital would not act as a way station for family disputes, the mother diluted the excited reports of her son's behavior. She volunteered that she had not done much to comfort the child since his return. Meanwhile, the admissions team thoroughly reviewed the case record and reacquainted the staff with the mother's history of frequent use of emergency facilities in the two years prior to her son's hospitalization.

Case 3: A woman in her early 20s is brought to the emergency room (ER) by her father and older brother following a wrist slashing episode. The woman is treated medically, cleared, and is seen by the clinical social worker covering the ER. The patient and her family demand that the patient be hospitalized. The patient says she will kill herself at the first opportunity. The family reports a previous wrist slashing three years earlier resulting in a six day psychiatric hospitalization. The present context appears to be a repeat of the first. The accompanying family disapproved of the patient's boyfriend, belittled him, and he broke up with the patient. The family feels the hospitalization will protect the patient. However, upon further exploration father and brother also believe it will teach her a lesson and keep her safely away from the boyfriend. Interviewed separately, the patient says her death would make her family regret their behavior. She more covertly implies that the hospitalization would serve the same purpose and cost her father some money as well.

The family is gathered together and told that a hospitalization would not solve their problem. The conflict is clarified that either the family must allow the young woman more dating freedom or the girl might consider living on her own. A shouting match ensues between patient and father. The patient says she cannot afford to live alone. The father says he will not allow his daughter to be a tramp. The family storms out leaving the patient in the ER. It became clear that the daughter had not considered leaving the family, even as a weapon. However, she was not working and had no immediate income. The social worker knew that the local women's shelter would not accept the patient because of the wrist slashing. The social worker was experienced enough to know not to ask directly in such an instance whether the patient could stay with other family or friends. Usually this feeds into the patient reporting helpless answers and providing no resources. Instead, the patient was engaged in dialogue about her extended family and friends. A grandmother emerged as a positive relationship and an available resource for temporary lodging. In a short period of time, the patient seemed to accept that this was the only alternative (especially considering that hospitalization was not allowed as an option) and that staying with the grandmother would provide enough drama to "show" her father. The grandmother was called to the ER and the patient discharged to her.

All of these so-called crises do not fit the usual conception of being in crisis. None include the disorientation and derealization that can follow the death of a close relationship or the loss of possessions following a fire or flood. The precipitating event in these cases was also repetitive rather than extraordinary. The contrast with traditional crisis concepts continues point by point (compare with page 73):

1. There appear to be no discernible stages to the development of the crisis with crisis-ridden characters and networks.
2. Often there is no identifiable precipitant. If there is, the precipitant is ordinary to the patient's life rather than extraordinary, for example, a spouse or lover who has left or returned several times. Or the patient's reaction to the precipitant appears to be greater than the precipitant might generally be considered to warrant.
3. The patient may not perceive the precipitating event as meaningful or threatening since often the patient cannot identify a precipitant. When the precipitant can be identified, the patient or social network often places greater significance on the latent agenda issue rather than the precipitant, for example, the wish for a revengeful hospitalization rather than reconciliation with the party who has abandoned the patient.
4. The crisis-ridden character's normal coping ability has not necessarily broken down. In fact, this patient's appearance at an emergency room or other crisis facility may be part of the routine coping style with his or her perpetual crises. As will be examined later in the chapter, however, there are times when this patient population is actually in crisis and coping skills have deteriorated.
5. The crisis character is not necessarily more accessible to intervention because he or she is often not technically in crisis in the traditional sense.
6. More accurately, the patient is more apt (although not consciously) to seek to influence the clinician in order to obtain satisfaction for the covert agenda, rather than to be influenced.
7. The crisis period for this population does not take the same course. With a clinician who is experienced with these patients, the turmoil can sometimes be resolved in minutes or hours. Instead of the crisis lasting four to six weeks, the crisis-ridden character or social network can sometimes present at emergency rooms or other crisis facilities several times in the same four to six week period, often with many different complaints.
8. The maladaptive adjustment for untreated crises described in traditional crisis theory does not necessarily apply to the crisis prone population because this group is seldom presenting at a time in which they are actually functioning below their own baseline. They are not, in summary, in a crisis state as it is meant in crisis theory.

Although crisis theory does not account for the above described circumstances, crisis workers and other health care providers can be frequently faced with such cases. The differences, in fact, are important to realize because they suggest different strategies and different interventions.

TREATING THE CRISIS CHARACTER

A primary technique utilized in the cases described involves finding out what the crisis personality or network is actually looking for, even if this expectation is out of the awareness of the patient, which it usually is. Another technique amounts to setting firm but benevolent limits when the covert request behind the patient's turmoil cannot be provided, as is also commonly the case. It is not often appreciated that such limits tend to reduce the anxiety and excitement because the patient no longer has to accelerate the behavior to obtain what is desired. It has been traditionally mistaken that such limits bring on rage. This is not the case when the limits are truly firm—that is, not negotiable even by tone of voice—and if the limits are clearly benevolent. If the crisis worker is on the defensive, the limits would instead sound angry and retaliative. It is possible with training for crisis practitioners to actually be benevolent with demanding, hostile patients if it can be appreciated to what a frantic level these patients work themselves in order to fulfill wishes for which they are often not even aware. Also, the rage tends to fizzle when the practitioner's boundary is solid and secure, and, therefore, comforting.

Realizing that crisis-prone patients present over and over again does not mean, however, that something helpful cannot be done. Since there is not a crisis in the usual sense, the crisis cannot be resolved. What can be accomplished are small, incremental changes in the patient and his or her social network over time, usually years. Also, the excited anxiety level of the crisis character can be reduced if the clinician can help the patient focus on the agenda that is behind the anxiety—and without necessarily meeting the demands of the latent agenda. The lack of large-scale problem solving will not be discouraging to the crisis worker if the short-term crisis concept is not applied to these patients. In that these patients are not so much psychologically disorganized as they are active participants in disorganized systems, it can be exciting and satisfying for the crisis worker who can relate to the patient's own network as well as the larger community system by knowing when to do something and what, as well as when to do nothing and why. Understanding that such patients live in turmoil makes benevolent helping possible because the helper does not expect the patient to change quickly, and sometimes not at all. The change that sometimes needs to occur is not in the patient but in the helper. Basic premises of what constitutes help need to be reappraised. Efforts directed at changing the helping network's attitude and expectations of the patient are often more indicated than changing the patient's behavior. As long as the helper does not add to the patient's turmoil by failing to provide appropriate limits or leading the patient to believe that frantic behavior will result in the satisfaction of unreasonable demands, help is indeed being rendered. The helper who can provide nonpunitive boundaries for the crisis-ridden character is often the one who the patient will return to for meaningful contact. "You are the only one who ever listens," is the description frequently given by the crisis personality to the helper who, from one perspective, never seems to have given anything to the patient at all. What the patient received was an unwillingness to feed into the patient's turmoil.

LEGAL VS. CLINICAL CONFLICT IN CRISIS INTERVENTION

The parameters of traditional crisis concepts are not the only limitations upon the crisis practitioner when servicing crisis personalities and systems. Misunderstanding legal statutes which were meant for the protection of patients but which do not have the foresight for every clinical situation can also result in a disservice to crisis-prone patients. It is a critical challenge for crisis workers today to provide the least restrictive intervention necessary for the patient's safety while avoiding lawsuits against the practitioner. Patient advocacy legislation was passed to protect patients from being in the hospital against their will as well as to put patients in the hospital who are a danger to themselves and others. The clinician who decides not to hospitalize a patient who reports to being suicidal is increasingly considered to be taking a legal risk. This is in spite of the earlier discussion that suicidal reports are often erroneous or exaggerated. As has been detailed, even suicidal behavior can be less an issue of individual depression than network conflict. Clinically, to hospitalize such a person can often feed into the network conflict and result in further suicidal, homicidal, or other forms of destructive behavior. Hospitalization in such cases would and could mean social and cost ineffectiveness. One study[16] randomly assigned 150 applicants for psychiatric hospitalization to outpatient family crisis intervention and then compared this group with another 150 who were hospitalized upon application. In 6 and 18 month follow-ups, the group treated with outpatient crisis work did as well as the hospitalized group in all respects, and better in some. For instance, those in the outpatient group who required later hospitalization, experienced fewer and shorter stays than the previously hospitalized group. From the cost perspective, the hospitalization group cost six and one-half times more on an average than the outpatient crisis group.

For those who believe that hospitalization in itself can prevent suicide, Decker and Stubblebine studied two groups of psychiatrically hospitalized patients.[17] One group (N-225) received crisis intervention prior to admission while the other group (N-315) was admitted directly. Follow-up in the two and one-half years after hospitalization revealed that the group who received crisis intervention spent significantly less time in the hospital and experienced one suicide while there were six suicides among the routinely hospitalized patients.

All of this is not to contradict that some patients do require hospitalization. It is to say that some patients' crises are ego-syntonic, that is, what appears to be a crisis is not a crisis for them. The so-called crisis-ridden characters or families require astute assessment to distinguish them from other patients who are in crisis, as it is conceptualized in crisis theory. For patients who are disorganized by a hazardous event and whose usual coping style has broken down, hospitalization may be indicated. But other criteria must be met to consider hospitalization as well. For instance, if the patient has thoughts of suicide, does he or she have a concrete plan? Is there a previous history of suicide attempts? What was the nature of the attempts? Does the patient have family or friends who could be with the patient at all times and helpful should the patient not be hospitalized? If the patient has serious suicidal intent and there are no reliable outpatient caretakers, hospitalization would usually be decided upon.

In keeping with the orientation of crisis theory and practice, the inpatient stay would be as brief as is safe for the patient's discharge. It is not that a patient would be discharged under traditional psychotherapeutic frameworks before he or she can manage but that from a crisis theory perspective the entire hospitalization would be geared toward getting the patient back to his or her normal environment as soon as possible. As with good clinical judgement on an outpatient basis, inpatient clinical management today is also hampered by legal concerns. For more than a generation, inpatient psychiatric hospital atmospheres have moved from a regressive, custodial environment to an open therapeutic milieu in which the patient has been treated as normally and responsibly as is safely possible. No undue constraints were put on the patient which would increase feelings of being infantile, helpless, and dependent; or other circumstances which might further separate a patient from normal, healthy community behavior. Staff relationships with patients replaced locked doors and physical restraints. Medication, of course, greatly enhanced the therapeutic milieu by chemically modifying excessive agitation and stress.

The emphasis on encouraging normality and preventing regression put pressure on inpatient staffs to increase their skills with the dynamics of patient interaction and ward management. As in outpatient crisis-oriented work, units fostering brief hospitalization have had to distinguish between crisis characters and patients experiencing decompensation. This work needs to continue. Suicide attempts which are a reflection of ward turmoil need to be identified as separate from patients who are individually feeling hopeless. Those who are reacting to ward conflict more than to internal despair require benevolent limits, while the isolated need continuous protection and ever-present interpersonal attempts to make contact. Nevertheless, legal considerations seem to be making reactionary inroads to the generation of progress toward the therapeutic milieu.

Inpatient psychiatric unit administrators need to be alert to not unilaterally return to old measures of protecting patients in order to protect against lawsuits. A return to safety conscious environments would tend to retreat from the challenge of differential patient assessment and care and provide a regressive impact on patients which is counter to the theory and intent of crisis intervention and patient advocacy.

On both an inpatient and outpatient basis clinicians need to make difficult differential assessments that are mindful of the law but not constricted by it. Clinical assessment and care, as has been illustrated, is complex and the complexity needs to be communicated to the present and future generations of lawmakers whose legislation should reflect a genuine understanding of patient protection and quality care. Only mental health professionals can contribute the clinical dimensions to this needed clarification.

To understand protection, one needs to learn to distinguish various manifestations of human behavior which may appear on the surface to be identical. As has been illustrated, many patients who appear to be in crisis may in fact not be in crisis, in the sense that the term has been defined. Patients perpetually in crisis require different interventions to be helped, and often hospitalization can produce more conflict, not less, for these patients. Similarly not all patients who potentially could and sometimes do kill themselves can be considered suicidal. Patients who fit into this potentially lethal category can include impulsive personalities, self-mutilators, individuals who report revengeful, angry thoughts of killing themselves as well as previous attempts, and persons who exhibit self-injurious ideas and/or behavior as a reaction to social network conflict. Unlike suicidal individuals who can be withdrawn, hopeless, preoccupied with death, and immersed in sad affect, this other group usually remains intensely object directed, that is, still heatedly involved in their social and familial relationships. While suicidal patients can require and benefit from inpatient protection and constant observation by staff, the crisis-ridden and reactive group can experience an acceleration of conflict and self-destructive behavior if hospitalized. The hospitalization can become only one of many which can be sought to obtain gains in the network conflict. The patient can learn to use suicidal threats or gestures as a vehicle to up the ante in a relationship dispute or to manipulate hospital admissions staff so as to gain leverage in obtaining resources from some other social agency. Subsequently, the health or mental health facility can wind up reinforcing the behavior rather than reducing or rechanneling the stress. Often times, crisis programs and inpatient units eventually refuse to treat the patient after repeated admissions and the patient is abandoned to another facility. By this time, however, the hospital which has allowed the initial admissions has become part of the patient's network, against which he or she is reacting. The patient ends up being at greatest risk when abandoned or when responsibility for treatment is tranferred.

In short, hospitalization even if brief, is often not the best protection for all patients who may seem suicidal. What is needed is the availability of an outpatient crisis program which will help the crisis-ridden patient to reduce turmoil within his and her social network. The cardinal rule is not to take responsibility for the suicidal threats. (This is equally true on inpatient units when too much emphasis on a suicide-proof environment can challenge some patients and inadvertently encourage suicidal behavior.) This would make the helper only one more object or target for the angry threats. What the patient thinks or fantasizes would be accomplished by the suicide needs to be explored and interpreted. On-the-spot family interviews may be required to expose and dilute the turmoil. If temporary separation of the most abrasive individuals seems indicated, the members will need help to realize this and then help to choose among other relatives or friends with whom to stay until tension subsides.

Because crisis-ridden patients by their nature tend to translate their anxiety and turmoil into behavior rather than words or neurotic symptom formations, work with this group also will inevitably mean involvement with the incidence of patient self-injury, suicide, homicide, and other forms of violence. Crisis programs and other health care facilities whose patients do not count among these statistics are not so much successful but are likely agencies which are avoiding case responsibility with this impulsive population.

WHEN THE CRISIS-RIDDEN CHARACTER IS IN CRISIS

Once the crisis worker can distinguish an individual in crisis from the person or network chronically in chaos, then it becomes possible to identify the most challenging and sophisticated situation in crisis intervention. This is the ability to accurately assess when the crisis-ridden character actually is in crisis, in the actual denotation of crisis theory. In other words, there are times when crisis personalities and networks, though accustomed to a life of turmoil and what is frequently mistakenly assessed as a crisis, do in fact reach a state of active crisis. It is at these times when crisis characters' usual coping styles break down and they *are* disorganized. It can be said that they would then be functioning below their own baseline behavior. In these instances, hospitalization and other shelter arrangements often do need to be used. Sometimes this assessment can be arrived at by noticing that the crisis character appears less reactive, less angry, genuinely agitated, and does seem hopeless and discouraged. At times the most pointed cue for concern with crisis-ridden characters can be their presentation without the usual demandedness, excitability, or covert agenda. The assessment, though difficult, is best made by a crisis worker who has known the patient and his or her social network over time. (This is a further argument for trying to maintain the same staff with the same patients. As previously noted, burn-out is avoided by training staff not to expect these patients to behave the same as other patients in crisis.)

When the crisis character is accurately assessed as being in crisis, social work skills are most needed in crisis work. This is because an intimate knowledge of the social environment is critical. With these patients, most community resources and often most hospital facilities already know these patients and want nothing to do with them. Crisis characters and their networks have had by their very nature excessive exposure to a multitude of community agencies. Usually, the agencies have previously overextended themselves for this patient and by this time have washed their hands of the patient. The earlier overinvolvement commonly includes the inappropriate dispensing of money, lodging, or other services. For hospitals, it typically means a past history of excessive and inappropriate admissions, both medically and psychiatrically. The crisis worker is aided if his program is attached to an inpatient facility. For outside resources, such as welfare programs, shelter homes for battered victims, and so on, the crisis worker has to resort to every skill and persuasion to obtain the necessary help.

Part of the dilemma of the lack of resources for the crisis character actually in crisis, is that the community programs are also constituted on the traditional conceptualization of crisis. Accordingly, many shelter facilities for rape, battering, financial distress, and the like have established rules that the need for the resource must be short-lived and that the resource can be used no more than twice. Crisis characters need to be limited from using the resource when inappropriate. Shelter staffs are usually not trained to make such assessments. Too often these patients have been allowed to use up their two admissions unnecessarily. Also, the limitation to use the facility no more than twice deprives the crisis character from benefiting from small, incremental changes over time. Even when crisis characters use such facilities appropriately, they would need to use them more than twice over a period of years.

All of this demonstrates that more training is needed not only in crisis intervention but in reappraised and further developed conceptions of crisis theory. Crisis practitioners and others who deal with individuals in crisis, need training to help those patients who do not fit the crisis model as presently constituted. Those social workers who have had experience with poor and chaotic individuals and social networks can and will undoubtedly contribute to this development. Social work expertise with the social environment can also aid in the expansion of crisis services to environments that are natural for potential crisis. In health settings, especially hospitals, the involvement of social workers with the entire host of patients who seek medical care demonstrates the need to provide preventative biopsychosocial services at the earliest possible time. For the health care industry and the consumer, this will mean realizing that the health care environment itself can be the hazardous event that precipitates crisis. The widespread use of social workers who understand the impact of the environment on the physical and mental health of the patient follows a historical continuum in health care which today embodies primary care. Recruiting enough trained social workers to be environmentally assessible throughout primary care medicine will mean understanding prevention from the perspective of crisis intervention.

SUMMARY

The tenets and techniques of crisis intervention are an integral part of the theory and practice of professional social work. The unique contribution of social work to crisis intervention and the brief psychotherapies derives from the particular knowledge and expertise with social networks and the social environment that is part of the social work tradition. Crisis intervention always includes an assessment and involvement of the social environment. The characteristic of social work that distinguishes it from other disciplines providing services to individuals with emotional problems is its unique experience in working with patients' families and significant others and its familiarity with community resources and expertise in negotiating these to resolve problems.

The special expertise of social workers is illustrated in the management of crisis-ridden characters. It is with these patients that the crisis pervades the social network as well as the individual. Family and friends are often less alleviators of turmoil than they are contributors to or partners in it. Because these patients and families to some degree require a different set of interventions, it is useful to distinguish them from the usual conceptualization of being "in crisis". It is inaccurate to say these patients are experiencing "an upset of a steady state," as is frequently seen in traditional crises. Relatively speaking, their turmoil may have increased, but their lifestyle itself is generally chaotic and not steady, if steady is to mean stable. What at first may appear to be a precipitating hazardous event, turns out to be an occurrence of some frequency. The usual coping mechanisms are not broken down as they are in others confronted with a crisis; the seeking of help from an emergency facility is part of the regular coping behavior of the chaotic style itself. These patients present in an excited fashion in nonemergency settings as well, commonly in most of the outpatient medical clinics of any general hospital, as well as during any phase of medical hospitalization. Since there is technically no actual crisis period for these patients, one cannot say that the crisis is time limited. For the patient or family that is intermittently though regularly in turmoil, the crisis atmosphere tends to be resolved only temporarily.

The primary technique in the management of such individuals involves finding out what the crisis personality or network is actually looking for, even if this expectation is out of the awareness of the patient. Firm but benevolent limits must be set when the covert request behind the patient's turmoil cannot be provided as is commonly the case. It is not often appreciated that such limits tend to reduce the anxiety and excitement because the patient no longer has to accelerate the behavior to obtain what is desired.

Realizing that the crisis-prone patient presents over and over again does not mean, however, that something cannot be done. Since there is not a crisis in the usual sense, the crisis cannot be resolved. What can be accomplished are small, incremental changes in the patient and his or her social network over time—usually years. Also, the excited anxiety level of the crisis character can be reduced if the clinician can help the patient focus on the agenda that is behind the anxiety—without necessarily meeting the demand's latent agenda. As long as the helper does not add to the patient's turmoil by failing to provide appropriate limits or leading the patient to believe that frantic behavior will result in the satisfaction of unreasonable demands, help is indeed being rendered.

NOTES

1. Lindeman, E., "Symptomatology and Management of Acute Grief," *American Journal of Psychiatry* (1944) 141-148.
2. Rapaport, Lydia, "Crisis-Oriented Short-Term Casework," *Social Service Review*, 41,1 (March 1967): 31-43.
3. Caplan, Gerald *Principles of Preventive Psychiatry* (New York: Basic Books, 1964).
.4. Golan, Naomi, "When Is a Client in Crisis?" *Social Casework* 50, 7, (July, 1969): 389-394.
5. Rapaport, Lydia, "The State of Crisis: Some Theoretical Considerations," *Crisis Intervention*, ed. Howard J. Parad (New York: Family Service Association of America, 1965): 22-31.
6. Berkman, B.G. and Helen Rehr "Early Social Service Case Finding for Hospitalized Patients: An Experiment," *The Social Service Review*, 47, 2 (June, 1973): 256-265.
7. Oppenheimer, Jeanette R., "Use of Crisis Intervention in Casework with the Cancer Patient and His Family," *Social Work* 12, 2, (April, 1967): 44-52.
8. Obier, Kathleen and Julian Harwood, "Role of the Medical Social Worker in a Coronary Care Unit," *Social Casework*, 53, 1 (January, 1972): 14-18.

9. Lipner, Joan and Etta Sherman, "Hip Fractures in the Elderly," *Social Casework*, 56, 2 (February, 1975): 97-103.
10. Farber, John M., "Emergency Department Social Work: A Program Description and Analysis," Social Work in Health Care 4, 1, (1978): 7-18.
11. Groner, Edith, "Delivery of Clinical Social Work Services in the Emergency Room," *Social Work in Health Care* 4, 1, (1978): 19-29.
12. Merton, Robert K., *Social Theory and Social Structure* (New York, Free Press, 1957).
13. Caplan, Gerald, "Patterns of Parent Response to the Crisis of Premature Birth," *Psychiatry*, 23, (1960): 365-374.
14. Ewing, Charles P., *Crisis Intervention as Psychotherapy*, (New York: Oxford University Press, 1978).
15. LaVietes, R. L., "Crisis Intervention for Ghetto Children: Contraindications and Alternative Considerations," *American Journal of Orthopsychiatry*, 44 (1974): 720-27.
16. Langsley, D. C. and D. Kaplan, *The Treatment of Families in Crisis* (New York, Grune and Stratton, 1968).
17. Decker, J.B. and J.M. Stubbline, "Crisis Intervention and Prevention of Psychiatric Disability: A Follow-up Study," *American Journal of Psychiatry*, 129 (1972): 725-29.

ADDITIONAL REFERENCES

Argles, P., and M. MacKenzie, "Crisis Intervention with a Multi-Problem Family: A Case Study," *Journal of Child Psychology and Psychiatry* 11 (1970): 187-95.
Bartlett, Harriet M., "The Widening Scope of Hospital Social Work," *Social Casework* 44, 1 (January, 1963): 3-10
Bartolucci, G., and C.S. Drayer, "An Overview of Crisis Intervention in the Emergency Rooms of General Hospitals," *American Journal of Psychiatry* 130 (1973): 953-60.
Bloom, B.L., "Definitional Aspects of the Crisis Concept," *Journal of Consulting Psychology* 27 (1963): 498-502.
Burgess, A., and L. Holmstrom, "Rape Trauma Syndrome," *American Journal of Psychiatry*, 131 (1974): 981-86.
Caplan, Gerald, *An Approach to Community Mental Health* (New York: Grune and Stratton, 1961).
Chandler, H.M., "Family Crisis Intervention," *Journal of the National Medical Association* 64 (1972): 211-16, 224.
Cowan, B., M. Currie, R. Krol, and J. Richardson, "Holding Unwilling Clients in Treatment," *Social Casework* 50 (1969): 146-51.
Duckworth, G.L., "A Project in Crisis Intervention," *Social Casework* 48 (1967): 227-31.
Eisler, R.M. and M. Hersen, "Behavioral Techniques in Family-Oriented Crisis Intervention," *Archives of General Psychiatry* 28 (1973): 111-16.
Ezra, Julia, "Casework in a Coronary Care Unit," *Social Casework* 50, 5 (May 1969): 276-82.

Fallon, C., "Providing Relevant Brief Service to Couples in Marital Crises," *American Journal of Orthopsychiatry* 43 (1973): 235-36.

Halpern, H., "Crisis Theory: A Definitional Study," *Community Mental Health Journal* 9 (1973): 342-49.

Hankoff, L.D., M.T. Mischorr, K.E. Tomlinson, and S.A. Joyce, "A Program of Crisis Intervention in the Emergency Medical Setting," *American Journal of Psychiatry* 131 (1974): 47-50.

Hoff, Lee Ann, *People in Crisis: Understanding and Helping* (Menlo Park, Calif.: Addison-Wesley California, 1978).

Hoffman, D.L., and M.L. Remmel, "Uncovering the Precipitant in Crisis Intervention," *Social Casework* 56 (1975): 259-67.

Kaplan, David, "A Concept of Acute Situational Disorders," *Social Work* 7, 2 (April 1962): 15-24.

Kaplan, David, "Observations on Crisis Theory and Practice," *Social Casework* 49 (1968): 151-55.

Langsley, D.G., "Crisis Intervention," *American Journal of Psychiatry* 129 (1972): 734-36.

Lindenberg, Ruth Ellen, "The Need for Crisis Intervention in Hospitals," *Hospitals* 46, 1 (January 1, 1972): 52-55, 110.

Lukton, Rosemary Creed, "Crisis Theory: Review and Critique," *Social Service Review* 48, 3 (September 1974): 384-402.

McGee, R.K., *Crisis Intervention in the Community* (Baltimore: University Park Press, 1974).

Nelson, Z.P., and D.D. Mowry, "Contracting in Crisis Intervention," *Community Mental Health Journal* 12 (1976): 37-43.

Parad, H.J., and G. Caplan, "A Framework for Studying Families in Crisis," *Social Work* 5 (1960): 3-15.

Parad, H.J., and L.G. Parad, "A Study of Crisis-Oriented Planned Short-Term Treatment: Part One," *Social Casework* 49 (1968): 346-55.

Parad, Howard J., "Crisis Intervention," *Encyclopedia of Social Work,* Vol. 1, (1971): 196-202.

Parad, L.G., and H.J. Parad, "A Study of Crisis-Oriented Planned Short-Term Treatment: Part Two," *Social Casework* 49 (1968): 418-26.

Parks, Ava, "Short-Term Casework in a Medical Setting," *Social Work* 8, 4 (October 1963): 89-94.

Pasewark, R.A., and D.A. Albers, "Crisis Intervention: Theory in Search of a Program," *Social Work* 17 (1972): 70-77.

Phillips, Beatrice, J. Wallace McCulloch, Malcolm J. Brown, and Naomi Hambro, "Social Work and Medical Practice," *Hospitals* 45, 4 (February 16, 1971): 76-79.

Porter, R.A., "Crisis Intervention and Social Work Models," *Community Mental Health Journal* 2 (1966): 13-21.

Puryear, Douglas A., Helping People in Crisis (San Francisco: Jossey-Bass 1980).

Rapaport, Rhona, "Normal Crises, Family Structure, and Mental Health," in *Crisis Intervention,* ed. Howard J. Parad (New York: Family Service Association of America, 1965) pp. 75-87.

Rubenstein, D., "Rehospitalization versus Family Crisis Intervention," *American Journal of Psychiatry* 129 (1972): 715-20.

Slaby, Andrew E., "Crisis Intervention," in *Textbook of Psychiatry*, ed. J. Lieb A.E. Slaby, and L.R. Tancredi, New York: Harper & Row, 1982).

Smith, Larry L., "A General Model of Crisis Intervention," *Clinical Social Work Journal*, 4, 3 (1976): 162-171.

Strickler, Martin, and Margaret Bonnefil, "Crisis Intervention and Social Casework: Similarities and Differences in Problem Solving," *Clinical Social Work Journal* 2, 1 (1974): 36-44.

Taplin, J.R., "Crisis Theory: Critique and Reformulation," *Community Mental Health Journal* 7 (1971): 13-24.

Chapter Four

On the Art of Engaging the Patient

In the crowded waiting room of a general hospital primary care clinic, a resident in internal medicine calls out the name of his next patient. A woman who appears to be in her sixties dressed in a worn overcoat and kerchief, gathers her belongings and follows the physician into the examining room.

"I'm Dr. Brown, Ruth. What brings you to the clinic today?"
"I used to see another doctor, but I guess he's not here anymore," answers Mrs. Ruth Jones.
"No, I'll be your new doctor. Let's review why you're here."

The patient describes the symptoms for which she has been treated in the past. The physician completes a review of systems, orders some lab tests, discontinues one medication and prescribes another. The patient is given a follow-up appointment for two weeks later. The physician assures her that her symptoms will improve, and the patient politely leaves although there is some sense of unfinished business.

Mrs. Jones returns in two weeks, reports that she wasn't able to get a ride to get the lab work, says that her symptoms haven't improved, and says that she couldn't take the new medication because of side effects. Somewhat irritated, Dr. Brown informs the patient that the lab tests are essential, tells her that the side effects will be reduced by dividing up the dose during the day, and gives her another biweekly follow-up appointment.

Mrs. Jones returns in two weeks and mentions in passing that the cab rides to the clinic are very costly and that she still has her symptoms. Dr. Brown and Mrs. Jones continue to meet intermittently over the following year. The patient consistently reports no symptom relief and continues to do what she wants with her medication. Could the outcome have been predicted? Could the course of treatment have proceeded differently? For anyone who has worked in an ambulatory medical setting, the general features of this case will seem quite familiar.

An analysis of how this relationship between patient and physician started is a prerequisite for corrections in this frustrating course of treatment. At the very first appointment Dr. Brown was aware that he was running an hour late but did not take this into account. Even though patients are often informed that hospital clinics are busy and waits are common, many experience the lateness as a personal insult. The inconvenience must be addressed directly in order to defuse this obstacle to an effective doctor-patient relationship. Once in the examining room, a more effective scenario might have begun as follows:

> "I'm sorry I'm running so late, Mrs. Jones; what was it like to be waiting there so long?"
> "That's OK, doctor, I've been coming here for years so I guess I'm getting used to it (jokingly)."
> "Well, I know it can be annoying, as you seemed a little upset when you first came in."

Whether the provider be physician, social worker, nurse, or psychiatrist, a general principle of engagement involves recognizing and addressing the patient's feelings about the treatment situation. This requires that the practitioner not take personally whatever feelings might be expressed even if these are directed at the provider. For example, another form of dialogue might have evolved as follows:

> "I'm sorry you had to wait so long," etc.
> "My last doctor never did this . . . "
> "I certainly didn't start off on the right foot, did I?"
> "Oh well, there's a lot of goings on to watch out there, anyway."

The technique in this instance amounts to dissipating the anger by accepting it as reasonable and not becoming defensive, as though criticism were inappropriate. The question of whether the criticism is appropriate or inappropriate misses the point in engaging the patient. The technique is one of not defending against the patient's statement even when the patient's criticism is unreasonable and not reflective of reality. The patient's anger is often about the past and often merely stimulated by the present. The patient really wants (unconsciously) evidence that the health care provider cares or at least is similar to or different from past unsatisfactory relationships. The provider is merely a stimulus for these associations, though the health care provider is certainly not immune from actually doing things that may appropriately incur the patient's displeasure.

This chapter will address itself to the art of engaging patients, particularly those who are most difficult and challenging. Primary attention will be paid to engagement in the medical setting, although the principles outlined here are applicable to any helping relationship. Many of the principles involved in engagement are derived from social work's traditional involvement with hard-to-reach clients.

THE CONCEPT OF ENGAGEMENT

Engagement is referred to as an art because (1) it has not as yet been fully conceptualized or systematized, and (2) its deployment depends in part on the personality of the helper. To become adept at engagement strategies, the capacity to become aware of one's feelings is required as well as a sense of humor and an appreciation for such things as reverse logic. The use of these elements will be demonstrated with clinical examples.

While there is currently no textbook plan of what to do in various situations, successful helpers do utilize a hierarchy of interventions. There has traditionally been a gap between observing clinical practice and conceptualizing what takes place. This chapter is intended as a contribution toward clarifying what happens in effective clinical practice—utilizing concepts from psychodynamic theory, interpersonal psychiatry, communication theory, social work practice, and systems analysis.

TECHNIQUES OF ENGAGEMENT

Recognize the patient's situation and attendant feelings

To return to the initial meeting between Dr. Brown and Mrs. Jones, the structure of the clinic waiting room can itself create potential problems. Large waiting rooms are usually impersonal and staff can easily overlook minor manuevers which could make the prospective client feel individually recognized. Dr. Brown could have asked the receptionist if she remembered who Mrs. Jones was. Often the receptionist can point out who and where the patient is. In this way, the physician or other provider can approach the patient directly and avoid calling out names in the middle of the waiting room. Clients are much more receptive to what help is available and possible when they are treated more personally at the onset. It can be a helpful training experience to have staff sit anonymously in a waiting room to acquire the patient's perspective.

Validate the patient's uniqueness and personal attributes

Dr. Brown initially addressed Mrs. Jones by her first name without having previously met the patient. Such presumptuous friendliness without a genuine basis for it can have an unsettling effect on patients. While it may be the intention to put the patient at ease, such remarks can be experienced as potential disrespect, and premature closeness is generally uncomfortable for many patients. Commenting on the patient's feelings about having waited in the reception room is a more effective way of establishing rapport with the patient and showing recognition of him or her as an individual.

Elucidate the patient's perception of previous treatment

Dr. Brown did not pursue Mrs. Jones' initial response about having had another doctor in the clinic. Allowing and even stimulating discussion about the previous practitioner can pay significant dividends in engaging the patient. As a general principle, it is important to find out the patient's perception of the previous treatment. While the details may not be historically accurate, they can foretell what is ahead in the present relationship. If the patient praises the previous doctor, find out specifically what he or she liked and listen for indication of what the patient hopes to obtain from the present treatment.

Allow for ventilation of feelings about previous providers of care

If the patient condemns aspects of earlier treatment, this is equally predictive of what the patient hopes to avoid. Listen to and elicit specifics. To forge a helping alliance, the physician must match his own expectations with those of the patient. The patient's specific likes and dislikes of previous treatment actually embody the patient's wishes and fears for the present. Encouraging the patient to ventilate feelings about previous providers also helps the patient to disengage from the earlier ties and to accept the new clinician. A further principle of engagement that usually occurs in the initial interview is found in the maxim: avoid being idealized or devalued. The interview might unfold as follows:

> "Mrs. Jones, I'm Dr. Brown. I will be your new doctor."
> "I'm so glad to meet you doctor. I was hoping to get a new doctor, and I've heard so much about you."
> "How are you feeling today?"
> "Well, I've been suffering like this (lists her complaints) but no one has been willing to give me any real medication for it."
> "I see from the record that your previous doctor treated you with medication X."
> "Yes, but he would never give me enough to help, but I understand that he wasn't too experienced."
> "Well, sometimes doctors are overly cautious. I suppose we could increase the dosage a bit."

What appears in this dialogue to start out as a promising relationship, deteriorated over the first few months as the patient's cooperative attitude and praise for her new physician declined and her demands for changes in the medical regimen shifted and expanded.

The key warning signal overlooked in the first exchange was the physician's willingness to accept the patient's hope and praise without any real basis for it. The helper who accepts being overvalued without having demonstrated as yet any reason to be valued at all, predictably faces criticism and an unsatisfied patient later. It is not so much the treatment offered but the acceptance of the role of savior which is destined for dismantling. He might say "I certainly hope I can be helpful as you say, but let's sit down and take a good look at this first."

Do not accept total responsibility for the treatment

The technique to avoid the above artificial semblance of engagement is to refuse to accept the implication that something special or extraordinary will take place. The physician, like any helper, can provide quality care only by maintaining the parameters of standard practice. While the outer boundaries of a helping relationship do not become an issue with most patients, the limitations of what help is possible commonly becomes tested by patients who by nature tend to devalue or idealize the practitioner and the treatment. Treatment involves alternatives for the patient to choose to follow. The patient's participation in the treatment is essential to a successful outcome. Total dependence on the clinician's "magic" precludes a mutual commitment and both the patient and the practitioner can fall into the trap of seeing all solutions and all responsibility for the care as resting with the practitioner.

The patient who does idealize the provider at the outset often harbors an agenda (almost always without the conscious awareness of the patient) to prove the "authority" wrong. The experienced clinician usually realizes that the patient who makes him feel extraordinarily special is inadvertently setting him up for a later problem.

Do not automatically ally with the patient for or against the previous treatment

Another oversight in the exchange between Dr. Brown and Mrs. Jones was Dr. Brown's inadvertent alliance with Mrs. Jones against her former treatment when he increased the dosage of medication after the patient criticized her previous doctor for not doing so. When Dr. Brown accepts the role as the one who will finally straighten things out, he accepts a task which can never be fulfilled. So, he must eventually and repeatedly be proven inadequate. The intensity with which help is initially sought is commonly proportionate to the degree to which it will later be devalued in time when offered. If the medical regimen does need to be changed at the outset, the physician should be careful to point out that the reasons for the change are in the context of the current situation. The converse of the above situation is presented with the patient who devalues any new help at the outset. The management, however, is identical to the initial experience of idealization. In summary, engagement is facilitated by (1) eliciting the specifics of the previous help, (2) side-stepping the role of either savior or villain, and (3) by keeping part of the responsibility for the treatment with the patient.

Ask the patient for a solution

Maintaining treatment as a shared responsibility between patient and practitioner is most challenged by the patient who seems to present with an insoluble problem. The most effective engagement technique for the patient who does present a problem which seems to include insurmountable barriers to effective care is to feed the problem back to the patient as presented and ask the patient for a possible solution. To illustrate, a case in point centered on a 20-year-old woman who wanted to be followed by a resident in a primary care clinic though she could neither afford the treatment nor was she able to visit the clinic during the hours it was open. The medical resident found himself frantic for how to accommodate her treatment. At day's end clinic conference, the resident's own presentation of the case demonstrated that he had taken it upon himself to solve the problem without asking the patient for any assistance. Consequently, he could not answer why the patient had recently switched services from a different hospital 30 miles away or how her treatment had been administered there. He was greatly relieved to hear that these parts of the puzzle were yet to be explored and that the patient could (1) choose a job with medical insurance, (2) take a job with different hours, and (3) in general, share some responsibility for her health care.

All of these cited examples are typical of problems in general hospital medical clinics for which social work consultation can be effective in assisting the primary care physicians to engage patients in effective helping relationships.

USEFULNESS OF ENGAGEMENT STRATEGIES: SOCIAL WORKER AS CONSULTANT

Primary care physicians, social workers, psychiatrists, nurses, physical therapists, and nutritionists—to name a few—experience daily encounters with patient care situations in which they could benefit from a knowledge of engagement principles and techniques. Of all of these helpers, the professional who assumes the role of consultant most keenly requires a mastery of engagement skills. On psychiatric consultation-liaison teams in general hospitals, for instance, the consultant role is usually filled by clinical social workers, psychiatrists, and psychiatric nurses. The consultation can take place either in ambulatory clinics or inpatient settings. Members of a hospital psychiatry consultation service are called in by medical staff to provide evaluations and recommendations for patients who present diagnostic questions or management problems. Patients referred to the consultation service have seldom requested these evaluations, often do not understand their purpose, and frequently are not initially receptive to the consultation process.

Many social workers can make a unique contribution in the role of consultant through their knowledge of the social environment and their awareness of its importance in engaging patients. Social work practice also underscores the functioning, healthy side of patients in developing helping relationships and interventions. Clinical examples of social work consultation will be used throughout the chapter.

THE FUNDAMENTAL PRINCIPLE OF ENGAGEMENT

The techniques which have been described so far generally concern the beginning phase of initial interviews. The consultation process as noted above is usually one of the most challenging encounters for engagement. The principle that underlies all techniques of engagement can be called *getting the patient's attention*. Patients bring with them established conceptions of almost every conceivable relationship. These vary from patient to patient but there do exist some universal stereotypes of what medical staff or mental health helpers are all about. For example, medical staff are often seen as impersonal and uninvolved while at the same time being expected to have immediate answers to all problems. Mental health professionals, on the other hand, are often assumed to be able to read people's minds, and to view all of their clients as "crazy." When these preconceptions are negative or constricted the interview will no doubt be greatly colored by them. It is the task of the consultant at the outset, therefore, to jostle the patient free from these negative value orientations and get the patient's attention, independent of them.

An example of getting the patient's attention involves Mrs. Petrocelli, a 59-year-old woman who was referred to a clinical social worker by two different medical specialty clinics after several attempts by health and other mental health professionals to relieve her depression. She had been extremely depressed since the death of her husband three years earlier. Two private psychiatric hospitalizations and repeated attempts at chemotherapy had been attempted as well as confrontative family therapy, the thrust of which was aimed at getting the patient to leave her dependent relationship with her husband behind and begin to take responsibility for herself. The patient's verbalized expectations of consultation were that the social worker would (1) help her obtain the right medication, and (2) allow her to continue to ventilate her feelings that her grown children were rotten and had deserted her. A consultation was obtained from a psychiatric physician on the issue of the medication; the conclusion was that much had been tried and she would be a difficult person to medicate. Regarding her children, the social work consultant told her—contrary to her expectations of a patient and empathetic listener—that if her children were that bad her situation did indeed seem hopeless. The consultant also voiced doubt that he could help her when other professionals had not succeeded in doing so. In essence, the social worker refused to be one more in a series of listeners. She seemed so surprised that the social worker did not fit her image of helper and did not try to get her to see the merits of her surviving family or attempt to offer her a new type of treatment, that *she* began to suggest solutions to her own dilemma. She regained her earlier abandoned mothering role and began to invite her children for nostalgic Italian dinners at home. She gave up her hope for a magic pill. She underwent job retraining and found a government agency position fielding consumer complaints. By changing the patient's expectations of how help might proceed, the patient was in turn able to shake herself loose from a self-defeating grief response, the angry and morose phase of which had become destructive.

Getting the patient's attention is the fundamental principle of engagement and it can take the form of many strategies simultaneously. The above example could be seen as including something similar to the technique of paradoxical intention as developed by the communication theorists. With paradoxical intention, the symptom of distress is actually assigned to the patient. A person who fears fainting in stores for instance is told to go and faint in the nearest store.[1]

ATTENTION GETTING AND THE RECOGNITION OF AMBIVALENCE

In the case of Mrs. Petrocelli, it may appear that her sense of hopelessness was confirmed by the consultant. However, this was not what actually happened. The more accurate translation of the process is that the situation would be hopeless and intervention would not be successful if her perceptions of her children and her expectations of getting help remained unchallenged. While only Mrs. Petrocelli could change her view of family and therapy, it was the consultant's job to give her the opportunity to do so. Attempts to persuade Mrs. Petrocelli to complete her mourning and relinquish her anger toward the other survivors had already proved unsuccessful. From a psychodynamic view, the strategy of getting Mrs. Petrocelli's attention consisted of avoiding entry into her struggle (acceptance of a destructive transference), that is, by not becoming an object of her grieving resentment.

The dynamic concept involved here is that of ambivalence, the recognition that human beings tend to have at least two opposite feelings about everything. Clinical practice substantiates that people are conscious of one side of their feelings and less aware or not at all aware of other thoughts or feelings that are different or even contradictory on the same subject. By not attempting to encourage Mrs. Petrocelli out of her hopelessness and anger, the consultant drew upon a commonly confirmed clinical hypothesis that Mrs. Petrocelli continued to possess a less obvious sense of hope as well as an array of suppressed positive feelings toward her children. In order to circumvent her resentment and not add unnecessarily to it, Mrs. Petrocelli was not engaged in a debate over her point of view and, therefore, was able to maintain a sense of control in the interview. This control made her less defensive and helped her to remind herself through the consultant that she also had the wish to live, and that she still cared for her family. The essence of getting Mrs. Petrocelli's attention amounted to side-stepping her fight and allowing her the independence to suggest her own solutions.

While a medical provider could not be expected to make so complicated a psychotherapeutic intervention, the above example is included in part to illustrate the potential value of seeking consultation from a clinical social worker or other mental health professional on the team even for situations that appear to be hopeless. The social worker might be able to draw upon these attention-getting maneuvers which could engage the apparently resistant or uncooperative patient in an effective treatment plan. The example is also intended to demonstrate the imaginative nature of the skills needed to be developed by social workers and other helping professionals who aspire to master the role of consultant in health and mental health settings. Other techniques which derive from understanding the concept of ambivalence will be further elucidated later in the chapter.

PROFESSIONAL ETHICS

The principle of getting the patient's attention can involve a spectrum of techniques that require professional maturity and ethics. Patients who are challenging to engage can generate angry and defensive affects in the inexperienced practitioner. Under such circumstances, the less experienced clinician can fail to appreciate the responsibilities which accompany the use of these techniques. Many engagement strategies can make the patient vulnerable to unguarded and unsuspecting affects which require the practitioner to limit and contain. Otherwise, the patient at best will be less open at the time of the next contact; at worst, the patient could suffer unnecessary emotional trauma from revealing unprotected affects without the benefit of a sustained and proven therapeutic relationship.

Getting the patient's attention goes far beyond simple surprise, though that may be part of it. The neophyte should beware of applying this technique in a wholesale manner. As in the case of Mrs. Petrocelli, the initial interview must end with confirmation of a helping relationship centered on hope.

The Origins of the Focus on Engagement

The capability and advisability of making a profound impact on a patient in an initial interview is a procedure of rather recent vintage. Freud did not think change was possible until well into a treatment relationship. As with Ben Franklin's "necessity is the mother of invention" many of the demands of health and mental health today do not allow for such time or for treating a selected population. Freud treated patients who both wanted his help and viewed themselves as having a problem. This is not the situation that commonly confronts most of health and mental health care professionals today in general hospitals, child welfare agencies, community mental health centers, visiting nurse associations, and the like. The clients served by these professionals often have not sought their services and are not at least initially open to them. For the clinical social worker on a psychiatric consultation-liaison service, for instance, there is not time to gradually develop a trusting relationship before an assessment can be completed. If the patient is resistant, whether it be on a conscious or unconscious level to the diagnostic information-gathering process, the consultant cannot wait for a long-term working through period. For the needs of both the referring medical staff and for the patient who may be at risk, the consultation service must often be provided in one or two interviews. In the emergency room setting, the psychiatric crisis assessment must be completed in the initial interview. This is also the case for the child welfare worker evaluating child abuse or for the visiting nurse making a protective assessment of the elderly at risk in the community.

No patients are easy to engage

The fact is that though some patients are less difficult to engage in a helping process than others, no patients are easy to engage. Freud contributed that even with his motivated, verbal patients, a time occurred when the patient would become uncooperative in the treatment, despite the patient's own conscious wishes to aid the helping process. Freud labeled this unwitting lack of cooperation "resistance" and described it as an unconscious phenomenon which signaled that the patient's central conflicts were emerging and being played out with the therapist. The difficult phase and how to manage it came later for Freud's patients, as it does for most patients who are candidates for psychoanalytic psychotherapy, not completely (if at all) because of the treatment, but because of the nature of the patients. These patients have the coping abilities, or defenses, to push out of their awareness or conscious mind whatever is at the root of their stress. This array of coping styles could take the form, for instance, of being very wordy or intellectual in order to bind or get away from painful emotions. Nevertheless, this type of person can tolerate more anxiety and is often able to be reflective about having problems without needing to blame others or transform the anxiety into a somatic complaint.

Many of the clients seen by child welfare workers or patients treated in primary care ambulatory clinics, however, differ from those described above both in personality and in the settings in which they commonly present. Psychodynamic concepts can be quite helpful with these patients and settings, but not in the form in which these concepts have been understood for psychoanalytic psychotherapy. For one thing, these patients tend to translate their anxieties less often into words than into action and behavior. Such manifestations can include the abusing parent in pediatric clinic, the overdose or wrist slasher in the emergency room, the patient with a behavioral component to an otherwise documented seizure disorder in neurology clinic, or the somatizing patient in primary care medical clinic. These situations call for active participation on the part of the helping clinician and a re-adaptation of dynamic concepts.

RECENT HISTORY

The reappraisal of dynamic theory and the quest to develop effective strategies to engage vastly different consumers of health and mental health services, has been a continual but spotty historical endeavor. In the last decade or so, William Glasser's *Reality Therapy*[2] experienced widespread popularity among helping professionals who were expected to develop therapeutic relationships with uncooperative clients. Glasser's book on delinquent teenage girls demonstrated that ventilation and permission giving help had often been applied to inappropriate populations, and that discipline-oriented, limit-setting intervention was more effective and what was needed. Essentially, Glasser's was an argument for better differential diagnosis and treatment, that is, selecting a therapeutic behavior suitable to the patient's behavior. It amounted to a call for more imaginative use of psychodynamic theory against a backdrop of what had become stereotypical analytic passivity.

FURTHER CONTRIBUTIONS TO ENGAGEMENT

The assault on the passive analytic position had come long before Glasser, however. In 1946, Franz Alexander departed from Freud's conception that the therapist had to wait until the patient was "ready" in order for the therapist to have a significant impact on the patient. Freud believed the patient had to fully project—or transfer onto the person of the therapist—the core of his inner conflicts and expectations, before the therapist could make a corrective or perception changing comment. Alexander coined the therapeutic encounter the "corrective emotional experience" and believed that the process could be substantially speeded up. "If the therapist knows what kind of problem is emerging into consciousness, he will find it simple to elicit such reactions deliberately. He may, for example, praise a patient for therapeutic progress in order to bring out a latent guilt feeling about receiving the father's approval. Or he may express approval of a friend of the patient's in order to bring out latent jealousy reactions."[3] When the patient thus aided became aware of the guilt or jealousy, the therapist could point out that though the therapy may have stimulated these feelings, their origins were within the life and perceptions of the patient. The patient, therefore, became more aware of his way of viewing events as was replicated in the therapy. The opportunity to reexperience these feelings and perceptions in a positive relationship was the other part of the healing process. This historical change to a more active interviewer provided theoretical credibility to today's needs of engaging patients in the medical setting who would likely never be around long enough for a passive helper to make successful entry.

An active involvement in the therapeutic process was also later advocated by Harry Stack Sullivan. A technique used by Sullivan to show the patient that the patient's feelings and/or perceptions of the therapist were derived from the patient's psyche and not from the reality of the encounter was called the "counter-projective statement".[4] Sullivan was fond of getting the patient's attention to this matter by referring to himself as the therapist in the third person. "Sounds like your therapist is giving you a hard time today," Sullivan would comment to demonstrate the transference of the patient's feelings onto the object of the therapist. This strategy served also for the therapist and the patient to experience an alliance against a side of the patient's feelings and perceptions which were often out of the awareness of the patient. This is an important understanding of the dynamic concept of the therapeutic alliance which will be discussed later in this chapter.

Another historical figure, more from the areas of hypnotism and communication theory than psychodynamics, who contributed to the strategy of getting the patient's attention was Milton Erickson. One of Erickson's intervention strategies was referred to as "the confusion technique."[5] This was designed to shake the person free very rapidly of his way of viewing the world. Erickson has used the example that if one were walking down the street at 10:00 A.M. and abruptly bumped into someone, the person would expect a nominal apology and then be on his way. If instead, the perpetrator looked down at his watch and announced "It's quarter to two," then turned and departed, the victim would be left baffled. Erickson would contend that half a block later, the person who left in confusion would still be trying to make sense of the experience. Not only was the usual polite apology replaced by the inappropriate citing of the time, but the time itself was nearly fours hours off. Erickson believed that in the midst of such confusion, the person would be highly suggestible to influence. Like the Freudian patient whose blossomed projections onto the enduring silent therapist were unexpectedly greeted with an unsuspecting and surprising interpretation, the baffled subject of Erickson might long remember the next words spoken following the startling event.

Humor and Paradox

Comedians commonly use similar psychological manuevers to shift our attention from serious predictability to the humorously unthinkable. The success of the comedy and our resultant laughter is due to a shift in our expected perceptions. The following interchange from a Marx Brothers movie demonstrates this:

> Chico: Where will we find the painting?
> Groucho: Search the house.
> Chico: What if it ain't in the house?
> Groucho: We'll search the house next door.
> Chico: What if there ain't no house next door?
> Groucho: We'll build one!

Similar thought processes are evident in the comedy of Woody Allen:

> If you think God is dead, try getting a plumber on weekends.
> If man were immortal, imagine his meat bill.[6]

All of the above examples, from Freud to Woody Allen, are testimony to attempts to engage an audience. It is not easy to be a comedian and it is also a challenge to initiate helping relationships. Similar to the audience for comedy, many of the helping situations described in this chapter do not provide the time or the captive audience that Freud experienced. The helping relationship is now brought regularly to persons who have not asked for it. This is so because quality health care—effective care—cannot be provided without supportive, facilitative psychosocial services. Nevertheless, the psychodynamic concepts initially developed by Freud, and the previously described variations contributed by later thinkers, can be useful if adapted to these new situations.

DYNAMIC CONCEPTS AND ENGAGEMENT

Therapeutic and Nontherapeutic Alliances

The therapeutic alliance essentially means establishing a relationship which is both helpful and healthy to the patient's interests. If this is accomplished,the relationship will be manageable for the clinician. Only untherapeutic alliances, established usually unintentionally, increase the patient's turmoil and cause havoc for the helper. The therapeutic alliance amounts to offering assistance only to the reasonable side of the patient, not the childlike or demanding, that is, regressive side.

Example 1: The angry parents in the emergency room who want to punish their drug-abusing, sullen adolescent by admitting him for psychiatric hospitalization can be told, "I know you want to do what is best for your son . . . hospitalization isn't really what you are looking for." An agreement for family-oriented outpatient care could consolidate what fabric the social system does possess and avoids emphasizing the separateness already rent by tension and disharmony. The critical time for this more healthy contractual arrangement is at the very beginning. Should outside referral be most appropriate, reach for the parent's healthy side (observing ego): "I can see how upset you are and you seem to want the best treatment available, so I'm referring you to Dr. Smith for regular help in the community." This allies with the parent's wish to do what is best, even though this wish has been covered by destructive resentment in the atmosphere of crisis or chaos.

Example 2: Another variation of this theme is the less organized family pervaded by narcissistic entitlement and vengeful rage. Repeating the same presentation as the first example, it would not be effective to try to ally with these parents' latent concerns for their child. These concerns would be too distant and buried beneath more deprived self-oriented needs. Accordingly, to avoid a hospitalization which would side with their rage, the alliance could focus purely on their self-interest but at a more adult or reasonable level. "I know you don't want to cause yourself any more grief than you've already been through, so let's figure out an outpatient plan you can live with."

Example 3: The patient who wants help but refuses to let the clinician seek records from previous agencies or practitioners. Agreeing to such an arrangement is untherapeutic and unreasonable. Moreover, the adult side of the patient knows this. To refuse such a bargain stimulates some initial patient anger but guarantees to preclude later, more unreasonable fury and gains the patient's respect as well. As noted earlier in the chapter, learning about previous help is an important diagnostic indicator of what the patient may expect in this encounter and may provide prognostic data as to how the present relationship may fare. The response to such an unreasonable request must be empathetic yet unwavering. "I can't treat you without that information. I know you don't want poor quality care . . . and I can't deliver it."

A similar example is the patient who tries to get the interviewer to promise not to share the contents of the interview with anyone. This request often confuses practitioners over the issue of confidentiality. Confidentiality cannot be unconditionally guaranteed should the withholding of information amount to a danger to self or others. Emergency intervention commonly involves, for instance, data that the patient is suicidal. To keep this data exclusively between the patient and the interviewer in an outpatient situation could result in unnecessary danger to the patient. Alerting family or friends to the patient's despondency could save the patient's life.

Erroneous applications of the concept of confidentiality are often confused with therapeutic alliance. Practitioners fear that the patient will sue the practitioner for a breach of confidentiality but they often forget that confidentiality was neither developed nor legislated to keep secret an emergency situation that could jeopardize the safety of the patient or others. A more serious lawsuit could result and be justified from the family or friends of a patient who had committed suicide and whose practitioner had entered into an untherapeutic agreement with the patient to keep between them the patient's suicidal intent.

Investigate the foundation of the requested untherapeutic alliance. The potential for an untherapeutic alliance which is illustrated by the withholding of information or secrets as described above can best be avoided by exploring what the patient or family's fantasies or fears are should the data be revealed. In general, finding out what the patient expects to gain from an untherapeutic alliance can usually circumvent the problem. In the cases of the threatened hospitalization of the adolescent, for instance, learning what effect the parents expect will be achieved can lead to their rescinding the request. Often those involved have not thought things out to this point or the latent agenda is out of their conscious awareness.

Example 4: A wife whose husband was being treated for narcotic withdrawal admitted to the clinician that she was aware that her husband had been hiding syringes around the house for years. She said her husband was not aware that she knew and refused to allow the consultant to bring this up in an upcoming marital diagnostic interview. When the clinician raised this problem in conference rounds, feedback was offered that accepting such terms would amount to an untherapeutic alliance. Most importantly, it was realized that the wife's fears of what would happen if the information emerged, had not been traced out and were only a matter of speculation. Did she fear that her husband would leave her? Hit her? Kill her? Was there any past history of abuse? Did she realize that covertly aiding his behavior could result in his death? Was this an unconscious wish? Had she ever fantasized that she would be rid of him? What was she getting out of the marriage at this point? Exploring any and all of these avenues often results in the request for the secret agreement to be abandoned.

While these questions are specifically explorative of this situation, the format can be generalized to any case in which a patient seeks to keep something secret. There is not as much a need to find out or share the actual secret, but to inquire of the patient what he or she imagines will result if the secret is revealed. It is usually fantasy, not reality, that inspires the patient to seek such a pact.

Ego Support

Support, as an engagement strategy, is a widely misunderstood concept and is often confused with simple encouragement. Offering reassurance may make the helper feel like he is doing something useful, but is often likely to underscore whatever self-doubt and feelings of inferiority the patient is harboring. For example, the patient who incessantly asks, "Tell me what to do" can better be supported by the statement, "You know that part of your problem is feeling you are incapable of making decisions. I would only be doing you a disservice to advise you here. This would only confirm your own sense of feeling inept." Rather than reassuring the patient, a more effective supportive strategy is to draw out the patient's skills at problem-solving that do exist (ego). These coping skills or problem-solving abilities are commonly forgotten by the patient at times of stress.

Example: A Vietnam veteran and his wife bring their 6-year-old son to a pediatric behavior clinic complaining that the boy does not obey them at home, has been mean to his pets, and has few peer relationships. The interviewing social worker mistakenly sees this presentation as an appropriate opportunity to provide some parent-child education. The parents appear to leave the initial session gratefully armed with a multitude of child guidance information about treating the child with more age appropriate expectations and advice to assume a more parent-like, less peer-like power stance with their son. The parents return the next week in discouragement, stating that nothing worked. The social worker experiences frustration but perseveringly provides further child guidance with some written parent education booklets. The parents return a week later with the same complaints, coupled with a growing resentment that is not verbally expressed—as is often the case. The clinician camouflages a fast developing sense of impatience, offers more advice and encouragement, and decides to go over the case with a supervisor. The supervisor paraphrases the parent's initial presentation as "We feel incompetent as parents...is it true?" The supervisor points out that the worker had agreed with the parents' unstated self-assessments by readily providing the corrective solutions. Under the guise of being supportive, the treatment in fact confirmed their sense of feeling inept. Subsequently, a truly supportive intervention involved exploring and emphasizing what skills the parents did possess. This soon led to the parents being able to express more directly how inferior as parents they had felt. They became more able to set limits and were less angry with the child. Not surprisingly, the child's behavior proportionately improved as the parents viewed themselves as more capable.

This example is not to say that some patients do not need information. But they often need far less than is commonly believed. Moreover, clients are more open to suggestions when appropriate if their own problem-solving skills are explored and helped to surface. This is the real meaning of ego support. This also takes a great deal of pressure off the helper to solve the problem. The clinician who can ask the patient who has presented a seemingly insoluble problem "What do you think you'll do?" will regularly discover that the patient will come up with a solution that the clinician may not have even imagined.

Avoid allowing inappropriate ventilation. A frequent misunderstanding of the concept of ego support involves the indiscriminate use of ventilation. It is often incorrectly believed that it is therapeutic to let a person in stress pour out his problems to a nonjudgmental listener. This is not only inaccurate, but such open-ended, limitless ventilation can leave the patient feeling that he or she is functioning more poorly than is actually the case. In this sense, unmonitored ventilation can be ego regressive rather than supportive. The patient can wind up feeling worse, and at times such could result in the patient being a danger to self or others. This can certainly happen with patients who are fearful of losing control or who think they have lost control.

Example: A 21-year-old man who was referred to the psychiatric consultation-liaison team by the primary care medical staff to evaluate the behavioral component of a suspected left temporal lobe seizure disorder. The patient had a history of a head injury, the EEG was unremarkable, but he did complain of recent temper outbursts. The psychiatric resident interviewed the patient with the supervision of the consultation service psychiatric social worker. The resident allowed the patient to ventilate virtually uninterrupted for much of the diagnostic session. The interviewer did ascertain that the temper outbursts were more situationally related to arguments with his young wife rather than at random. However, the patient vented a stream of self-condemnation over his past violence with his wife, his fears of hitting her again, of this causing her to leave him, and so on. Soon the patient began to sob, expressed little hope for the future, but doubted he would ever take his own life. Near the end of the session, the resident asked the social worker if he wanted to make any inquiries. The social worker elected to restrict the ventilation and pursue ego supportive strategies, as will be illustrated in the forthcoming dialogue. Specifics were elicited as to exactly what the nature and frequency of the violence with the wife had been. It turned out that the history of violence amounted to one slap in the face. This discovery was painstakingly arrived at since the patient's self-condemnation made the violence sound frequent and physically injurious. In part, the ego-supportive dialogue went as follows:

Social Worker:	"When did you last hit your wife?"
Patient:	"Just the other day (crying)."
Social Worker:	"This week?"
Patient:	(drying his tears) "Well...no, I guess it was the beginning of the month."
Social Worker:	"You mean three weeks ago?"
Patient:	"Yes" (now quiet, not crying, starting to make eye contact).
Social Worker:	"When did you hit her before that?"
Patient:	"Before that?" (looking surprised).
Social Worker:	"Yes, when was the time before this incident?"
Patient:	"Well...I didn't ever do it before."
Social Worker:	"I see. And did she require medical treatment?"
Patient:	"Oh, no!" (looking very surprised at the question).
Social Worker:	"How did you hit her?"
Patient:	"With my hand." (looking down ashamedly).
Social Worker:	"Your hand? Show me what kind of fist you made."
Patient:	"I slapped her...I didn't use my fist."
Social Worker:	"Why didn't you use your fist?"
Patient:	"I wouldn't do that!" (looking a bit shocked).
Social Worker:	"And were there not any objects around to hit her with...a stick maybe, or a bottle?"
Patient:	"I couldn't do that!"
Social Worker:	"It sounds as if even in the midst of your anger you had a great deal of control. Do you notice that?"
Patient:	"I hadn't thought about it that way." (for the first time appearing a bit hopeful) "I don't think I really ever could hurt her. I didn't intend to."
Social Worker:	"It sounds like you were pretty down on yourself. You didn't give yourself much credit for the control you had even when very angry. Did you notice that?"
Patient:	"No, not until you mentioned it."

By finding out what coping skills the patient did possess and by reinforcing them, there was no need for the interviewer to provide solutions. By pointing out the patient's own self-criticism there was equally no need to provide false reassurance, especially without the actual data of the patient's behavior. While limitless ventilation could in this case have left the patient to become a victim of his own self-condemnation and resultant underevaluation of his own self-control (both unintentionally endorsed by the silence of the interviewer), contrarily, premature reassurance can result in the support of ego capacities or personality strengths that are nonexistent. The interviewer must obtain the specifics of the patient's behavior, what coping skills are within the patient's possession, and offer an intervention suited to the differential needs of the patient in question.

Ego lending vs. ego support. Ego support is not possible or appropriate in some situations. Some patients have few coping skills or developed ego available to support—and this requires concrete input or ego lending by the interviewer. The following vignette illustrates a personality structure possessing with less self-control and a genuine need for suggestions by the interviewer.

Example: A 48-year-old woman, twice divorced, with two children from each of the marriages and one child from a relationship between the marriages, complained of anger toward her boyfriend and wishes to be rid of him. The patient was referred for help with these relationship problems by a primary care resident who was treating the patient for a bladder infection. The patient had recently discovered that this current live-in boyfriend was cheating on her. The patient said she was disgusted with him and wasn't sure what she would do. Unlike the previous patient with suspected violent tendencies, exploration revealed that this patient did indeed have a pronounced history of violence and poor impulse control. In the past, she had been in arguments using broken bottles, on one occasion a steel pipe, and several times a knife. When the specifics of one recent argument with the boyfriend were solicited, the patient freely volunteered that she almost "got him" with an icepick but he moved and "I just missed him here," she said pointing to a spot on her throat. This is a patient for whom it would have been inappropriate to point out any "unfair" criticism of herself, had she expressed any remorse over the incident. Persons like this sometimes do express remorse or fear of losing control but the guilt is usually so intense that it cannot be worked with in a short-term contact and there is commonly too little self-control to reinforce.

Such patients require what might be called "ego supplementing" intervention. There is a need for reminding them that the behavior they are contemplating is unlawful and its employment would result in arrest and jail. Alternative concrete suggestions may be helpful, including advice to stay with a friend or relative until this rageful period cools down or to leave the house whenever they feel murderous thoughts and anger emerging. Twenty-four hour emergency services can also be helpful with such crisis-prone patients. However, the prognosis for preventing violence in these cases in not good for the very fact that there is not much ego or developed coping capacities with which to work. The life histories of such persons are filled with extensive early childhood deprivation, life-long, unsatisfactory, chaotic relationships, and little or no tolerance for dissatisfaction without having to translate this perpetual frustration into behavior which is destructive to self or others. The bottom line for the helping professional in these instances, is that ventilation without focus is not helpful, clearly untherapeutic, and often dangerous.

The Role of Defenses and the Engagement Process

The concept of defenses, which is derived from psychoanalytic thought, has also been subject to misunderstanding among helping professionals, and similarly deserves further attention for the effective engagement of patients in medical settings. The key problem is that difficult to engage patients usually present with obvious and annoying traits which are all too often directly confronted by practitioners. Consequently, such dilemmas as medical compliance or even regularly kept appointments remain unimproved. Before further illustrating these problems and recommending some strategies to better engage patients with certain defenses, some discussion of the notion of defenses might be helpful.

In common language, defenses essentially mean the psychological mechanisms through which people cope with anxiety in particular, and the elements of their world in general. For some people, one defense may be predominant. For instance, the generally obsessive person may utilize intellectualization to create a sense of order when events, feelings, or relationships seem uncertain. Defenses are simply ways of coping and are not necessarily unhealthy or maladaptive. A defense becomes an issue only if it prevents the person from taking part in mutual discourse or isolates the person from feeling that may be essential to carry on a relationship.

Some defenses are considered more effective for a satisfactory life and are usually associated with the person who has had a more emotionally fortunate development. The person who can resort to intellect to explain and thereby tolerate dissatisfaction, for example, is usually considered to be more adaptive to the world and to suffer less turmoil than the person who must physically strike out against others or take drugs to cope with disappointment. The latter person tends to project all responsibility for disharmony onto others. The person who predominantly utilizes projection as a defense is thought to do so because his or her covert self-blame (originating in early childhood deprivation) is so intense that its emergent experience would be intolerably devastating to the person.

Do not challenge defenses. The importance of understanding the role of defenses and personality type lies in realizing the purpose they serve: to bind anxiety and to cope with it. A cardinal rule of engagement is to allow the person to maintain his or her defenses and particular style of relating and not attempt to challenge them. This is emphatically the case in the medical setting in which patients commonly view themselves as exclusively experiencing the biological problems without any psychological and/or social components. Often interviewers in the medical setting will become quickly disenchanted with patients who have "converted" grief reactions into somatic complaints by telling them "It's all in your head. There's nothing wrong with you." The patient is often not relieved by this diagnosis and returns soon with identical or additional medically unremarkable somatic symptoms. A more effective helping process would be to allow this patient to report the somatic distress and then also stimulate some discussion on the suspected psychological and/or social precipitants, by saying, for example, "Have you been able to talk about this with anyone else?" This will elicit, for instance, ventilation of lonely feelings.

It is also tempting for psychosocial helping professionals to become impatient with clients whose defenses and coping styles make the interview laborious. Attempts to cut through or take away the defenses, however, only add to the difficulty and often result in a failure of engagement.[7] To use the obsessive and typically wordy evasive patient as an example again, respect for the defense is far more constructive. With politeness, the clinician can focus and structure the interview without embarrassing the patient or engaging in a struggle for control. The clinician could remark, "I know you have a lot to tell me, but let me just ask you this." Remarks that address the patient's penchant for detail can be employed repeatedly and with variety throughout the diagnostic process, "This information you are sharing is helpful to understand your problem. By the way, what about . . . etc." If the interviewer can understand the purpose the patient's defense serves, tolerance for the defense is more likely and genuine empathy is possible. The greater the respect for the patient's style, the greater the chance the patient will become more comfortable, and hence more engageable.

Further examples of defenses such as repression, reaction formation, doing and undoing, and displacement will be elaborated in the following segment.

Understanding Ambivalence and Its Associated Strategies

Ambivalence is a fundamental psychodynamic concept that when understood and constructively adapted to the medical setting provides the basis for developing further engagement strategies. In simple language, ambivalence means that individuals experience at least two feelings about any given event, idea, or relationship. These feelings are usually contradictory, such as love and hate, but the individual is commonly aware of only one of the feelings. The other feeling is considered to be out of the awareness of the individual although it may be accessible with some suggestion (preconscious). The contradictory feelings, which can be manifested in thoughts, fantasies, or daydreams, do not necessarily cause the individual stress or conflict unless awareness or potential awareness of these opposing feelings is experienced as threatening or intolerable to the individual. If one becomes aware, for instance, that in an otherwise positive relationship, one also has been harboring negative feelings, such a realization could be stressful if it is equated with being abnormal or malevolent. Illustrations of this in primary care medicine will be provided below. For some people, becoming aware of these unintentionally hidden (that is repressed) feelings can cause unbearable anxiety. The latter might take the form of extreme guilt, shame, or self-condemnation. The person can confuse feelings and thoughts with action and may fear losing control and acting out the feelings.

If an individual's mixed feelings do include a component which would be intolerable should it threaten to surface into awareness, some alternative conflict resolution tends to occur. In analytic terms, this process is called symptom formation. For some persons, the intolerable affects are avoided by converting the conflict into a preoccupation with somatic distress. Other individuals might unwittingly manage the fear of their own unconscious resentment by being overly sweet or invariably optimistic (reaction formation). Still others may unknowingly play out the source of their conflict with other parties. The employee who harbors wishes for long lost nurturance from a parent, may feel perpetually unsupported by the boss. The businessman who is only partially aware of an uncomfortable fantasy to leave his family and start anew, may instead express this in the form of unfair criticism and impatience with his office staff or general disillusionment with his business (displacement). The need to transfer the conflict to other persons or objects, such as somatic concerns, serves to avoid not only the anxiety-provoking, unconscious affects, but also the tension of experiencing at least two opposing, contradictory feelings on the same matter.

The concept of ambivalence can be applied to couples, groups, families, and larger social systems as well. As with many individuals, often two or more person systems similarly avoid stress when threatened with the experience of contradictory feelings. A marital couple may seek to "project" their disharmony onto a child or an in-law. A family may cope with the dissatisfaction of several members by unknowingly colluding to blame one member for all the trouble (scapegoating). In any workplace, competition among employees (sibling rivalry) may be shifted to discontent with administrators. All of these manuevers represent attempts to cope with mixed feelings. If the marital couple could tolerate and balance both affectionate and resentful affects toward each other, they would not need to project one set of these feelings outside their marital dyad. Even when the feelings are intense, as with the individual who may be frightened by fleeting fantasies of hate and doing away with a loved one, the awareness of the feeling can be tolerable when it is understood and not confused with action or behavior. Conflict is resolved and tolerance for the affects is increased, as well, when the individual or group is helped to realize that opposing feelings do not have to negate each other. It is possible or quite ordinary, in fact, to have both affectionate and resentful or dissatisfied feelings in a relationship, without one canceling out or overwhelming the other.

A thorough understanding of the concept of ambivalence is not essential for medical providers who wish to achieve more effectively engaged relationships with their patients (especially for compliance), but a basic grasp of the issue cannot be avoided to accomplish this task.

An understanding of ambivalence and its associated strategies is critical in engaging patients. While everyone experiences mixed feelings, the intensity of the ambivalence and the amount of energy devoted to avoiding conscious awareness of one or more sides of the ambivalence are diagnostic of how much affect an individual or system can bear. In general, the greater the tolerance of consciously experienced mixed feelings or the more the individual can live with ambiguity, the less there will be evidence of conflict and the presence of various defenses against conflict. The skillful interviewer will observe these diagnostic indicators and will rely upon them in order to engage patients. The nature of the contradictory affects as well as how much these are guarded against, will be data upon which fundamental engagement strategies can be developed. The following techniques of engagement are derived from the concept of ambivalence and its adaptation to the medical setting, consultation and so on.

Siding with the defenses is the primary technique of engagement that derives from understanding ambivalence and the one that is most effective in settings in which the patient is resistant to help of any kind. Siding with the defenses will be illustrated after its opposite, confronting the defenses, is demonstrated below. The importance of allowing patients to maintain their defenses and style of relating has been mentioned earlier. *Confronting defenses* and/or identifying defenses can be facilitating and therapeutic in psychotherapy but not in an evaluation interview or consultation in the medical setting. This is the case because in psychotherapy the patient has the already established helping relationship to contain the emergence of unprotected feelings and to act as a replacement for the challenged defenses. No similar safety has been constructed in a diagnostic interview in which the patient may not even be seeking help or may not view himself or herself as experiencing psychological or social problems. The examples below will illustrate the difference between confronting defenses and siding with them.

Example: A 36-year-old woman was referred to the medical clinic social worker by the primary care resident for a consultative evaluation of the patient's request for temporary disability. The woman had been working with some satisfaction as an office clerk for the past six years but developed gastric distress in recent months and had been treated so far in the medical clinic without symptom alleviation. The patient was now asking that a form be signed for temporary disability but the physician did not think there was enough medical evidence to justify the disability. He liked the patient and was concerned that being out of work would not be the answer, especially in that he was aware there were some family problems at home. The resident had taken a thorough history of the presenting illness, including substantial psychosocial data. He noticed that the gastric distress developed shortly after the patient's mother moved in with the patient, her husband and two young teenage daughters. The patient would mildly complain that her husband was spending less time at home and that her mother was now supervising all of the patient's housework; but the patient would quickly take back her resentment when the physician tried to focus on these complaints (doing and undoing). The physician painstakingly attempted to show the patient that her dissatisfaction with her home life was being expressed in the form of her intestinal disturbance. This direct confrontation of the patient's defenses resulted only in the patient wanting to dwell on her somatic complaints.

It should be said that in psychotherapy the interviewer would proceed a step further and with more exploration might be able to identify for the patient not only the defense but the purpose of the defense. Commonly, the purpose here is that the patient fears the intensity and power of her resentment, that is, she confuses it unconsciously with childhood murderous rage and the wish to kill off her adversaries. Awareness of such a wish would be emotionally frightening, so her "minimumization" of her resentment and the "conversion" of it into the compromise of the somatic complaint makes the conflict more palatable. There are a multitude of other interpretations that could be made within the atmosphere of psychotherapy but the point is the interviewer needs to know the patient better to make reasonably accurate identifications and to know if that patient could handle hearing these. The established relationship would also provide a feeling of safety for the patient.

Though the resident in the medical setting does not have the time nor training to make elaborate psychotherapeutic interventions, it might be noted that even psychosocial professionals often overestimate the appropriateness and effectiveness of directly confronting defenses. Without patients viewing themselves as experiencing psychosocial and/or social problems for which they are seeking help, and without established helping relationships, confrontation will seldom prove successful. Rarely, if ever, are these described circumstances present for the clinician in the medical setting.

Siding with the Defenses

Example (siding): The referral to the medical clinic social worker as a member of the consultation-liaison team was made to seek an opinion on the justification for temporary disability and to see what could be done with the suspected behavioral component to the physical illness. The social worker approached the interview by letting the patient describe what she saw as the problem. The patient was informed at the outset in rather global terms why she was seeing the social worker:

Social Worker: "Mrs. G., what is your understanding of why you are seeing me today?"

Mrs. G.: "Dr. C. thinks I have family problems that cause this stomach condition so he thought I should talk to you."

Social Worker: "How do you feel about that kind of referral?"

Mrs. G.: "That's OK with me . . . Dr. C. has been very understanding . . . it doesn't bother me."

Social Worker: "Tell me what you've been going through . . . how do you see the problem?"

Mrs. G's acceptance of the referral without much debate was typical, even diagnostic, of how she covered her resentment. However, this did not mean she was engaged in the helping process by any means. Other patients may be more reluctant to accept such a referral and their mixed feelings may need to be explored at the outset. Starting from a global level of clarification of the consultant's role, then becoming more specific as needed per patient seems to work best.

Initially, Mrs. G. focused exclusively on her medical problem, detailing the complaints at length. After ten minutes of showing interest in these complaints, the interviewer asked for some details on the family situation.

Social Worker; "Tell me about your home and family."

Mrs. G.: "Oh, they're all very understanding and helpful. My husband works regularly and my mother has been very helpful since she moved in."

The social worker obtains a description of the mother and the background as to when and why she moved in, then comments:

Social Worker: "It must be so comforting to have such a helpful mother so close by!"

Mrs. G.: "Yes, it is . . . (hesitating) but sometimes she does get a little on my nerves."

Social Worker: "Really?"

By expressing mild interest, the social worker allows the patient to express her dissatisfaction at a pace which does not aggravate her conscience. By siding with the patient's need to defend her mother and family and thereby guard against unleashing the patient's aggression, the patient can begin to ventilate some of the unconscious resentment which may be churning her insides. Individuals and systems that protect against negative affects can be helped to tolerate the release of some of these if first they are allowed to share positive affects and thereby build up stores against a harsh conscience.

If the patient noted above should persist in protecting her negative feelings toward her mother and husband the interviewer can equally continue to express interest in such a "harmonious" family life until the patient gets tired of hearing herself say this and begins to express some dissatisfaction, if only toward the interviewer. The fact is that usually only a couple of exchanges of siding with the defenses produces some affects which the defenses are protecting.

The same technique of siding with the defense can be employed effectively with individuals and systems that are uncomfortable with and guarded against positive feelings. This arrangement is common for patients presenting in crisis in emergency rooms. In these circumstances, some patients will initially reveal only their anger and dissatisfaction with their family and social relationships. Siding with this way of coping circumvents a struggle with the patient and prevents the clinician from becoming yet another target for the rage. Contrarily, reassuring comments such as "Surely things can't be that bad," or "I'm sure the storm will blow over," tend to increase the resentment and disequilibrium because these statements are experienced as disconfirming of the patient's perspective and seriousness.

Most importantly, siding with the defense gives the patient the opportunity to give up the fighting mood and recall or become aware of the other side of the feelings, in this latter case, more affectionate affects. For example, the interviewer might more profitably say, "How awful to always be treated that way," or "How unfair to wind up with such a family." Remarkably, patients begin to educate the interviewer that "Well, it's not always that bad," or "Sometimes they're not like that." As patients inform helpers, they inform themselves as well.

Sometimes helping professionals express concern that siding with such affects will only make the person worse. If done properly, there is no evidence of this. A guideline to remember is never to assume responsibility for the problem or the cure. Even after siding with the defense, and after some ventilation, the cardinal rule of seeking solutions from the patient ("So what do you think you'll do?" or "What have you done with this situation in the past?") must not be forgotten. Moreover, providing an opportunity for the emergence of repressed or forgotten feelings can be affectively and cognitively restoring. This is one of the contributions of crisis theory. Finally, as explained earlier in the chapter, no individual or social system should be allowed to ventilate an array of affects in an unlimited way. Such would not be supportive intervention, but rather regressive.

FURTHER TECHNIQUES OF ENGAGEMENT

Establishing Benevolent Parameters

By the use of the phrase "establishing benevolent parameters," the term "set appropriate limits" is avoided. Limit setting has gotten as bad a name as confrontation, and both are as widely misunderstood as the concept of support. Nevertheless, individuals and social systems in need of help will sometimes seek to negotiate agendas which are not within the therapeutic parameters of the helping relationship. The protective service social worker investigating child abuse, for instance, cannot grant a family's wish to abandon the assessment. Similarly, the psychiatric consultation-liaison clinician cannot meet the needs of general hospital staff or the patient's if the clinician does not pursue the evaluation beyond the patient's initial refusal to respond. Limits can be set in a benevolent way, however, if it is realized that some requests, such as refusing the evaluation, should not be part of the negotiation. This dilemma comes up regularly in child therapy when an aggressive youngster who threatens to destroy a room is told, "You can't run around the room but you can draw on this paper." The options of what is possible are clarified and laid out. Usually, if an individual or social system knows what is negotiable, territorial bargaining will be kept within the specified parameters. Also, as was explained earlier in the chapter, finding out what is behind the objections may even obviate the need for limits.

An illustration of engaging a patient by establishing benevolent parameters involved a 44-year-old man who presented nearly 15 times in the emergency room over a period of 60 days, each time with pain and palpitations of the heart. Initially, when no medical basis could be found for his complaints, the patient also requested a doctor's letter to get a phone paid for by the welfare office so he wouldn't need to wake up his neighbors at night to call the ambulance. After the physician provided the letter, the patient continued to present in the ER, soon making another request, this time for an air conditioner. Even before this, the ER had several times encouraged the patient to be seen in the medical clinic and not the ER. The medical clinic social worker coordinated a plan that no more letters would be provided by the ER staff. The patient next refused to go to the medical clinic and attempted to engage the social worker in a debate over what appointment times he could make. The patient was given two different times from which to choose. The patient gave different reasons why he could not make either time, one being because of transportation. "I guess you won't be able to make it then," said the social worker with a tone of concern. "Well, come to think of it the landlord could give me a ride," countered the patient. Once the boundaries of negotiation were clear, the patient chose within them. The patient never has come regularly enough for staff to complete an evaluation and provide treatment for the apparent behavioral component of his somatic distress, but his trips to the ER have stopped. It could be suggested that the establishment of the benevolent parameters was the treatment the patient could handle at this point.

Establishing successful parameters with some individuals and social networks is not possible unless the helping system of which the clinician is a part, in this case the general hospital, is cohesive and not fragmented. Helping systems whose staff members do not work in concert usually inadvertently reinforce and unintentionally reward the type of behavior exemplified by the patient described above.

Providing a Sample of the Treatment

All too often it is expected that the patient will be open to help if it is cognitively explained what the help is and why the clinician thinks it is needed. The purpose of an evaluation is not to offer help but for the clinician and the patient to come to an understanding of what problem, if any, exists and what plan might be appropriate and mutually desirable. Neither party can make an assessment until the patient expresses his thoughts and feelings, even if only in response to the interviewer's inquiries, and has the opportunity to experience in turn the clinician's responses. If the patient is able to express some difficulty or if the clinician is able to elicit it, this ventilation when met with the interviewer's facilitating, shaping, and confirming comments amounts to a sample of the treatment. It is more often the case in consultative work, in fact, that the burden of providing the sample treatment must originate with the interviewer and depends on what array of engagement strategies are within the interviewer's training and experience.

Making Use of the Social Environment

In this case, the principle of engagement is the use of a medium or transitional object between the patient and the interviewer to ease the patient into a more comfortable and accessible frame of mind. The medium could be one of allowing the patient to bring a friend or family member into the interview or examining room for the early part of the contact. This may be suitable for patients who appear hesitant to leave their companions in the waiting room. Or engagement could be facilitated by focusing on a need or problem in the patient's social environment. Discussion centered on a patient's expressed concern about money or job can pave the way to soon explore areas which may be more sensitive for the patient. In some cases, offering to make a telephone call to a social agency to clarify a patient's confusion over a form may be helpful.

The idea of doing something concrete to engage children in helping relationships has been employed commonly but this has been overlooked and often devalued with adults. It has been thought that adults do not need tangible efforts or that performing such tasks could later stimulate childish demands or dependency in adults. The fact is that while a patient's impressions can be adjusted later, no efforts will be of value if the patient does not participate in the first interview and return for follow-up sessions, if indicated. The same can be said for allowing the patient to involve companions in the process. Children's attachments and problems of separation anxiety have been widely appreciated while adults have been routinely expected to present as autonomous individuals, even when it is otherwise realized that many adults live within enmeshed, entangled social systems of two or more persons. The spouse who allows the partner to do all the talking, for instance, can be a well-established style. Such an alignment cannot be altered any more immediately than one might expect the hysterical person to abandon a style of theatrics in a first encounter. As the latter patient tends to calm down once he or she becomes comfortable with the interviewer, so might the former patient later be at ease alone if earlier allowed to speak through or with the security of a companion.

A corollary to this principle of engagement is simply tolerance for how both individuals singularly and systems of individuals collectively present themselves. The importance of respecting the individual's defenses and personality style was described earlier. The same must be said about understanding and respecting how systems present. Though an individual may be by role and/or biology a member of a social group or family, the individual may initially relate and communicate neither as an individual nor in association with the whole group or family. Some individuals can be engaged only as a subset of the group, that is, in the presence of or literally through the speech of, one or more but not all the members of his or her social group or family. This reality is sometimes no more appreciated by practitioners of family and systems therapy than the mistake of the unseasoned one-to-one helper who at the outset directly confronts the defenses and personality style of the individual. Equally unseasoned systems-oriented clinicians fail to engage families and social networks by requiring an initial diagnostic interview in which all family members are expected to attend and participate. Many social systems do not have the coping style of presenting as a whole group. Accordingly, such fixed rules will guarantee engagement failures.

ENGAGEMENT AND THE MENTAL STATUS EXAM

The number of professional disciplines and helping settings in which the mental status exam has been included as a routine part of the interviewing process is progressively on the increase. Residents and nurses in medical training are being taught to test for orientation, record data on neurovegetative signs, and to inquire about suicidal ideation. As social workers become part of multidisciplinary teams in primary care medicine, consultation-liaison psychiatry and emergency room crisis programs, they are relying on the usefulness of the mental status exam as social workers have in community mental health for more than a decade. However, while the substance and content of the mental status exam is being taught, not enough attention has been paid to the process of employing the exam.

If the mental status exam is followed verbatim according to its usual structure, the impact on the patient and the interviewer can be one of feeling quite mechanical and artificial. The patient can be left feeling as an object or specimen rather than a person. Under these circumstances, the information gained from the mental status exam could be faulty and erroneous, being more a reflection of an uncomfortable experience between patient and interviewer. While the nature and content of mental status examination questions can be awkward in themselves, the patient's responses can be colored as well by feeling embarrassed or insulted by the manner in which the questions are asked.

The object of the mental status exam is to obtain information by observation, rudimentary tests, and inquiries as to the level of the patient's mental functioning. Since an accurate outcome is in the interests of the patient's health, adequately engaging the patient in the process should be a primary goal. As with most other helping interventions, success and/or effectiveness cannot be achieved without securing the patient's assistance.

The most basic point to realize is that the part of the interview in which the mental status exam is employed is usually more formal than what seems to happen before or after its use. This may not always have to be the case, but to date the helping professions have not come up with a way of blending all parts of the mental status into the more fluid flow of the interview. Nevertheless, some recommendations can be made to ease the transition so as to engage the patient in the process and thereby avoid faulty data.

If the mental status exam will be a noticeable transition to an account of the history of the presenting illness or the gathering of sociodemographic information, it would be more facilitating for the interviewer to comment on the transition. Just as the interviewer might courteously explain to the patient why he switched his chair in midsession (for example, to avoid a draft or escape a ray of sunlight), so should the clinician make note of an abrupt change in the nature of the questions. "The questions I now need to ask you may seem rather out of the ordinary, but bear with me—they will help me understand how you are doing . . . What day is it today?" Or, if the patient is on medication, the clinician could explain that this can cause confusion so questions about time and place are asked to check for this.

Depending upon the discomfort of the patient, several transitional statements may need to be made. Even after a patient has given an answer, the interviewer should become comfortable to ask the question again, especially if the clinician suspects the answer is more a reflection of the patient's unease than his or her functioning. This technique can be quite effective in obtaining information on auditory hallucinations when the patient is not blatantly or obviously psychotic. "I know it may be embarrassing to say you've been hearing voices, but we do have medication for that nowadays." If the interviewer even remotely suspects present or past psychotic processes, he or she could follow-up the patient's initial denial of the question, "Have you been hearing sounds or voices?" with "When did you last hear the voices?" Remarkably, the second question will sometimes result in reports that voices were heard earlier that day or last week, etc.

Should the patient become angry or insulted by such questions, this could also be significant data. The interviewer could empathetically respond that "Sometimes people do feel insulted by these questions. Has anyone ever put you through this before?" The latter question may bring out previous personal or psychiatric history that earlier had been withheld. At the very least, it would reveal the patient's feelings about such questions. Being aware of and sensitive to these feelings is imperative to obtaining an accurate mental status.

An illustration of this was a 56-year-old woman on the inpatient psychiatric unit who had had several admissions for depression and had been treated with ECT. A consult was requested of the psychiatric consultation-liaison team to assess organic mental disorder. When asked to copy a bender-gestalt cross, the patient drew such a distorted figure that organic dysfunction seemed confirmed. However, the interviewing psychiatrist noted the patient's mildly resentful affect as well as her verbal allusion to having been made to draw pictures when in grade school. *The principle here is identifying the patient's affect.* Subsequently, the interviewer solicited some ventilation about the patient's negative relationship with teachers and commented how this request on the mental status might seem unintentionally reminiscent of being treated like a child. Following this dialogue, the request was repeated and the patient drew the figure in perfect detail.

With cleverness and creativity, some parts of the mental status can be tested in ways that are not abruptly out of character with the rest of the interview. For instance, a social worker who wants to test the memory of an elderly medical inpatient awaiting nursing home placement could look at the nurse's data sheet on what the patient ate for breakfast, then casually ask the patient what she had had. If there is significant memory dysfunction which is not noted in the medical chart or whose etiology has not been established, this could be critical to bring up for medical team review. The memory disturbance could be evidence of a reversible, untreated organic mental disorder, or may be one symptom of a cluster suggestive of a treatable major depression. By employing parts of the mental status in the social worker's routine interview, data could emerge that could significantly affect the health care of the patient.

Questions that are not technically part of the mental status exam also require sensitivity to their impact on the patient. Examples include obtaining information on past psychiatric history or seeking data on drug and/or alcohol use. When the interviewer suspects alcohol abuse, for instance, why ask the patient if he or she drinks? The patient is left to "confess" the obvious. This barrier invites unnecessary denials and sets the stage for otherwise avoidable tension and struggle. Accordingly, the engagement principle here is to avoid soliciting confessions. A more effective engagement technique would be to ask, "What do you like to drink? Wine? Beer? Liquor?" If the patient reports gin as the drink of choice, it will be next easier to ascertain the quantity and frequency by starting out high and allowing the patient to reduce the figures as needed, "Do you drink a quart a day or a pint?" The patient can then respond, "Oh, no. More like a quart a week . . . maybe a pint on payday but then I sober up for the weekend."

TERMINATION AND ENGAGEMENT

Terminate the interview without controlling the patient. Patients who either have not asked for help, are unsure about what they want, or who seem to have mixed feelings about accepting involvement with the practitioner, are best engaged if the clinician maneuvers the closing minutes of the interview so that the patient feels in control. Allow patients to assess for themselves the value and meaning of the session and whether continuing contact would be in their interest. Ask, for instance, "How was this meeting for you today?" If the patient needs further clarification, add "Was it helpful to you or not helpful?" If the patient says it was helpful ask in what way and enlist their recommendations for future contact, frequency of contact, and the content focus of what would serve their needs. If the needs or requests of the patient are not within the realm of what the clinician feels he or she can or should provide, this needs to be clearly stated. Even if that is the case, the interviewer can then ask what other help the patient may want which could be provided.

If the patient says the session was not helpful, do not become defensive but seek the specifics as to what did not meet which needs of the patient. The patient's feelings can be empathized with and identified for the patient without the clinician needing to experience the dissatisfaction personally. Often, once the patient has expressed the dissatisfaction without retaliation from the practitioner, this is evidence enough for the patient that the professional is a person with whom the patient can entrust his or her own concerns without fear of undue criticism or punishment. Such responses could be quite different from what the patient has become accustomed to expect, especially since the patient's own critical style is probably attracting counteroffensive reactions in his or her other personal and professional relationships. After the patient has expressed the dissatisfaction with the contact and specifics have been gathered, this information will usually clarify both for the clinician and the patient whether a treatment plan can be offered to more pointedly address the patient's needs. If this is not yet clear, then ask the patient, "What do you think would be helpful?" And the patient can be queried directly, "Do you think coming back again would be helpful or not?" If the patient is particularly oppositional, siding with the defense is often facilitative—with the practitioner openly concluding, "It sounds as if not returning would be most to your liking then?" At this, the most oppositional patient will sometimes remain consistent in his or her contrariness and thereby switch to complying with the treatment just to feel in opposition to the clinician.

For the patient who remains adamant to the end that he (or she) will not return, accept the patient's decision and tell the patient that he can make contact in the future should he change his mind. Sometimes this works out for the best because it does not force patients into contracts to which they will not be bound and cuts down on unkept appointments in often already overcrowded clinics. Also, these patients commonly recontact when they are ready to do so anyway. Others can only be treated on a crisis basis.

At any rate, once the patient feels more trusting and comfortable with the practitioner, these tactics become unnecessary. For very wary patients who may have particularly deprived past relationships, this testing phase goes on for quite some time, while for others it lasts only a few contacts. Nevertheless, these strategies in the closing minutes of early interviews with difficult patients are indispensable if the practitioner wants to become more effective at engaging difficult patients and increasing the rate of compliance with treatment plans.

SUMMARY

Principles of engaging patients in helping relationships, primarily in the medical setting, were discussed in this chapter. The principles elucidated included:

Recognize the patient's situation and identify for the patient what feelings might likely be generated by this situation. This necessitates that social workers, physicians, and other helping professionals not take personally the feelings that might be expressed, even if they are directed at the caregiver.

Elucidate the patient's perception of previous treatment. Even when the details are not historically accurate, the account can be a harbinger of what is ahead in a new therapeutic relationship.

Allow the ventilation of feelings about previous providers of care. This helps the patient disengage from earlier ties and sees the new caregiver as different and not necessarily an extension of the past.

Refuse to accept total responsibility for care. Caregivers can provide quality care only by offering the parameters of standard practice. This includes reasonable alternatives for the patient to choose to follow. The patient's participation is essential to a successful outcome. If this dual commitment is not recognized, both the patient and the practitioner fall into the trap of seeing all solutions and all responsibility for care as resting with the practitioner. The patient who idealizes the caregiver at the outset usually harbors an agenda (almost always out of conscious awareness of the patient) to prove the "authority" wrong.

Do not ally with or against the previous treatment. Cast the plans and prescriptions of the treatment in a current context. Do not endorse or defend earlier treatment until the patient is better known.

Ask the patient for a solution. The most effective engagement technique for the patient who does present a problem which seems to include insurmountable barriers to effective care is to feed the problem back to the patient as presented and ask the patient for a possible solution.

Get the patient's attention. This does not mean making sure the patient encounters the consultant visually or auditorily. Patients bring with them from their past experiences already established conceptions of almost every conceivable new relationship. These vary from patient to patient but there do exist some universal stereotypes of what medical staff or psychosocial helpers are about. When these preconceptions are negative or constrictive, the interview will no doubt be greatly colored by these. It is the task of the consultant at the outset to jostle the patient free from these orientations and get the patient's attention independent of them.

No patients are easy to engage. The question always is one of when resistance will happen, not whether it will. Patients have resistances imbedded in a number of psychological conflicts which militate against easy involvement in any helping relationship.

The therapeutic alliance. The therapeutic alliance essentially means establishing a relationship which is both helpful and healthy to the patient's interest. If this is established, the relationship will be manageable for the clinician. Untherapeutic alliances, established usually unintentionally, increase the patient's turmoil and cause havoc for the helper. The therapeutic alliance amounts to offering assistance only to the reasonable side of the patient, not the childlike, demanding, regressive side.

Ego support. This principle is not to be confused with encouragement. Offering unnecessary reassurance may make the helper feel better but is more likely to result in underscoring whatever self-doubt and feelings of inferiority the patient is already harboring. A more effective "supportive" strategy is to draw out the "ego" strengths or self-skills at problem solving that *do* exist within the patient's developed personality and life experiences. These coping skills or problem-solving abilities are commonly forgotten by a patient at a time of stress.

Understand the role of defenses and personality types. Defenses are necessary to bind anxiety and to cope with it. A cardinal rule of engagement is to allow patients to maintain their defenses and particular style of relating and not attempt to challenge them. This is emphatically the case in medical settings in which patients commonly view themselves as exclusively experiencing biological problems without any psychological or social components.

Understand ambivalence and its associated strategies. While everyone experiences mixed feelings, the intensity of the ambivalence and the amount of energy devoted to avoiding conscious awareness of one or more sides of ambivalence are diagnostic of how much affect an individual or system can bear. In general, the greater tolerance of consciously experienced mixed feelings or the more the individual can live with ambiguity, the less there will be evidence of conflict in the presence of various defenses against conflict. The skillful interviewer will observe these diagnostic indicators and will rely upon them in order to engage patients.

Side with the defense. This is the most effective technique and most underused psychological maneuver with resistive patients.

Establish benevolent parameters. Indivduals and social systems that are in need of help will sometimes seek to negotiate agendas which are not within the therapeutic parameters of the helping relationship. Limits can be set in a benevolent way if it is realized that some requests should not be part of the negotiation. The options of what is possible should be clarified and laid out. Usually if an individual or social system knows what is negotiable, territorial bargaining will keep within the specified parameters. Also, finding out what is behind the objections may even obviate the need for limits.

Provide a sample of the treatment. All too often it is expected that patients will be open to help if it is cognitively explained what the help is and why the clinician thinks it is needed. Contrarily, if the patient is able to express some difficulty or if the clinician is able to elicit the difficulty, this ventilation when met with the interviewer's facilitating, shaping, and confirming comments amounts to a sample of the treatment, which is commonly required to engage difficult patients. Some affective confirmation of the patient must be a part of the process in order to engage the patient.

Make use of the social environment. Using tangible mediums such as concrete services, or involving the patient's companions in the interview can help to engage less talkative, less reflective patients and those who appear uncomfortable being seen alone.

Identify the patient's affect. This is the most basic technique of all helping relationships, yet it is often forgotten in the most awkward situations, such as during a mental status exam when it could be so helpful.

Avoid soliciting confessions. This is particularly true when the information is obvious, such as not asking if the patient drinks alcohol when the smell of liquor is on the patient's breath. Specific questions cultivate more accurate answers and facilitate engagement.

Terminate the interview without controlling the patient. This is a crucial technique for helping to insure continued contact with the patient. It amounts to allowing the patient to assess the interview which is coming to a close and to enlist the patient's recommendations for the nature of future contact and its frequency. It is the opposite of the clinician summing up the session and telling the patient what is advisable.

NOTES

1. Watzlawick, Paul, John Weakland and Richard Fisch, *Change: Principles of Problem Formation and Problem Resolution* (New York: Norton, 1974).
2. Glasser, William, *Reality Therapy* (New York: Harper & Row, 1965).
3. Alexander, Franz, and Thomas French, *Psychoanalytic Therapy* (New York: Ronald Press, 1946), 83.
4. Havens, Lester, *Participant Observation* (New York: Jason Aaronson, 1976).
5. Watzlawick, Paul, *How Real Is Real* (New York, Random House, 1976).
6. Allen, Woody, *Getting Even* (New York: Vintage Books, 1978).
7. For further discussion of personality types in primary care medicine see R. J. Goldberg, "Personality Disorders," Chapter VI in *Psychiatry in Primary Care Medicine*, ed. H. Leigh (Menlo Park, California: Addison-Wesley, 1983). Also, R. J. Kahana and G. L. Bibring, "Personality Types in Medical Management," in *Psychiatry and Medical Practice in a General Hospital*, ed. N. Zinberg (New York: International University Press, 1974), 108-23.

ADDITIONAL REFERENCES

Aronson, H., and B. Overall, "Treatment Expectations of Patients in Two Social Classes," *Social Work* 11 (1966): 35-42.

Borghi, J., "Premature Termination of Psychotherapy and Patient-therapist Expectations," *American Journal of Psychotherapy*, 22 (1968): 460-73.

Eisenthal, S. and A. Lazare "Evaluation of the Initial Interview in a Walk-in Clinic: Social and Psychiatric Variables," *American Journal of Orthopsychiatry* 46 (1976): 503-09.

Frank, A., S. Eisenthal, and A. Lazare, "Are There Social Class Differences in Patients' Treatment Conceptions? Myths and Facts," *Archives of General Psychiatry* 35 (1977): 61-69.

Freud, Sigmund, "On Beginning the Treatment," in *Collected Papers by Sigmund Freud*, Vol. II (London: Hogarth Press and the Institute of Psycho-Analysis, 1946).

Freud, Sigmund, "Transference" in *Collected Papers by Sigmund Freud*, Vol. II (London: Hogarth Press and the Institute of Psycho-Analysis, 1946).

Goin, M., J. Yamamoto, and J. Silverman, "Therapy Congruent with Class-linked Expectations," *Archives of General Psychiatry* 13 (1975): 133-37.

Golan, Naomi, "When Is a Client in Crisis?" *Social Casework* 50, 7, (July 1969): 389-94.

Goldstein, A.P., "Participant Expectancies in Psychotherapy," *Psychiatry* 25 (1962): 72-79

Gottlieb, W. and J.H. Stanley, "Mutual Goals and Goalsetting in Casework," *Social Casework* 48 (1967): 471-77.

Hass, Walter, "Reaching Out: A Dynamic Concept in Casework," *Social Work* 4, 3 (July 1959): 41-45.

Heine, R.W., and A. Trosman, "Initial Expectations of the Doctor-Patient Interaction as a Factor in the Continuance in Psychotherapy," *Psychiatry*, 23 (1960) 275-78.

Hornstra, R.K., B. Lubin, R.V. Lewis, and B.S. Willis, "Worlds Apart: Patients and Professionals," *Archives of General Psychiatry* 27 (1972): 553-57.

Kounin, J., N. Polansky, B. Biddle, H. Coburn, and A. Fenn, "Experimental Studies of Clients' Reactions to Initial Interviews," *Human Relations* 9 (1956): 256-92.

Lazare, Aaron, and Sherman Eisenthal, "A Negotiated Approach to the Clinical Encounter I: Attending the Patient's Perspective", Chapter 7, *Outpatient Psychiatry*, ed. Aaron Lazare, M. D., Williams & Wilkins Co., Baltimore, Md., (1979): 141-56.

Lazare, Aaron, Sherman Eisenthal, and Arlene Frank, "Disposition Decisions in a Walk in Clinic: Social and Psychiatric Variables," *American Journal of Orthopsychiatry* 46 (1976): 503-09.

Lazare, Aaron, Sherman Eisenthal, and Arlene Frank, "Negotiated Approach to the Clinical Encounter II: Conflict in Negotiation," *Outpatient Psychiatry*, ed. Aaron Lazare (Baltimore: Williams and Wilkins, 1979): 157-71.

Overall, B., and H. Aronson, "Expectations of Psychotherapy in Patients of Lower Socio-economic Class," *American Journal of Orthopsychiatry* 33 (1963): 421-30.

Platt, F. W., and J. C. McMath, "Clinical Hypocompetence: The Interview," *Annals of Internal Medicine* 91, 6 (1979): 989-92.

Polak, P., "Patterns of Discord: Goals of Patients, Therapists and Community Members," *Archives of General Psychiatry* 23, (1970): 277-83.

Polansky, N. and J. Kounin, "Clients' Reactions to Initial Interview and Field Study," *Human Relations* 9, (1956): 237-64.

Sullivan, Harry Stack, *Psychiatric Interview* (New York: W.W. Norton, 1970).

Wallace, Stephen R., *The Origins of "Getting the Patient's Attention." Some Thoughts on Transference, Countertransference, the Repetition Compulsion, and Therapy,* unpublished (1980) (copies available through R. I. Hospital Outpatient Psychiatry, Providence, R. I.).

Williams, H., R. S. Lipman, E.H. Uhlenhuth, K. Rickels, L. Covi, and J. Mock, "Some Factors Influencing the Treatment Expectations of Anxious Neurotic Outpatients," *Journal of Nervous and Mental Diseases* 145 (1967): 208-20.

Chapter Five

The Biopsychosocial Data Base

Primary medical care takes place at the confluence of biologic, psychologic, and social systems. Physical symptoms alone do not determine why a patient seeks medical care[1] nor does the presentation of a seemingly psychological or social complaint assure that an underlying medical disorder is not a direct or aggravating cause.[2] As far as we can uncover, no one has yet systematically studied the patterns of referral to social work in a primary care setting or clarified the role that the social worker actually fulfills in that setting. Preliminary data from one such study completed at the Rhode Island Hospital Medical Primary Care Unit[3] adds additional evidence to the claim that patients with unrecognized major psychiatric disorders are often referred to social work and that the role of medical factors in psychosocial distress is often not adequately appreciated by the physician[4]. Such findings imply that the clinical social worker who aspires to practice the comprehensive primary care approach should be trained to recognize such problems. Other studies have revealed that social workers are almost universally unaware of underlying medical disorders relevant to the psychologic or social symptoms being evaluated.[5] In order to become a significant colleague in a team of professionals involved in primary medical care, the social worker must be prepared to speak the language of the biomedical as well as the psychosocial disciplines, must be aware of those medical disorders which present as psychological symptoms, and must learn to conceptualize patient problems in a biopsychosocial model.[6] The biopsychosocial data base is the fundamental clinical tool to assure a systematic approach to such patient care. Without such a data base, it is too easy for clinicians to make assumptions about the etiology of a patient's problems according to their particular bias or predisposition. Examples in this chapter will show how initial presumptions are often unwarranted and how improved patient care can result from balanced data gathering in every situation.

The biomedical knowledge necessary to use this data base does not require that the social worker become a "minipsychiatrist." The intent is not to convert the social worker into a psychiatrist but to augment the traditional knowledge base of the social worker with information necessary for the social worker to become a more comprehensive clinician and consultant to the primary care team. Rather than resulting in a deviation of social work from its psychosocial orientation, the augmentation of skills outlined in this chapter will enable the social worker to participate as a valuable mental health professional who is able to make a unique contribution to primary patient care.

The data base is not an end in itself but a means to an end. It is not meant to be used as a rigid outline which must be filled out sequentially at the risk of alienating the patient and destroying the therapeutic relationship. As one becomes familiar with its contents, it is not difficult to gather all the appropriate information in the course of a clinical interview while remaining sensitive to interpersonal nuances. The contents of this data base represent information which a majority of the competent clinicians routinely gather during each and every evaluation. The particular order of the questions and the format is somewhat arbitrary and the inclusion or omission of some items can serve as the basis for constructive revision. However, when one takes up the task of organizing and writing a data base within certain time and space limitations, decisions about what to include or exclude have to be made. This particular data base remains a living document that is altered as warranted by growing clinical experience of its usefulness in settings in which the primary care approach is practiced. This chapter will discuss the rationale for the inclusion of questions in the biologic dimension. Since a clinician's time is so limited, he or she should understand the purpose of every question asked and should feel that each question can bring a high yield with a potential to significantly alter further clinical decisions about the patient.

A systematized data base simultaneously serves a number of needs in any comprehensive health care setting. It facilitates communication among a variety of disciplines by organizing information into an identifiable format that becomes familiar to participating staff. Too often, information obtained in a psychosocial interview is organized in idiosyncratic ways, is illegible, or has significant errors of omission or commission which make the clinical effort much less useful to the rest of the treatment team. Further, since patients treated in settings in which the primary care approach is practiced are often seen longitudinally, this format establishes a true data base which lends itself to problem-oriented record keeping—increasingly a part of health care. Naturally, patients do not need a total new data base each visit. Once a good data base has been established, the need for only minor revisions rather than complete review actually saves clinician time in the long run. Finally, health care settings are often staffed by a variety of disciplines (including physicians, physicians-in-training, nurse practitioners, psychiatric nurses, clinical social workers, social work interns, psychologists, and so on). The data base serves not only as a uniform approach to patient evaluation but also becomes an important teaching tool that can be used interchangeably by a variety of disciplines.

THE DATA BASE

Patient Identification and Sociodemographics

The first half of page one contains information regarding patient identification and sociodemographics. It is useful to have such information located in one place and also can remind the clinician of important clinical aspects that are sometimes overlooked. The identification of a primary clinician can lead to a gathering of adjunctive information which is crucial to current management. Current therapists or physicians should always be contacted as part of the evaluation, at least to clarify the purpose of the meeting. Likewise, the identified responsible person is often appropriate to include in an evaluation. The patient who has no "responsible person" is, of course, subject to all the risks associated with low levels of social support.[7,8] Sociodemographics are not inert details but should be thought of as epidemiologic risk factors. For example, schizophrenia or drug abuse are much less likely to account for psychosocial problems in a 68-year-old recently retired man than they are in a 15-year-old adolescent who dropped out of the tenth grade six months previously. Much has been written on the use of sociodemographics to predict suicidal risk.[9] Particular occupations should bring to mind certain possible risks such as alcohol use in bartenders, substance abuse in nurses or other medical professionals, toxic exposures in certain factory workers, and so forth.

Finally, the usefulness of information is limited if it cannot be concisely and accurately communicated to another professional. The data base serves as a format for coherently organized oral presentations among professionals and becomes the basis for more complex discussion of evaluation or management issues.

The beginning of every patient presentation should be patient identification and sociodemographics. We often have found that discussion of a patient presentation can be disrupted by a seemingly never ending flow of small details that the presenter often forgot to include. "How old was she? . . . Is she married? . . . Are there any children? . . . How far did she go in school? . . . Is she working? . . . etc." It is virtually impossible to listen intelligently to a case presentation without this type of information presented initially since the experienced clinical listener will be constantly processing possibilities and formulations from the very beginning of the presentation and the likelihood of clinical hypotheses are to a large extent determined by sociodemographics. It is recommended that at the beginning of an oral case presentation, the presenter should take a deep breath and try to include patient identification and sociodemographics in one extended sentence which can set the stage for the remainder of the case presentation. For example, "This is a 32-year-old white Roman Catholic woman who is divorced, has no children, is currently living alone and working as a nurse's aide."

Vital Signs

The following discussion depends on an understanding that organic mental disorders resulting from impaired neuronal function in the brain, regardless of cause, can produce disturbances of mood, thought, or behavior which are indistinguishable from so-called "functional" disturbances.[10] Organic mental disorders can masquerade as psychological symptoms or disrupted social systems in ways that are indistinguishable on the surface. The checking of vital signs is useful as an initial gross screening to rule out some of the most basic medical disturbances that can lead to altered mood, thought, or behavior.

Vital signs, including blood pressure, temperature, heart rate, and respiratory rate, are crucial factors in the biopsychosocial data base which are almost universally neglected in the nonmedical setting and are often overlooked in the medical setting because of the bifurcation of thinking about patients into "physical" or "psychosocial" categories. The following examples illustrate how such a bias is fraught with danger for clinical care.

Temperature

Elevated temperature can significantly alter brain function to the point of producing a variety of behavioral or personality changes.[11, 12] For example:

A Puerto Rican Spanish-speaking family brought in their 18-year-old son because he had stopped going to work a week before. With some difficulty translating through an interpreter, it was determined from the mother and sisters that his behavior had significantly changed. Instead of going out with his friends, he began to spend most of his time on the living room couch, falling asleep frequently and at times waking up and starting to laugh for no apparent reason. He seemed inaccessible and often would not join the family for meals. At other

times, however, he seemed alert and more like his normal self. On examination, he was withdrawn and appeared to be responding to internal cues as if he were hallucinating. There was no history of drug or
alcohol abuse. On routine vital signs he was found to have a temperature of 101.6° with no apparent source. Because of the elevated
temperature and fluctuating state of consciousness a spinal tap was
performed which revealed evidence of a central nervous system
infection.

Had it not been for the careful history and awareness of the elevated
temperature, this patient easily could have been misdiagnosed as schizophrenic and treated incorrectly. Patients with diabetes or cancer or who are
on immunosuppressive medication are at special risk for development of
these infections.

Of course, not every elevated temperature will be associated with
encephalitis (brain infection) and more commonly will be secondary to
more common maladies such as viral, upper respiratory, or urinary tract
infection. However, a source must be sought for every elevated temperature
in a patient with psychosocial symptoms.

Blood Pressure

Patients with extremely high elevations of blood pressure (usually in
the range of 200/140) can develop "hypertensive encephalopathy" which
along with headache and visual changes can be accompanied by a variety of
personality changes. It is equally important to check for low blood
pressure, or hypotension. Social workers in inpatient medical settings may
be frequently called to see patients who complain of a sense of uneasiness or
anxiety during the hospital stay. Such nonspecific symptoms (which could
appear to be due to any number of psychological adjustment issues in the
hospital) are sometimes the very first signs of an impending medical catastrophe such as loss of blood pressure secondary to internal bleeding or
cardiac arrhythmia. Such medical catastrophes will often be signaled by
loss of blood pressure leading to autonomic nervous system discharge and
feelings of anxiety. Furthermore, because so many of the commonly used
psychotropic drugs, especially the tricyclic antidepressants, and neuroleptics can lower blood pressure, it is important to make sure that some
member of the health care team is documenting blood pressure in both the
sitting and standing positions to see whether there is a significant change with
posture. Hypotension secondary to postural change, known as orthostatic
hypotension, is often secondary to medication and frequently accounts for a
variety of nonspecific complaints including lightheadedness, dizziness, or just
not feeling right while taking medication. Failure to recognize the basis

for such symptoms can lead to noncompliance, feelings of frustration in the patient, or in some cases to medical consequences such as a serious fall. For example, it has been estimated that as many as 40 percent of patients on imipramine (Tofranil) have clinically significant orthostatic hypotension (with symptoms) and that a few patients fall with resultant injuries, such as hip fractures.[13]

Pulse Rate

During a diagnostic interview, patients are often anxious and will have a somewhat elevated pulse of over 100. However, there are certain specific conditions mistakenly directed to a mental health professional which are actually secondary to pulse abnormalities. An entity known as paroxysmal atrial tachycardia causes a pulse in the range of 180 per minute and can cause the patient to experience intermittent episodes of anxiety which can be incorrectly ascribed to some psychosocial precipitants. Patients with mitral valve prolapse may also be predisposed to pulse irregularities associated with panic.[14] Anxious patients with hyperthyroidism can present with an elevated pulse rate.[14] At other times, irregularities in the pulse can be signs of toxicity due to medication or cardiac problems which are impairing blood circulation to the brain and therefore resulting in a wide variety of "psychiatric" symptoms, that is, alterations of mood, thought and/or behavior.

Respiratory Rate

Increased respiratory rate can represent a nonspecific symptom of anxiety or can result from impaired cardiac or pulmonary function (such as pulmonary embolus) or from salicylate toxicity from excessive aspirin ingestion. A patient who has prolonged periods of excessively rapid respiration should be medically screened for a wide variety of possible underlying medical causes. Labeling a patient as having "hyperventilation" is not adequate without proper medical evaluation.[15]

Past Psychiatric History

Documentation of past treatment experiences can be an important predictor of current treatment response and future prognosis. Old treatment records should be requested with a signed release of information for all past mental health treatment contacts. When possible, it is important to find out what psychotropics a person has been given in the past including the reasons for the medication, the dose, duration, and response or lack of it. Frequently, patients who say they did not respond to a particular medication actually did not have an adequate trial of the drug at a high enough dose for a long enough duration of time. It is always helpful to find out the nature of a past treatment relationship, what took place, what sort of experience it was for the patient, what was helpful about it, and how it ended. From such a history, the alert therapist will note warning signs that may be likely to repeat in the current treatment context. More detail is presented on this topic in Chapter 4, "On the Art of Engaging the Patient." While it is important to recognize that history often repeats itself, even chronic psychiatric patients can develop new or additional medical disorders. All symptoms cannot automatically be ascribed to a chronic condition.

Family History

A careful family history can provide the key to the diagnosis and management of a patient referred to social work in the primary care setting. Some psychiatric researchers feel that a comprehensive family history is the single most important tool in making a psychiatric diagnosis since such disorders as unipolar depression, bipolar depression, schizophrenia, anxiety disorders, alcoholism, seizure disorders, or even hysteria have some hereditary basis. Equally important, this history can reveal medical mythologies of psychiatric or medical illness which run in the family and therefore influence the interpretation of symptoms by the patient.

Mr. R.S. was a 52-year-old typesetter who had had no previous medical or psychiatric history until he began to make multiple visits to the medical clinic with a variety of nonspecific physical complaints. The primary physician became increasingly frustrated, being unable to uncover any underlying medical disorder or obvious psychosocial precipitant. The patient had finally begun to miss work so much that he was finally referred to social work to assist in processing an application for temporary disability. Rather than take the case at face value, the social worker completed a biopsychosocial data base. While reviewing the family history he found that the patient's father had died of a heart attack at age 52 while at work. In exploring this important information, the social worker tapped into a vast well of unresolved affect relating to the father and uncovered a myth held by the patient that he too would die at work if he continued.

Significant past relationships not uncommonly surface in a medical setting because of unresolved grief. It appears clinically that many somatizing medical patients have some unresolved grief situation which contributes to depression and somatic preoccupation.[16] Such information cannot be obtained by asking the patient questions like, "Has there been some death in your family that you haven't yet gotten over?" Rather, a careful family history which elicits some detail about each member of the family will tipoff the carefully listening clinician to problematic or unresolved relationships because such relationships will be talked about in ways distinctly different from the usually bland, matter-of-fact descriptions given less crucial relationships.

Substance Use

Alcohol

The effects of alcohol, acutely or chronically, are ubiquitous in the medical setting. It is important to carefully review alcohol use. Even the most careful clinician will from time to time get fooled by a patient whose symptoms are actually secondary to covert alcoholism. The social worker or other health care team member should be aware that early morning symptoms of anxiety or shakiness are often due to minor withdrawal in a heavy drinker. This is important enough that the clinician should consult other texts to become familiar with the toxic and withdrawal effects of alcohol.[17, 18]

Illicit Drugs

Drug use and abuse can account for virtually every known psychosocial symptom. In many parts of the country today there is an epidemic of phencyclidine (PCP or "angel dust") abuse. Use of this drug can result in dramatic and frightening personality distortions including violent, destructive episodes.[19] While the effects of marijuana (or THC) are less dramatic, chronic marijuana use may lead to an amotivational syndrome or chronic memory and thought disturbance. Cocaine use may be associated with severe anxiety or depression during withdrawal.[20] The social worker is not expected to become an encyclopedia of street drug abuse but should become conversant in the terminology necessary to take a street drug history.

Caffeine

Caffeinism is indistinguishable from anxiety neurosis.[21] In addition, many patients who complain of insomnia are simply suffering from caffeinism. Withdrawal from chronic caffeine use can also lead to symptoms including headache, anxiety, or irritability.[22] Many patients use excessive caffeine without being aware of it. Table 5.1 lists the amounts of caffeine in commonly used products. Since symptoms can result from fairly small amounts, the interviewer should ask specifically for the amount of coffee, tea, and cola drunk each day.

TABLE 5.1. Caffeine

Source	Approximate Amounts of Caffeine per Unit
Beverages	
Brewed coffee	100-150 mg per cup
Cola drinks	40- 60 mg per cup
Decaffeinated coffee	2- 4 mg per cup
Instant coffee	86- 99 mg per cup
Tea	60- 75 mg per cup
Over-the-counter analgesics	
Anacin, aspirin compound, Bromo Seltzer	32 mg per tablet
Cope, Empirin compound, Midol	32 mg per tablet
Excedrin	60 mg per tablet
Vanquish	32 mg per tablet
Prescription medications	
APCs (aspirin, phenacetin, caffeine)	32 mg per tablet
Cafergot	100 mg per tablet
Darvon compound	32 mg per tablet
Fiorinal	40 mg per tablet
Typical over-the-counter cold preparations	30 mg per tablet
Typical over-the-counter stimulants	100 mg per tablet

Source: R. Goldberg, *Anxiety Biobehavioral Diagnosis and Therapy*. Reprinted with permission.

Nicotine

Nicotine is a stimulant which may lead, in heavy users, to insomnia,[23] while the other psychiatric sequelae of addiction are less well specified.[24]

Current and Recently Discontinued Medication

Every medically prescribed drug should be suspected of being involved in the onset of psychosocial difficulties because of secondary effects on the central nervous system.[25] There is no way that a social worker (or for that matter most psychiatric clinicians who are not working in the midst of the medical setting) can develop an intimate and up-to-date knowledge of the psychiatric consequences of medical drugs; however, the way to begin is to write down the names and doses of the prescribed medical drugs the patient is on or has recently discontinued. By discussing each one in ongoing consultation with the psychiatric member of the primary care team, the social worker will eventually learn those drugs which are most likely to have secondary psychological consequences. (See Table 7.2 which lists drugs that commonly produce psychiatric symptoms. Obviously, any drug that directly effects the central nervous system can produce disturbances in mood, thought, or behavior. Such drugs would include L-dopa that is used for Parkinsonism, amphetamines that are used for stimulant or dietary reasons, narcotics, central nervous system sedatives such as the barbiturates, or benzodiazepines such as Valium or Librium.

Mrs. L.W. was a 54-year-old married woman living with her husband. She had the onset of asthma at age 50 and her breathing status had become progressively worse until she required intermittent use of oxygen and her activity became fairly limited. Until this latter stage she had cared for herself; however, at this point she was referred to a social worker for a nursing home placement. She had, according to her physician, become increasingly demanding about her care and after utilization of several home health aides she had alienated her husband with her excessive anxiety and increasing dependence. Aware of the possible psychiatric effects of theophylline (a drug commonly used to treat bronchospasm) from a previous case, the social worker asked for a psychiatric consultant to see this patient. A theophylline blood level was obtained which confirmed it to be excessively high and probably directly responsible for her increased anxiety, decreased ability to care for herself, and her general functional deterioration. Downward adjustment of the dose led to re-equilibration in the patient's personality function and avoided unnecessary nursing home placement.

Mr. T.R. was a 43-year-old accountant who had been followed for two years in medical clinic because of stomach pain associated with an ulcer. He had been treated with dietary alteration, antacids, and was placed on cimetidine (Tagamet) for three months with relief of his symptoms. On his most recent visit to his primary care physician, the patient was accompanied by his wife who complained of increasing marital tension. She said that her husband has always been an obsessional and demanding individual whose chronic criticism of her has been difficult to deal with. However, over the past several months, he had become even more abrasive and difficult to tolerate.

The patient, himself, was willing to discuss the marital problem not because he felt anything was different in the marriage, but because his performance in work had been declining. He described his poor job performance as being secondary to increased tension because of the marriage and felt that if his wife would just leave him alone things would be better. Before launching into a major intervention with the couple, the social worker to whom the couple had been referred recognized that cimetidine is commonly associated with changes in mental status including confusion and irritability. Following the presentation of this case to the primary care team, the patient's cimetidine dose was cut in half with rapid subsequent improvement in his behavior and a return to the former equilibrium in the marriage. At the same time, his work performance improved markedly. As it turned out, both his personality abrasiveness and poor work performance were probably secondary to central nervous system effects of the cimetidine, although the patient, his wife, and the primary physician had constructed plausible stories to account for these symptoms on the basis of interpersonal and personality issues.

Mini-medical Data Base

Allergies

It is important for medical and legal reasons to be aware of allergies a patient might have. In addition, one will sometimes hear that the patient feels certain allergies account for a variety of personal difficulties. Unless such a myth is uncovered and discussed, it can undermine other attempted treatment.

When Is the Next Period Expected

Anxiety over the possibility of pregnancy can account for a wide variety of otherwise puzzling behavioral changes. Clinicians should also be aware that loss of menstrual cycle can accompany anorexic disorders.

Head Injuries

It is important to ask the patient "Have you ever had a head injury in which you have been knocked unconscious?" A history of such head injury may predispose the patient to the onset of temporal lobe seizures which can present years later with symptoms that include changes in behavior or personality,[26] or may result in a postconcussion syndrome with symptoms of insomnia, irritability, and mood change.[27]

Acute and Chronic Medical Conditions

Again, it is impossible for the social worker to appreciate the experience of a medical patient without being aware of the medical conditions the patient has. As incredible as it may seem, patients are seen in the health care setting by mental health professionals and engaged in ongoing interventions without even discussing or touching upon the medical illness which accounted for bringing the patient into that setting. It is not uncommon to see counselors work with cancer patients without ever discussing the disease itself. Such a discussion is often avoided by mental health professionals who feel uncomfortable with the subject area. It is not necessary to be an expert in medical disorders to discuss their psychological and social impact on the patient. The application of basic clinical interviewing skills are often the most fruitful means of initiating a helpful psychosocial intervention. Such typical questions might, for example, include, "Before your diagnosis of cancer, what were the first symptoms that you noticed? What did you think of doing about them?. What made you finally seek medical help? What was your experience with the doctor like? What did he tell you and/or your family about the illness? What is the most difficult thing for you about this illness?" And so on. Naturally, while any illness may have a psychological impact on the patient's mood and behavior, some will specifically damage the central nervous system thereby creating special difficulties for understanding the patient.

Consider the following example of a patient whose depressive symptoms were mistakenly ascribed to psychogenic causes.

Mr. E.R. was a 47-year-old math teacher, married and the father of three children. He had been in good health his entire life until one morning he awoke with a major seizure. Shortly afterwards, his physician arranged for a CAT scan of his brain which revealed a large tumor located in an area in which surgery could not be done. The patient received a course of brain irradiation and several months later a repeat of his CAT scan showed disappearance of the brain tumor. With great relief and some cautious optimism, both the patient's family and physician looked forward to a return of the patient to his normal level of functioning. However, over the following several months, the patient became more withdrawn, irritable, appeared to lose interest in his usual activities, and stopped going to work. Finally, under the assumption that he was simply unable to adjust to his medical misfortune, the patient was referred for psychiatric treatment of his depression. During the initial interview with the psychiatrist, the patient appeared withdrawn, exhibited little spontaneity, and looked depressed. He would not respond to prompting from his wife to talk about his feelings. While his wife was describing the situation, the patient would begin to gaze blankly out the window, a behavior which the wife felt confirmed his inability to face the situation. It would have been quite understandable if this patient had been treated as a psychological casualty. Certainly, the appearance of a brain tumor in a middle-aged family man is a catastrophe which could account for any number of possible reactions including depression. However, a more thorough medical and neuropsychiatric evaluation revealed several additional problems. Of some significance was the fact that measurement of his levels of anticonvulsant medication revealed that they were excessively high and probably accounted for some of the feelings of fatigue and lethargy which the patient experienced. In addition, careful assessment by a neuropsychologist of the patient's brain function revealed some significant impairment that was probably secondary to the tumor or to the radiation treatment or both. Specifically, the patient had an exceedingly short attention span, could not organize visual information sequentially in an efficient manner, and had lost some of his ability to rapidly think of the words to name objects. When these deficits were revealed, it slowly became clear that they accounted for many of the patient's symptoms. The patient reported that he did not not go to work due to a lack of motivation, but because of his frustration with the inability to perform work tasks which were formerly so straightforward for him. He gazed out the window not because of a lack of interest in solving his problems, but because his attention span was so brief that he could not follow a prolonged conversation. Recognition that the patient's symptoms were not due to depression but were rather the consequences of some physical brain impairment had important implications for his management and rehabilitation. Both the patient and family stopped thinking of him as being a "bad person" or a "psychological casualty" but began to think of him as a person with some specific deficits who needed to develop alternative strategies to function. For example, the wife and family realized that "pushing" the patient to do more only served to stress certain already diminished capacities and that it was more efficient to help the patient focus at first on some limited goals. Trying to do less became an eventual means of accomplishing more. By a concrete problem-solving approach to limited aspects of his work, he was slowly able to return on a part-time basis to his former job within a few months. His positive feelings as a result of these accomplishments contributed to improvement of his mood as well.

Surgery

Surgical procedures can alter body image as well as a patient's sense of identity. Procedures such as hysterectomy, mastectomy, and bowel surgery can drastically affect a patient's behavior and social interactions. It is less important to know about the technical name of the surgery than to know about the psychological impact of the event and its conceivable psychosocial consequences.

Significant Medical and Neurologic Findings

The information for this section of the data base is usually obtained by a review of the medical record in addition to the interview. It is important for the social worker in the health care setting to be aware of significant medical or neurologic symptoms. There are obvious psychosocial consequences which follow such disturbances as visual impairment following a stroke, loss of sensation or motor function in some part of the body, a congenital defect, cataracts, and so on. The list is endless and it should be quite obvious that such conditions alter the patient's self-image and potentially affect interpersonal behavior. As discussed in the chapter on "The Art of Engaging the Patient," many medical patients in the primary care setting are not easily engaged even by the professionally trained social worker. Nevertheless, even when the patient's medical problem is not seen as the central issue for a particular evaluation, it often serves as the entree into the world of patients who may otherwise resent or do not see the point of a psychosocial line of questioning. For example, a patient with arthritis who may not give a reasonable answer to a question such as "Do you feel depressed?" may be engaged by saying, "It seems like you have been coming to clinic for quite a while for treatment of the arthritis and despite the best medical efforts you are still left with a lot of pain. Do you find that discouraging at times?" The positive answer that usually follows such a question can usually be followed up by a much more prolonged discussion of the impact of the illness on the patient. Likewise, a denial of the situation as discouraging will provide data about the patient's coping style.

Developmental History:

Perinatal Complications

The interviewer may ask, "As far as you know, are there any family stories about your birth? For example, did you hear anything unusual about your delivery? Were you able to go home from the hospital right away or did you need to be in a special care nursery? Were there any problems with your breathing? Did you ever need to go to the hospital or did you have any serious illnesses when you were an infant?" Such questions are significant in many patients because perinatal complications which cause a lack of adequate oxygen to the brain can result in mood or behavioral disturbances in childhood and into adulthood. Many children who have some birth anoxia will have learning or behavioral problems during school and may end up with an adult form of minimal brain dysfunction which can be characterized by difficulty concentrating and/or impulsivity, resulting in a variety of disturbances in interpersonal and vocational development.[28]

For the same reason, it is important to ask about a history of minimal brain dysfunction during early schooling. Appropriate questions would include: "Were you in any special classes in school? If there were no special classes, did you have any special problems learning to read? Were you known as the kind of child who couldn't sit still? Were you a special behavior problem in school or did you have to be kept behind for any reason?" These questions are selected for the developmental history because of their neuropsychiatric implications for symptoms in adulthood. Obviously they are not appropriate to ask in all situations. If one were evaluating an 80-year-old woman who is beginning to argue with her landlady they may not be appropriate; however, in a 28-year-old chronically unemployed man in his third marriage who is being seen for anxiety over marital discord, it is quite appropriate and in fact clinically indicated to review such a developmental history. Adult patients can be successfully treated for symptoms of minimal brain dysfunction by stimulant medications.[29,30]

Mental Status Examination:

Most clinicians become overly casual about eliciting specific information about the mental status. Again, premature assumptions are often made about the explanation for psychosocial disturbances. The following section discusses selected important aspects of the mental status exam with some examples of how they are relevant to the social worker's role in the health care setting. Even though a comprehensive review of the mental status examination will not be included here, a basic knowledge of its content and implementation should be fundamental to the social worker's battery of skills. The social worker may be the only one involved in a patient evaluation who is in a position to uncover significant alterations in mental status.

Organic Mental Disorder:

Confusion, impaired memory, judgment, disorientation, impaired intellectual function, or performance difficulties can obviously lead to a variety of consequences including job loss, social withdrawal, irritability, argumentation, and so on. Disorientation or impaired memory may not be obvious to the casual interviewer. In fact, patients with a certain form of alcoholic degeneration known as Wernicke Korsakoff Syndrome can confabulate a history which seems so realistic that the unwary clinician can be caught off-guard and fail to uncover that the patient has virtually no intact memory. Patients are usually embarrassed or frightened when they are aware of decreased mental faculties and usually do not volunteer such information. In fact, they are usually guarded and often resentful when asked questions that may uncover such deficits. The clinician must develop a tactful strategy for finding out whether the patient is disoriented. For example, the interviewer might say, "You know, patients who are on the kind of medication you are on often develop some confusion and lose track of time. Has that happened to you?" By the time the clinician has given such an introduction, the patient no longer feels threatened by his confusion and is more likely to answer the question because it now makes sense in a medically reasonable context. No mental status is complete without asking the patient to write or copy something, such as a cross or clock to assess right hemisphere dysfunction. For further details of the mental status exam for organic mental disorder, refer to Chapter 1 of *Strategies in Psychiatry for the Primary Physician*.[31]

Depression

In health and mental health care settings, social workers will see a great number of patients with depressive symptoms. The clinician must sort out whether such symptoms represent:

A. features of a chronic depressive personality
B. temporary discouragement associated with the intermittent trials and tribulations of everyday life
C. adjustment to some loss, whether it be physical or interpersonal or symbolic
D. depression secondary to some medical problem
E. a primary affective disorder

In the real world with an increasing shortage of psychiatrists and referral patterns of other specialties in primary care roles, the social worker must be prepared to make competent triaging decisions about such matters and should recognize when symptoms warrant the consultation of a psychiatrist. One of the important tasks of the social worker on the health care team is to determine whether discouragement, which appears on the surface to be a simple adjustment problem, is actually part of a symptom complex of a primary affective disorder. It is important to recognize this entity because of the implications for both psychologic and pharmacologic management. The list of questions which should be asked in any patient with depression include the criteria for major depression taken from the current Diagnostic and Statistical Manual III of the American Psychiatric Association.* An inquiry about suicidal ideation must always be included. In fact, application of these criteria to a medical population is problematic because many of the symptoms if present may be secondary to the medical illness or its treatment. A method of accurately diagnosing a major depression in a medical population remains unresolved at this time and can be problematic in patients with major medical illness.[32]

Multi-Axial Diagnosis

The biopsychosocial approach to patient care allows for different dimensions of problems to be present simultaneously and to interact to produce the manifest clinical picture.[33] For example, a patient can have a particular kind of personality disorder, as well as a psychiatric diagnosis such as major depression, as well as a medical diagnosis such as congestive heart failure which produces an organic mental disorder, as well as a problem in the social system with the family, as well as some concrete social problem. The role of the social worker as a representative of the mental health team in primary care medical delivery should not be as an exclusionist or an isolationist but should rather be as a coordinator who speaks to the interplay of the various dimensions which are woven into the patient's problem. The use of the biopsychosocial data base will allow the social worker in primary care medicine to play this critical role which remains as yet unfulfilled. The use of this data base will also maximize the efficiency with which the social worker can interact with the psychiatric consultant on the primary care team. By uncovering potential problem areas in this data base, the social worker will discover areas that require further psychiatric consultation. Rather than entirely reviewing the data base, the psychiatric consultant can then utilize the information which the social worker has obtained in the comprehensive data base and focus more specifically on a problem area such as the possibility of temporal lobe seizures (because of past head injury), the possibility of behavioral consequences of medical drugs or street drugs, or the possible use of psychopharmacologic agents. Finally, by taking this data base, the social worker can serve as a model for the primary care medical clinician in terms

---

* For a review of the mental status examination for depression refer to chapter 2 of Goldberg, *Strategies in Psychiatry for the Primary Physician.*

of a biopsychosocial approach to patient care that represents the true spirit of primary care practice.

NOTES

1. D. Mechanic, Social Psychologic Factors Affecting the Presentation of Bodily Complaints" *N. Engl. J. Med.* 286 (1972): 1132-39.
2. R. C. Hall, M. K. Popkin, R. A. Devaul, et al:, "Physical Illness Presenting as Psychiatric Disease," *Arch. Gen. Psychiatry* 35 (1978): 1315-20.
3. R. J. Goldberg, S. Wallace, J. Rothney, and S. Wartman, "Medical Clinic Referrals to Social Work: A Review of 100 Cases," *General Hospital Psychiatry* (In press).
4. T. L. Thompson, A. Stoudemire, W. D. Mitchell, and R. L. Grant, "Under-recognition of Patients' Psychosocial Distress in a University Hospital Mental Clinic," *Am. J. Psychiatry* 140 (1983): 158-61.
5. E. K. Koranyi, "Morbidity and Rate of Undiagnosed Physical Illnesses in a Psychiatric Clinic Population," *Arch. Gen. Psychiatry* 36 (1979): 414-19.
6. G. L. Engel, "The Need for a New Medical Model: A Challenge for Biomedicine," *Science* 196 (1977): 129-36.
7. J. A. Flaherty, G. Moises, E. Black, E. Altman, and T. Mitchell, "The Role of Social Support in the Functioning of Patients with Unipolar Depression," *AM. J. Psychiatry* 140 no. 4 (1983): 473-76.
8. F. J. Haggerty, "Life Stress, Illness and Social Supports," *Develop. Med. Child Neurol.* 22 (1980): 391-400.
9. W. M. Patterson, H. H. Dohn, J. Bird, and G. A. Patterson, "Evaluation of Suicidal Patients: The Sad Persons Scale," *Psychosomatics* 24, 4 (1983): 343-49.
10. G. L. Engel, and J. Romano, "Delirium, A Syndrome of Cerebral Insufficiency," *J. of Chronic Dis.*, 9 (1959): 260-77.
11. P. C. Misra, and G. G. Hay, "Encephalitis Presenting as Acute Schizophrenia," *Br. Med. J.* 1 (1971): 532-33.
12. G. H. Glaser and J. H. Pincus, "Limbic Encephalitis," *J. Nerv. & Mental Dis.* 149, no. 1 (1969): 59-67.
13. A. H. Glassman, E. V. Giardina, J. M. Perel, J. T. Bigger, S. J. Kantor, and M. Davies, "Clinical Characteristics of Imipramine-Induced Orthostatic Hypotension," *Lancet* (March 1979): 468-72.
14. S. F. Pariser, E. R. Pinta, and B. A. Jones, "Mitral Valve Prolapse Syndrome and Anxiety Neurosis/Panic Disorder," *Am. J. Psychiatry* 135, 2 (February 1978): 246-47.
15. Ibid., Chapter 8.
16. S. Zisook and R. A. DeVaul "Grief, Unresolved Grief, and Depression," *Psychosomatics* 24, 3, (1983): 247-56.
17. E. M. Sellers and H. Kalant, "Alcohol Intoxication and Withdrawal," *NE. J. of Med.*, 294, 14 (1976): 757-62.

18. A. E. Slaby, J. Lieb, and L. R. Tancredi, *Handbook of Psychiatric Emergencies* 2 ed. (Garden City, N.Y.: Medical Examination Publishing Co., 1981)

19. M. A. Fauman and B. J. Fauman, "Violence Associated with Phencyclidine Abuse," *Am. J. Psychiatry* 136, 12 (1979): 1584-86.

20. R. Byck, B. L. Weiss, D. R. Wesson, S. R. Scott, and D. E. Smith, "Cocaine: Chic, Costly, and What Else?" *Patient Care* (September 15, 1980): 136-54.

21. B. S. Victor, M. Lubetsky, and J. F. Greden, "Somatic Manifestations of Caffeinism," *J. Clin. Psychiatry* 42 (1981): 185-88.

22. B. C. White, et al, "Anxiety and Muscle Tension as Consequences of Caffeine Withdrawal," *Science* 209 (1980): 1547-48.

23. C. R. Soldatos, J. D. Kales, M. B. Scharf, E. O. Bixler,and A. Kales, "Cigarette Smoking Associated with Sleep Difficulty," *Science* 207, 1 (1980): 551-53.

24. E. Garfield, "Nicotine Addiction Is a Major Medical Problem: Why So Much Government Inertia?" *Current Comments*, 31 (1979): 5-13.

25. M. Abramowicz, "Drugs That Cause Psychiatric Symptoms," *The Medical Letter* 23 (1981): 9-12.

26. D. Blumer "Temporal Lobe Epilepsy and Its Psychiatric Significance," in D. F. Benson and D. Plumer, eds. *Psychiatric Aspects of Neurologic Disease* (new York: Grune and Stratton, 1975).

27. R. J. Goldberg, *Anxiety: Biobehavioral Diagnosis and Therapy* (Garden City, N.Y.: Medical Examination Publishing Co., 1982).

28. H. B. Mann, and S. I. Greenspan, "The Identification and Treatment of Adult Brain Dysfunction," *Am. J. Psychiatry* 133, 9 (September 1976): 1013-17.

29. D. R. Wood, F. W. Reimherr, P. H. Wender, and G. F. Johnson, "Diagnosis and Treatment of Minimal Brain Dysfunction in Adults," *Archives of Surgery* 111 (December 1976): 1453-59.

30. P. H. Wender, F. W. Reimherr, and D. R. Wood, "Attention Deficit Disorder ('Minimal Brain Dysfunction') in Adults," *Arch. Gen. Psychiatry* 38 (April 1981): 449-56.

31. R. J. Goldberg, *Strategies in Psychiatry for the Primary Physician*. Patient Care Publications. (Darien Connecticut, 1980).

32. R. J. Goldberg, *Anxiety: Biobehavioral Diagnosis and Therapy*, (Medical Examination Publishing Co. 1981).

33. H. Leigh, A. R. Feinstein, and M. F. Reiser, "The Patient Evaluation Grid," *General Hospital Psychiatry* 2 (1980): 3-9.

Chapter Six
Medicine for Social Workers

A 30-year-old recently certified internist becomes morose and self-effacing. He feels his marriage of 10 years is stale, his 3 children ungratifying, his skills as a physician less than mediocre and his future without promise or hope. Despite the fact that until two weeks prior, he felt he had a very good marriage, was happy, his children were doing extremely well at school, and he was pleased to have been offered the faculty position at a prestigious university he very much wanted. He commits suicide by a self-inflicted gunshot wound. Three weeks prior to his suicide, he had been placed on reserpine, an antihypertensive medication, for high blood pressure.

A 42-year old school teacher was brought to the emergency room of a large city hospital after awakening at three o'clock in the morning grossly psychotic. She was confused, agitated, paranoid, hallucinating visually, and complaining of severe headache and nausea. Her husband of 22 years and 21-year-old son and 19-year-old daughter accompanied the police ambulance that brought her in. According to her husband, she had no personal or family history of psychiatric illness. She was employed as a teacher in the same school for the past 14 years and, in fact, had taught class the day before. She had several close friends and had been active in community organizations such as her church and local preservation society. She had seen her internist about six months prior for headache and he prescribed Valium. In the emergency room she was examined by an internist who found her to have a normal physical examination and diagnosed her as schizophrenic. She was then referred to the psychiatric clinician in the emergency room who felt she had an organic disorder because of the suddenness of onset in a 42-year-old person who had no personal or family history of psychiatric illness

151

and had functioned well at home, work, and in the community until the day prior. The psychiatric clinician then called in a neurologist for consultation. The neurologist found the patient confused and psychotic with a normal physical examination and used the patient to demonstrate to a group of medical students the difference between organic illness (which he felt the patient did not have) and psychogenic illness. Because of the disagreement in opinion by medicine and neurology on the one hand and psychiatry on the other the Directors of Emergency Medicine and Emergency Psychiatry were called in for consultation. The Director of Medicine deferred to the Director of Psychiatry because a behavioral disturbance was the presenting complaint. The Director of Psychiatry concurred with his staff person's opinion and recommended admission to a medical ward for observation. Three hours after admission to the medical service, the symptoms completely remitted and the patient returned home. A diagnosis of migraine equivalent was made. This was consistent with the patient's history of headache and presenting symptoms of visual disturbances, severe headache, and nausea. There were no further episodes on two-year follow-up.

A 34-year-old dentist came for consultation because of difficulty sleeping, overwhelming anxiety, palpitations, diarrhea, and agitation. She had begun couples therapy four weeks prior with her husband of eight years. They had had prior difficulty and therapy had helped. This time her anxiety was becoming worse rather than better with therapy and she sought counsel as to whether she should terminate couples therapy, the marriage, or both, feeling that one or both might be contributing to her problem. The consulting clinician took the patient's pulse and found it to be 130 beats per minute and ordered thyroid studies. The results of the study were interpreted as abnormal and the patient commenced on appropriate medication. On five year follow-up, she was still married to the same man, had had a child, and was without further symptoms.

A 40-year-old, divorced real estate agent was referred to the emergency psychiatric service of a large general medical hospital by his internist because of a rapidly decreasing ability to talk over a period of hours. His internist, a specialist in hypertension, diagnosed him as having conversion hysteria. He was seen by a clinical social worker as a member of the ER crisis team who felt that the decreasing ability to talk coupled with a decreasing level of consciousness was not consistent with a diagnosis of hysteria. Furthermore, he was accompanied by his sister, a school social worker, who stated that the patient had never been psychiatrically ill. The crisis clinician asked for the patient to be* seen by both an internist and neurologist in the emergency room who found his examination within normal limits save for the fact he did not speak or attend. Blood studies, including blood gases, and glucose, chest, and skull x-rays, and results of a lumbar puncture and an electrocardiogram were all within normal limits. The consulting internist, as well as the patient's specialist, concluded that the original diagnosis of hysteria was correct and pressed the psychiatric clinician to admit him to a psychiatric ward. The psychiatric clinician refused to accept the patient stating that it is her opinion that the patient's symptoms could not be explained on a psychological basis alone. The patient was, therefore, reluctantly admitted to a medical ward as "probable hysteria, which psychiatry will not believe." Eight hours after admission, the patient was intubated and transferred to a neurosurgical intensive care unit with the diagnosis of brain stem infarct. It was found that the patient had a clot in a blood vessel in the brain stem.

In all of the above examples, a clue to the organic nature of a patient's problem is apparent to a seasoned clinician in the health setting. Medical and neurological sophistication may be needed to obtain the exact diagnosis, but the exclusion of a predominant psychological explanation for the alteration in mood, thought, or behavior can be made without such knowledge even by non–medically trained team members such as clinical social workers or psychologists as long as they receive appropriate training. A medical disorder masquerading as psychiatric symptoms should be suspected whenever there is a *sudden onset* of symptoms in individuals without previous psychiatric histories and with good premorbid functioning. As people get older, it is possible to develop unipolar or bipolar affective illness despite a high level of functioning, especially if one has a history of depression, mania, bankruptcy, alcoholism, suicide, or sociopathy in the family; however, the onset of affective illness is more insidious, generally over many weeks or months. The onset of schizophrenia and the major affective disorders is not sudden and there is a concomitant alteration in social functioning.[1,2,3]

Diagnosis and differential diagnosis are cornerstones of therapy and needed for the development of an integrated treatment plan. A symptom or sign is just that and *not* the illness. Just as a neurologist does not merely label a seizure "epilepsy" and commence treatment without seeking a cause for the seizures such as alcohol withdrawal, a cardiac arrythmia, hypoglycemia (low blood sugar), or a brain tumor, so too a psychiatric physician seeks a cause for disorders of mood, thought, and behavior. Even if the clinician providing a front line assessment in an emergency room or a primary care clinic is not a psychiatrist but perhaps a nurse, clinical social worker, or psychologist, there is a need to acquire a basic competency in the biomedical dimension of the biopsychosocial differential diagnosis. There are a great number of medical, surgical, and psychological causes for depression, mania, disorganized thoughts, memory disturbances, difficulty concentrating, and self- and other destructive behavior of which nonmedical practitioners must become more aware. Failure to identify these causes not only leads to inappropriate treatment, but can be the source of considerable pain to patients and, in the extreme, perhaps lead to their deaths, as in the case of the internist who became depressed on antihypertensive medication. Many of the medications used for the management of high blood pressure have the potentiality of causing depression. This is because they either cause changes in brain neurotransmitters similar to those changes associated with depression, or because they deplete the body of chemical substances which can result in symptoms associated with depression. Antihypertensive drugs such as reserpine and alphamethyldopa (Aldomet) may produce profound depression as a side effect by causing changes in brain neurochemistry. Other antihypertensives, such as Diuril, sometimes referred to as a "fluid pill," depletes the body of potassium, a vital salt. If the lost potasium is not replaced in the diet or by supplements, potassium depletion can produce weakness and malaise which can be confused with depression. In both instances, an individual on such medication may become more and more depressed and develop a distorted perception of life. Happy marriages become troubled, wanted children become burdens and occupational success, failure. Social workers or other clinicians (including some psychiatrists) who are not aware of the biomedical basis in such cases may inappropriately attribute a causal relationship to psychosocial events that are not actually the basis of the person's problem. A sister of a 22-year-old student, who committed suicide during a biologically based depression, said angrily of her brother's therapist "He (the therapist) tried to analyze him. He refused to give him drugs because my brother said his depression began four years ago when he met his girlfriend. My brother wasn't depressed then; even if he were, however, one month later he said he had been depressed for six years previously; two months later, he claimed to have been depressed for twelve years and just before his suicide he said he could not remember a day in his life when he wasn't depressed." Being depressed is like taking a mood-altering drug. It distorts perception and leads to actions that would never occur if the person were not so. What is reported as factual by a depressed person may not be and if it is, it may be decidedly distorted.

In the example of the school teacher with migraine, an absence of diagnosis would have not been as extreme as death but, nonetheless, dire. If the woman had not been diagnosed as having a migraine equivalent, and if the psychiatric consultant had been willing to accept the diagnosis of schizophrenia by the internist and neurologist, the patient would have been admitted unnecessarily to a psychiatric ward. She would most likely have been given several doses of antipsychotic medication for the emergency management of her acutely agitated state. Recall that she was in four point restraints, paranoid, agitated, and visually hallucinating. The behavior would have ceased in about three to four hours, not because of the medication but because the natural course of a migraine equivalent is time-limited. The amelioration of symptoms coincident with the use of high-dosage antipsychotic medication would have been misinterpreted as further evidence of her being an acutely psychotic schizophrenic patient. The patient's affect on antipsychotic medication would appear somewhat flattened. Individuals given antipsychotic medication may appear "spacey" or "zombie-like" and resemble schizophrenics in behavior and emotion, further confusing the diagnostic picture. One wonders how many people such as this woman have been labeled as good prognostic schizophrenics who were actually *forme frustes* of medical illnesses presenting as schizophrenia.

In addition to the deplorable mistreatment, a number of other sad implications would have accrued to the patient and family of an individual with migraine or any other medical illness (for example, temporal lobe epilepsy) mislabeled as schizophrenia. These consequences have been discussed in the literature under the topics of "labeling" and "attributional theory." In both instances, the patient is given a diagnosis, and all further unexplicable behavior is attributed to it. If such an individual comes into an emergency room and complains of stomach pains, there is a danger the patient's symptoms will be seen as "mental" and a less comprehensive evaluation provided. If the patient is ill and stays home from work, the employer or family may fear "another breakdown." In some instances, in fact, an individual may be passed by for a promotion or a new job because of fear they will "not be able to handle it." The patient often feels tainted or damaged and less able to handle what others, who had not "broken down under stress," are able to handle.

To sum up: (1) schizophrenic and major affective disorders rarely have a sudden onset; and (2) a diagnosis of schizophrenia should not be made on the initial admission of any patient with a good premorbid social and occupational history, no personal or family psychiatric history, and an affective component.

In the following sections, we will review some of the relatively common medical and surgical illnesses that may present with depression, thought disorders, anxiety, and homicidal behavior.

COMMON MEDICAL AND SURGICAL ILLNESSES

Depression

Depresion is a common human affliction. It has been estimated from community surveys that one out of five people during their lifetime will experience the type of depression that responds to antidepressant drugs.[4] Such depressions are called "endogenous" or "primary major affective disorders" and are accompanied by sleep and appetite disturbance, decreased libido, weight loss, and a diurnal (day to night) variation in mood.

When a person is depressed, he or she looks at the world through blue-tinted glasses. Regardless of the reality of their situation, such people feel worthless, helpless, and hopeless. Nothing about them satisfies them and nothing, including themselves, is valued. In the depth of any depression, regardless of its etiology, an individual is in an abyss of nihilistic despair. Suicide is a real possibility. The risk of suicide among depressed people is 500 times that of the rest of the population. One out of 100 people will end their life by their own hand.[5,6]

The medical causes of depressive symptoms are myriad [5,7,8,9,10,11,12,13,14,15] and we say only semifacetiously that Table 6.1 represents an abbreviated list of such illnesses. As mentioned earlier, most of the medications that are used to treat high blood pressure have depression implicated as a potential side-effect. These include methyldopa, propranolol, reserpine, and hydrodiuril. Comparably, a number of other commonly prescribed medications have depressive symptoms as a potential side effect. These include the benzodiazepines (for example, Valium, Librium, Serax, Ativan, Tranxene), cimetidine (Tagamet)[16,17,18]; steriods (for example, Prednisone), digitalis,[19] disulfiram (Antabuse), and levodopa (L-Dopa). Serum levels of some drugs can be helpful in diagnosing toxicity with some drugs, such as Digoxin; however, others such as Valium may contribute to depressive symptoms even within the therapeutic range.

The various diseases of the endocrine system (the endocrinopathies) are also associated with alterations in mood. Addison's disease, due to decreased adrenocorticosteroid output, may cause the picture of depression, schizophrenia, or dementia. Cushing's disease, the obverse, (that is, excess secretion of adrenocorticosteroids) may present as depression, mania, thought disorder, or dementia. The syndromes seen with Cushing's disease resemble those seen with the use of exogenous steroids such as Prednisone. Both hyper- and hypothyroidism, due to excessive and deficient secretion of thyroid hormones, may present with depression as the predominant feature. In the case of hyperthyroidism, the picture is of an agitated depression; with hypothyroid disturbances, the

TABLE 6.1 Some Medical Disorders Presenting with Depression

Addison's disease
Alcohol intoxication
Antihypertensive medication toxicity (e.g., Inderal)
Arteriosclerosis
Barbiturate intoxication (Phenobarbital)
Benzodiazepine intoxication (Valium, Librium)
Carbon disulfide intoxication
Carcinoma of pancreas
Cerebral tuberculosis
Cerebrovascular syphilis
Cessation of amphetamine or cocaine use
Cirrhosis of the liver
Corticosteroid toxicity (e.g., Prednisone)
Cushing's syndrome
Degenerative diseases of the central nervous
    system (e.g., Alzheimer's disease)
Diabetes
Digitalis toxicity (e.g., Digoxin)
Distal effects of cancer
Disulfiram (Antabuse) intoxication
Encephalitis
General paresis
Hepatic failure
Hepatitis
Hyperparathyroidism
Hyperthyroidism
Hypoglycemia
Hypokalemia
Hyponatremia
Hypothyroidism
Infectious mononucleosis
Levodopa (L-Dopa) intoxication
Multiple sclerosis
Occult malignancy
Pernicious anemia
Post-viral infection syndrome
Renal failure
Subdural hematoma
Thallium intoxication

depression appears as a retarded one. Hyperparathyroidism, due to excessive secretion of the hormone of the parathyroid glands—which leads to alterations in calcium—can also create depressed mood.

Intoxication caused by a number of sedative substances may make a person appear depressed as well. These include barbiturates (taken both for seizure disorders and recreationally), carbon disulfide, and the benzodiazepines (such as Librium or Valium). Tumors may cause a patient to seem depressed with or without direct invasion of the brain. Tumors in a number of locations in the brain can alter the personality. The tumor may be primary, that is originating in the brain itself, or metastatic, originating outside of the brain but spreading to the brain as a secondary site. In some instances, a tumor may grow outside of the brain and cause changes in it without actually invading it. This phenomenon is called distal, that is, remote effects of a tumor. There are cellular changes in the brain but the tumor itself is not growing in it. Cancer of the pancreas can cause a person to seem profoundly depressed without a person being aware they have the tumor and without direct invasion by metastasis or cellular change. Such a situation can be terribly misleading since the loss of weight and appetite seen with cancer before it is diagnosed may be mistaken as due to affective illness.

A number of infections can make a person appear depressed. Following a severe viral infection, a person may feel down and neuroasthenic for weeks or months. Both viral and bacterial pneumonias may present with depressed mood and weight loss. Cerebral tuberculosis and cerebrovascular syphilis and general paresis (syphilis of the brain without primary vascular involvement) may present as depression, dementia, and schizophrenia. Encephalitis (infection of the brain) of a number of other etiologies and sarcoidosis of the brain, a disease of unknown origin which somewhat resembles tuberculosis in its pathological picture, also may present with depression. Infectious mononucleosis, a common disease of younger people often is misdiagnosed as depression and should be sought as a basis for depression in this age group using the appropriate test.

Alcohol intoxicaion may make a person look depressed. In addition, alcoholics are prone to a number of other disorders which may make them seem depressed and can go undiagnosed because they are alcoholic and the clinician mistakenly attributes the change in affect to alcohol rather than to a more serious cause such as subdural hematoma (blood clot on the brain). Cerebral arteriosclerosis may cause changes in the personality resembling affective illness, thought disorder, and dementia. The cessation of amphetamines or cocaine may result in "crashing," accompanied by a depression so profound that antidepressant medication or electroshock may be needed to prevent suicide. Both liver disease, such as cirrhosis and hepatitis, and kidney disease, such as renal failure, may alter mood. All the degenerative diseases of the brain (for example, Alzheimer's disease, Pick's disease, and Huntington's chorea) may be associated with depressed mood.[20] Diabetes and hypoglycemia may have depression as a symptom. In the latter, violent outbursts and anxiety may also be part of the picture. A five-hour glucose tolerance curve is usually needed to diagnose hypoglycemia. Multiple sclerosis and the vitamin deficiencies such as pernicious anemia (a vitamin B_{12} deficiency) are also associated with affective change.

Anxiety

When anxiety is associated with pronounced physiologic changes such as persistently increased heart rate and diarrhea or when it presents as well-circumscribed intense episodes with feelings of impending doom or panic in individuals who are otherwise quite normal or healthy, the clinician should consider an underlying medical cause. (See Table 6.2.) One social worker (the assistant director of a primary care psychiatric service) initiated an evaluation that led to the diagnosis of two cases of temporal lobe epilepsy by suspicion raised by seeing well-circumscribed episodes of intense anxiety in individuals in their mid-thirties and forties with close friends and normal development and work history without any previous problems with anxiety. Causes of isolated episodes of intense anxiety in addition to temporal lobe (psychomotor) epilepsy include other temporal lobe diseases (for example, tumors), mitral valve prolapse[21,22] (vascular disease of the heart sometimes presenting as agorophobia, that is, fear of open spaces), paroxysmal atrial tachycardia (runs of very rapid heart beats) and other disturbances of the heart rhythm, and pheochromocytomas (tumor of the adrenal glands). Overwhelming anxiety and a feeling that a person is imminently about to die may be seen with pulmonary emboli (blood clots to the lungs often from the leg veins), impending myocardial infarction (heart attack), internal bleeding (for example, secondary to a bleeding ulcer or ruptured spleen), shock due to blood loss or overwhelming infection, and subacute bacterial endocarditis (infection of the heart).[23]

Withdrawal from, as well as intoxication with, a variety of chemical substances is associated with overwhelming anxiety. Delirium secondary to withdrawal from sedatives, known as delirium tremens, is accompanied by, and sometimes preceded by, intense anxiety and fear. The fear may reach panic proportions and in an agitated and confused state patients may jump out of bed or a window and harm themselves in an attempt to escape the ill-defined source of fear. Hallucinogens and other substances taken for recreational purposes may be associated with overwhelming anxiety. LSD (lysergic acid diethylamide) may result in self-destructive behavior either because an individual on it may feel he or she can fly and, therefore, jumps

TABLE 6.2 Some Medical Disorders Presenting with Anxiety

Alcohol withdrawal
Amphetamine and similar-acting sympathomimetic
    intoxication
Atropine psychosis
Barbiturate and similar-acting substance withdrawal
Caffeine intoxication
Cannabis intoxication
Cerebroarteriosclerosis
Cocaine intoxication
Encephalitis
Glue sniffing
Hallucinogen intoxication
Hypertension
Hyperthyroidism
Hyperventilation syndrome
Hypocalcemia
Hypoglycemia
Hypokalemia
Impending myocardial infarction
Insecticide organophosphate intoxication
Internal hemorrhage
Lead intoxication
Mitral valve prolapse
Paroxysmal atrial tachycardia and other cardiac
    arrhythmias
Phencyclidine intoxication
Pheochromocytoma
Post-concussion syndrome
Pulmonary embolism
Subacute bacterial endocarditis
Temporal lobe disease (other)
Temporal lobe epilepsy

from a high spot or the individual may in panic leap from a window or car. Amphetamines and other stimulant sympathomimetic substances, such as those used in the treatment of asthma, may leave a person anxious and fearful. PCP (phencyclidine), also known as "angel dust," not only makes one anxious, but in addition, at times outwardly destructive, leading to violent and sometimes gruesome physical abuse of others, including murder. Marijuana usually calms one and is most frequently euphorogenic. In some people, however, especially those with need for control, the relaxation of defenses is accompanied by considerable anxiety. Atropine toxicity secondary to use of both prescribed drugs such as the antipsychotics and antidepressants or from recreational drugs can lead to anxiety, dry skin, flushing, psychosis, and elevated temperature. Sniffing glue, snorting or injecting cocaine, insecticides, and solvent toxicity or lead toxicity are other sources of anxiety. Finally, excessive use of caffeine leads to caffeinism of which anxiety is the predominant feature.

A sustained feeling of anxiety accompanied by sleep disturbance and palpitations may be seen with hyperthyoidism (Grave's disease). This is documented by measuring blood levels of thyroid hormone in its forms T_3 and T_4.

Vascular and infectious diseases of the brain may be accompanied by irritability and the subjective feeling of anxiety. Examples of such diseases are hypertensive encephalopathy, cerebral arteriosclerosis, and encephalitis (brain inflammation). In all instances, the intensity of anxiety may fluctuate. In the case of encephalitis, one would expect to find bilateral slowing on the electroencephalogram and increased cells in the cerebrospinal fluid.

Alterations in serum electrolytes (sodium and potassium) and blood glucose levels also may lead to anxiety. This is especially dramatic in instances of hypoglycemia due either to abnormal production of insulin by a tumor or inappropriate doses of insulin taken for diabetes. Hypoglycemia is often manifested by feelings of irritability, anxiety, and sometimes a sense of "going crazy" about three to four hours after eating. This feeling is eliminated by the ingestion of food and treatment entails dietary regulation if there is not a cause such as an insulinoma (a tumor that produces insulin) that needs to be surgically extirpated. Low serum potassium (hypokalemia) is accompanied by a more sustained sense of anxiety. Finally, the hyperventilation syndrome secondary to rapid overbreathing is accompanied by anxiety, light-headedness, and a feeling the individual is going to faint. Breathing into a paper bag so that a person rebreathes air rich in carbon dioxide is the treatment of this condition. Ironically, chronically anxious people tend to drink an abundance of coffee leading to caffeinism,[24] a condition that worsens anxiety. Educating patients about how these conditions may contribute to their neurotic symptoms may lead to an alteration in behavior and some relief.

Thought Disorders

Schizophrenia is usually insidious in onset and predominantly a disease of younger people with a personal history of impaired interpersonal relationships and a family history of schizophrenia and/or long unexplained hospitalizations. The usual course is months to years of increasing withdrawal and difficulty in functioning at school, at work, and at home. A previously talented student becomes increasingly interested in religion and philosophy and no longer attends to studies or friends. A factory worker is more concerned about the fact that someone is either putting thoughts into his or her head, withdrawing them, or controlling them. It is unusual to have the onset of schizophrenia after the third decade of life with the exception of the paranoid subtype. The mean age of onset of this variety has been reported to be 35. The deterioration of personality is less, the I.Q. greater, and the likelihood of hospitalization less than with other forms of disorder. While it is true that schizophrenia can occur in families without a history of psychiatric illness, when there are, in fact, no other family members who may have been schizophrenic (e.g., individuals who withdrew and never worked again; people who abandoned their family for a religious movement and were never again seen or heard of; individuals who committed suicide but were not manifestly depressed) and when there is no personal history of impaired social functioning, one should question the diagnosis of schizophrenia. The diagnosis in such instances is much in doubt and the likelihood of a organic mental disorder or of an affective disorder is greater.

There are no features that are pathognomonic (i.e., definitively diagnostic) of so-called psychogenic schizophrenia. Symptoms such as thought control, thought insertion, thought withdrawal, hearing voices commenting and arguing, and somatic delusions which, in some cases, are referred to as Schneiderian First Rank symptoms of schizophrenia (used for research purposes) may be seen with a number of other disorders.[25,26,27,28,29] Sleep deprivation associated with manic illness can also be mistaken for schizophrenia because the lack of sleep can lead to hallucinations and delusions. In addition, the alterations caused in personality by amphetamine-like substances, [30,31] cocaine,[32] and phencyclidine ("angel dust", PCP)[33,34] can perfectly simulate a schizophrenic psychosis. With the psychoses seen with the hallucinogens[35,36,37,38,39,40] such as mescaline, LSD, and psilocybin,[41] there are characteristic distortions of perception as well as synesthesias. The latter, frequently felt diagnostic of hallucinogenic psychoses, consist of the condensation of two sensory perceptions. For example, one tastes or smells color. A patient tastes green or smells black. Visual alterations are common and a patient who is "tripping" may see windows melt into the floor or try to become convergent with infinite sky. In some instances, there may be overwhelming panic or a feeling one is superhuman and indestructible. The danger of the latter is self-harm from the delusion of ability to fly or remain under water indefinitely.

Every major mode of pathologic deterioration of body systems may manifest itself in disorders of thought (see Table 6.3). Degenerative diseases of the central nervous system such as Huntington's chorea, Alzheimer's

TABLE 6.3. Some Medical Disorders Presenting with Disordered Thought

Addison's disease
Alcohol hallucinosis
Alcohol paranoia
Alcohol withdrawal
Amphetamine intoxication
Atropine psychosis
Bacterial meningitis
Barbiturate and similar-acting substance withdrawal
Cerebral neoplasm
Cerebroarteriosclerosis
Cerebrovascular syphilis
Corticosteroid toxicity
Cushing's disease
Degenerative diseases of the central nervous system (e.g.,
    Alzheimer's disease, Huntington's chorea)
Digitalis toxicity
Disulfiram (Antabuse) intoxication
General paresis
Hyperparathyroidism
Hyperthyroidism
Hypoparathyroidism
Hypothyroidism
Idiosyncratic alcohol intoxication
Insecticide (organophosphate) intoxication
Isoniazid intoxication
Lead intoxication
Levodopa (L-Dopa) intoxication
Manganese intoxication
Mercury intoxication
Methyldopa (Aldomet) toxicity
Multiple sclerosis
Niacin deficiency
Normal pressure hydrocephalus
Pernicious anemia
Pheochromocytoma
Phencyclidine intoxication
Porphyria
Pyridoxine deficiency
Schilder's disease
Systemic lupus erythematosus
Temporal lobe epilepsy
Thallium intoxication
Thiamine deficiency
Tubercular meningitis
Wilson's disease (hepatolenticular degeneration)

disease, Schilder's disease, and Pick's disease are insidious in onset. The flattening of affect, social withdrawal, alterations of thought (e.g., paucity of associations), and delusions (e.g., paranoia) frequently seen with these disorders may be mistaken for schizophrenia. The onset is usually but not always considerably later than schizophrenic disorders with the exception of the paranoid subtype. The onset of Huntington's chorea is said to be usually in the fourth decade of life much as paranoid schizophrenia. Both are associated with the occurrence of delusions of persecution. Toxic, metabolic, and endocrine disorders have a number of *formes frustes* which resemble acute and chronic schizophrenia. Addison's disease (adrenocortical insufficiency) may present as a thought disorder, depression, and dementia. Corticosteroid excess due to endogenous steroids with Cushing's disease (due to excessive production of cortiocosteroids) or from exogenous steroids such as prednisone used in the management of a number of disorders may produce a thought disorder, in addition to symptoms resembling depression, mania, dementia, or an anxiety neurosis. Other endocrine disturbances which may present as schizophrenia include hyperparathyroidism (due to excessive production of the secretion of the parathyroid glands) and hyperthyroidism (Grave's disease).

Vitamin deficiency diseases that may also result in altered thought include niacin deficiency, pernicious anemia (vitamin B_{12} deficiency), pyridoxine deficiency and thiamine deficiency. Sadly, prior to the advent of recognition of these illnesses and a knowledge of how to most effectively manage them, not only were these patients misdiagnosed as schizophrenic or more broadly as "insane", but, in addition, they went on to have brain damage which never would have occurred if the diseases were recognized early in the course and effectively treated.

Disorders of thought may occur both as a toxic effect of a variety of medicinal and nonmedicinal substances as well as from drug withdrawal.[42,43,44,45,46,47,48,49,50,51,52,53,54,55,56,57,58,59] The latter may so resemble a schizophrenic disorder that the patient may go untreated for withdrawal until grosser signs of withdrawal are manifest such as seizure tremors and elevated temperature. Alcohol withdrawal, alcohol hallucinosis, and alcohol paranoia from chronic alcohol use may result in a thought disorder. In the first instance (alcohol withdrawal) these are seen only transiently and usually as a harbinger of delirium tremens. Following withdrawal, the symptoms remit. In the latter instances (alcohol hallucinosis and alcohol paranoia) the symptoms may last longer. Some people, in fact, feel that alcoholic paranoia may only occur in those genetically or otherwise predisposed to schizophrenia and, therefore, may not be a separate disorder. Disorganized thought may be seen with both toxicity from central nervous system depressants such as barbiturates, Placidyl, Quaaludes, and meprobamate (Equinil, Miltown) as well as with complete or partial withdrawal from these substances. It should be remembered that individuals may abuse more than one substance such that a person may be successfully withdrawn from alcohol in which the symptoms of withdrawal appear relatively soon, within two to three days after cessation of use, but go on to develop symptoms of a thought disorder and ultimately of delirium tremens a week or two later from the concomitant withdrawal of longer acting central nervous system depressants such as phenobarbital. Since delirium tremens has a significant fatality rate, this is not a point of mere academic interest. Intoxication from atropine-like substances, amphetamine-like substances, bromides, digitalis, disulfiram (Antabuse[60]), insecticides, isoniazid, lead, levodopa (L-Dopa[61,62]), manganese, mercury, methyldopa (Aldomet), phencyclidine, and thallium are yet other potential medical causes of a schizophreniform disorder. In most instances, a careful drug use and occupational history will reveal the exposure to such an agent. Another disorder in which a person becomes grossly disturbed and often violent after drinking a small dose of alcohol (e.g., as little as a glass of wine) is idiosyncratic alcohol intoxication, sometimes referred to as pathologic intoxication. Serum alcohol level is low and the patient usually recovers in 24 hours. Sometimes, but not invariably, the symptoms may be reproduced by subsequent ingestion of alcohol and an electroencephalogram (EEG) appears abnormal at the time of symptoms. This disorder is felt to be epileptic equivalent and due to a lowered seizure threshold.

Infections of the brain and its covering (the meninges) are also associated with schizophrenic symptoms. In instances where disorganized thought is part of the picture of encephalitis (inflammation of the brain) or meningitis (inflammation of the coverings of the brain), antipsychotic medication is given to control symptoms. Comparably, antipsychotic medication may be used for schizophrenic-like symptoms due to tumors or vascular diseases (e.g., lupus erythematosus, cerebrovascular syphilis, cerebroarteriosclerosis) of the brain. In the instances of a collagen disease, such as lupus erythematosus and periarteritis nodosa, the alterations in personality may occur before the disease is diagnosed. The treatment (for example, steroids) may further contribute to the problem by causing alteration of thought. Cerebral syphilis (general paresis) and cerebral tuberculosis have long been known as great masqueraders and may present with disorders of mood, thought, and behavior resembling a great number of psychotic syndromes. Studies of the cerebrospinal fluid obtained by lumbar puncture (e.g., call count, cultures, serology) generally reveal the etiology of the disturbance.

Multiple sclerosis is an illness with a high morbidity (considerable impairment of functioning) but low mortality (seldom do people die of the disease itself). Plaques in certain parts of the brain may produce alteration in personality and affect. Hydrocephalus in which the ventricles of the brain expand causing destruction of brain cells by pressure following infection or hemorrhage with resultant impairment of cerebrospinal fluid flow may cause a person to look "spacey" and to withdraw from people much as a schizophrenic. Neurosurgical intervention with placement of a shunt to drain the fluid of the brain is curable if the disease is recognized early and intervention is prompt. Pheochromocytomas and temporal lobe epilepsy, both mentioned in regard to episodic anxiety, may also alter thought and personality. Not only may intense feelings of anxiety and impending doom be caused by discharges in the temporal lobe, but continuous discharges (sometimes referred to as "psychomotor status") may cause an oneiroid (dream-like) state that resembles schizophrenia. Finally, both porphyria, the disease George III of England was reported to have, and Wilson's disease (hepatolenticular degeneration), both metabolic diseases, cause alterations of personality, affect, and thought. With porphyria, there is a defect in the metabolism of porphyrins; in the case of Wilson's disease, the genetically determined defect is in copper metabolism.

Violent Behavior

Violent behavior, and perhaps even more so the anticipation of violent behavior is always frightening. This is always true of the observer and sometimes may also be true of the individual who may be feeling such impulses but who may not have previously been aware of such aggressive behavior or acted out hostile impulses. Psychiatric clinicians including clinical social workers and particularly those on diagnostic services and working in crisis or emergency units, are called upon to look for psychological or medical explanations for the abusive behavior associated with medical disorders which may lead to violent behavior and sometimes to murder in people not so inclined. (For other social workers, whether they be called clinical or generic, as well as other psychiatric clinicians who have not had regular exposure to emergency services, the prospect of being called upon to make such an evaluation can provoke enough anxiety to make what skills are developed effectively unreliable.) The change in the patient's behavior tends to be sudden, dramatic, bizarre, and unexpected in individuals with a healthy nonviolent premorbid history. Phencyclidine (PCP) and amphetamines can lead to violence. In the former instance, the murders are sometimes quite bizarre and gruesome. "Speed kills" is an expression used in the drug culture and it is true. Amphetamines ("speed") cause a paranoid psychosis which leads the intoxicated person to attack his or her believed assailants.

Disturbances deep within the temporal lobe where the primitive centers of the brain are, due to tumor, infection, or epilepsy, can also lead to violent outbursts and sometimes homicidal behavior. Encephalitis, alcohol intoxication (either in excess or in small amounts as in the case of idiosyncratic alcoholic intoxication), hypoglycemia, and delirium tremens are other disorders which at times are associated with other-directed violence. An evaluation of a patient with a history of violent outbursts should include physical examination coupled with appropriate clinical and laboratory tests to determine the potential causes of the violent behavior. (See the section on "ego support" in Chapter 4 for a discussion of assessing violence in addition to biomedical considerations.)

TABLE 6.4:   Some Medical Disorders Presenting with Violent Behavior

---

Alcohol intoxication (excess)
Amphetamine and other sympathomimetic intoxication
Encephalitis
Delirium tremens
Hypoglycemia
Idiosyncratic alcoholic intoxication (pathologic intoxication)
Phencyclidine (PCP, angel dust) intoxication
Psychomotor epilepsy
Temporal lobe tumors

LABORATORY STUDIES

In most instances, laboratory studies are supplementary to history, physical, and mental status examination[63] rather than the primary mode of diagnosis. In some instances, however, the clinical picture of a physical illness may simulate an affective disorder or schizophrenia in such a way that non-behavioral physical signs and symptoms are absent and there is no evidence on mental status examination of an organic mental syndrome. In these cases, such as with syphilis and vitamin B_{12} deficiency, laboratory tests may be the only way a diagnosis may be confirmed or ruled out.

Electroencephalography (EEG), the so-called brain wave test, is used to identify seizure disorders, although in most instances it is normal between seizures (the interictal period). Patients with encephalitis and dementias associated with degenerative diseases of the brain commonly show generalized disturbance usually with a slowing of the rhythm, sometimes called "generalized slowing." Space-occupying lesions, such as brain tumors, meningiomas (tumors of the coverings of the brain), subdural hematomas, and abscesses generally cause "localized slowing." Skull x-rays can reveal fractures of the skull, abnormal bone growth or erosion over a tumor, calcium deposits in some lesions—such as certain brain tumors and cysts, and space-occupying lesions. "CAT" (computerized axial tomography) scans of the brain are especially helpful and to a large degree have replaced the more painful and less useful pneumoencephalogram where fluid was removed from around the spinal cord and brain and replaced with air.[64] CAT scans (also called CT scans) using the principle that structures of different densities will appear differently when beams are reflected off them reveal not only distortions of normal structures much as the pneumoencephalogram did but also the nature of the change (for example, a tumor, or abscess).

Blood studies provide an easy and relatively nontraumatic means of confirming a diagnostic impression obtained by history and physical and mental status examination. Most prescription and nonprescription drugs can influence behavior at therapeutic or more frequently at nontherapeutic toxic levels. Normal therapeutic values for commonly used drugs in a general medical hospital are given in Table 6.5. These include barbiturates, bromides, flurazepam (Dalmane), lidocaine, digoxin, propanolol (Inderal), phenytoin (Dilantin), glutethimide (Doriden), chlordiazepoxide (Librium), lithium, meprobamate (Miltown, Equanil), mysoline (Primidone), methyprylon (Noludar), phenobarbital, ethchlorvynol (Placidyl), procainamide (Pronestyl), methaqualone (Quaalude), quinidine, salicylate (aspirin), sulfonamides, carbamazepine (Tegretol), aminophyline (theophyline), diazepam (Valium), valproic acid (Depakene), and ethosuximide (Zarontin). In all instances, changes in mood, thought processes, and behavior may occur at either therapeutic or toxic level. The frequency and intensity of psychiatric symptoms increase with increasing serum levels. Even at therapeutic doses drugs such as the benzodiazepines can make a person look as if he had a stroke. It is not that nonpsychiatric physicians do not encounter behavioral changes frequently but rather that, being unaware that alterations in personality commonly accompany toxic levels of various therapeutic agents, they fail to recognize the changes in personality as due to such.

Other drugs used recreationally can frequently cause changes in personality at low levels. This is the rationalization for their use as "social facilitators," relaxants or "mind expanders." Even at low doses (for example serum levels of 100 milligrams percent is considered intoxicated) alcohol can cause violent outbursts as part of the syndrome referred to as idiosyncratic alcoholic intoxication. Abnormal liver function is reflected by changes in alkaline phosphatase, bilirubin, and serum transaminase levels. Abnormal kidney function is evidenced by changes in serum creatinine levels, blood urea nitrogen (BUN) urinalysis. Serum amylase levels and insulin levels reflect functioning of the pancreas and the latter, specifically, of the islet cells that produce insulin. Levels of vitamins such as folate and B_{12} are easily

TABLE 6.5: Normal Laboratory Values*

Alcohol		0 reading
Alkaline phosphotase (serum)		40-130 IU/L
Amylase (serum)		10-160 U/21
Arterial blood gases		pH 7.35-7.48
		pO_2 78-92 mm Hg
		O_2 Sat 93-98%
		p CO_2 35-45mm Hg
Ascorbic acid (vitamin C)		0.7-1.5 mg %
Barbiturate		Therapeutic range dependent on barbiturate ingested.
Bilirubin		Total 0.2-1.0 mg/dl
		Direct 0-0.5 mg/dl
Bromide		0-50 mcg/ml
Calcium (serum)		8.4-10.4 mg/dl
Catecholamines - Total (or fractionated to norepinephrine, epinephrine, and dopamine (24 hour urine)		0-135 mcg/24 hr.
Coulter blood count (CBC)	White cell count (WBC)	$7.8\pm3\times10^3$/cu mm
	Red cell count (CBC)	
	Male	$5.4\pm0.7\times10^6$/cu mm
	Female	$4.8\pm0.6\times10^6$/cu mm
	Hemoglobin (HGB)	
	Male	16.0 ± 2 gm
	Female	14.0 ± 2 gm
	Hematocrit (HCT)	
	Male	$47 \pm 5\%$
	Female	$42 \pm 5\%$
Cerebrospinal fluid	Cell count	0-10 mononuclear cells
	Glucose	38-85 mg/dl
	Protein	20.0-55.0 mg/dl
Ceruloplasmin		20-60 mg/dl
Cholesterol fractionation	LDH	62.0-185.0 mg/dl
	HDL	29.0-77.0 mg/dl
	Triglyceride	30.0-135.0 mg/dl
Chromosome study	Male	46xy
	Female	46xx
Copper (24 hour urine)	Adult	15.0-60.0 mcg/24 hr.
	Child	32.0-64.0 mcg/24 hr.

(continued)

Cortisol (serum)	a.m.	7.0-25.0 µg/dl
	p.m.	2.0-9.0 µg/dl
Creatinine (serum)		0.5-1.5 mg/dl
Dalmane (flurazepam)	Method does not distinguish between flurazepam, diazepam (Valium), Tranxene or other metabolites	
Digoxin (dose 0.25 mg/day)	Therapeutic range	0.8-1.6 mg/ml
Dilantin (phenytoin)	Therapeutic range	10.0-20.0 mcg/ml
Doriden (glutethimide)	Therapeutic range	up to 7.0 mcg/ml
Drug screen	Alcohol alkaloids, cocaine and amphetamines are obtained in a usual drug screen. Chromatography and mass spectroscopy are employed.	
Electrolyte	Sodium	135.0-145.0 mcg/l
	Potassium	3.5-5.0 mcg/l
	Chloride	96.0-105.0 mcg/l
	Carbon dioxide	22.0-32.0 mcg/l
5-HIAA (five hydroxy indole acetic acid) (24 hour urine)	Adult	2.0-8.0 mg/24 hr
Free T_3 (includes total T_3)		80.0-350.0 pg/dl
Free T_4		0.8-2.4 ng/dl
FTA (fluorescent treponema antibody)		non-reactive
Glucose (serum)	Fasting	61.0-102.0 mg/dl
Inderal (propanolol)	Therapeutic range	40.0-85.0 ng/ml
Insulin (fasting)		5.0-25.0 uU/ml
Iron binding capacity		75.0-150.0 mcg/dl
Iron		150.0-300.0 mcg/dl
Lead (serum)		up to 30.0 mcg/dl
Librium	Therapeutic range	1.0-3.0 mcg/ml
Lidocaine	Therapeutic range	1.5-5.0 mcg/ml
Lithium	Therapeutic range	0.8-1.4 mcg/l
Meprobamate	Therapeutic range	up to 10 mcg/ml
Mysoline (primidone)	Therapeutic range	5.0-12.0 mcg/ml
Noludar	Therapeutic range	up to 10.0 mcg/ml
Phenobarbital	Therapeutic range	15.0-40.0 mcg/ml
Phosphorous		2.0-4.0 mg/dl
Placidyl	Therapeutic level	5 mcg/ml
Platelets		$140\text{-}400 \times 10^3$/cu.mm
Porphobilinogen (random urine)		negative
Porphyrins (24 hour urine)	Coproporphyrin	0-95.0 mcg/24 hr.
	Uroporphyrin	0-20.0 mcg/23 hr.
Prolactin	Male	165.0-495.0 IU/ml
	Female	165.0-825.0 IU/ml

Pronestyl (procainamide)	Therapeutic range	4.0-10.0 mcg/ml
Quaalude (methaqualone)	Therapeutic range	1.0-8.0 mcg/ml
Quinidine	Therapeutic range	3.0-6.0 mcg/ml
Reticulocytes		0.5-1.5%
Salicylate	Therapeutic range:	
	Analgesic	20.0-100.0 mcg.ml
	Antiinflammatory	100.0-250.0 mcg.ml
Sedimentation rate		
(Westergren)	Male	0-10 mm/hr
	Female	0-20 mm/hr
17-ketogenic steroids (24 hour		
urine)		Based on weight and sex
17-ketosteroids (24 hour urine)		Based on weight and sex
SGOT (serum glutamic-oxalo-		
acetic transaminase)		5.0-31.0 IU/L
SGPT (serum glutamic-pyru-		
vic transaminase)		5.0-31.0 IU/L
Sickle Cell Preparation		negative
Sulfonamides	Therapeutic range	100.0-150.0 mcg/ml
Tegretol (carbamazepine)	Therapeutic range	8.0-12.0 mcg/ml
Theophyline (Aminophyline)	Therapeutic range	10.0-20.0 mcg/ml
Total Thyroxine T$_4$ by RIA	Male	5.0-11.5 mcg/dl
	Female	5.0-12.5 mcg.dl
Triiodothyronine		80.0-350.0 pg/dl
TSH (thyroid stimulating		
hormone)		0-9.5 mU/ml
Urea nitrogen (BUN)		7.0-25.0 mg/dl
Uric acid	Male	3.5-7.8 mg/dl
	Female	2.5-6.6 mg/dl
Urine (routine)	Specific gravity	1.010-1.030
	Ph	5.0-9.0
	Protein	negative
	Sugar	negative
	Blood	negative
	Ketones	negative
	R.B.C.	0-1/HPF
	W.B.C.	0-5/HPF
	Casts	0/HPF
Valium (diazepam)	Therapeutic range	0.5-2.5 mcg/ml
Valproic acid (depakene)	Therapeutic range	50-100.0 mcg/ml
Zarontin (ethosuximide)	Therapeutic range	40.0-100.0 mcg/ml

* Values may vary somewhat from laboratory to laboratory depending on procedures used.

detected and should be checked in anyone suspicious of poor dietary intake or severe illness compromising absorption, and in individuals with a symptom picture suggestive of a deficiency disease.

Abnormalities of the thyroid gland are revealed by alterations in levels of T_3 and T_4. However, normal levels of T_3 & T_4 do not guarantee that thyroid status is normal. Especially in individuals with depression, a more subtle form of hypothyroidism may be revealed by measurement of thyroid stimulation hormone (TSH). Serum cholesterol levels change with abnormal thyroid function. Abnormalities of parathyroid function is revealed by changes in calcium and phosphorus levels. Changes in behavior secondary to illnesses impairing pulmonary functioning such as emphysema and cystic fibrosis are indicated by changes in blood gas levels. Catecholamine levels change in illness affecting the medulla or care of the adrenal glands such as pheochromocytomas associated with periodic episodes of overwhelming fear and anxiety. Vitamin deficiencies, infections, blood loss and toxic illnesses such as plumbism (lead poisoning) are among the diseases that may alter personality that are reflected in blood changes. Examination of the cerebrospinal fluid may reveal evidence of tumor (by increase in protein), infections (by presence of white cells) and bleeding (by presence of red cells). Changes in ceruloplasmin and urinary copper are an indicant of Wilson's disease, a disease associated with an alteration in copper metabolism. Chromosome studies are used to detect chromosomally determined forms of mental deficiency and some of the syndromes associated with gender disturbance and violent outbursts. Drug screens are used in evaluation of patients in coma or confusion who have overdosed or are suspected of drug abuse. Alterations in serum electrolytes may be caused by a number of illnesses and associated with behavioral changes, especially depression. The fluorescent treponemal antibody test is used to confirm a diagnosis of syphilis. Changes in the erythrocyte sedimentation rate ("SED rate") may occur with severe infections and tumors. Changes in 17-ketosteroids and electrolytes indicate alteration of adrenal cortical functioning. Alterations in uric acid levels occur with gout. Sickle cell disease is detected by examination of a patient's hemoglobins and by sickle cell preparation.

DOSES OF COMMONLY USED PSYCHOTROPIC DRUGS

The daily doses of commonly used psychotropic drugs are given in Table 6.6. In individual instances, considerably greater doses may be given when clinically indicated and potential side-effects are monitored. Serum levels can be monitored in a number of cases and may be found to be

TABLE 6.6: Usual Daily Doses of Some Commonly Used Psychotropic Agents

Antipsychotics (Neuroleptics)

Halperidol (Haldol)	2-40	mg.
Thioridazine (Mellaril)	200-800	mg.
Thiothixene (Navane)	10-40	mg.
Fluphenazine (Prolixin)	15-60	mg.
Trifluoperazine (Stelazine)	15-40	mg.
Chlorpromazine (Thorazine)	300-800	mg.
Perphenazine (Trilafon)	24-80	mg.

Minor Tranquilizers (Benzodiazepines)

Alprazolam (Xanax)	0.50-3.0	mg.
Chlordiazepoxide (Librium)	10-75	mg.
Clorazepate Dipotassium (Tranxene)	7.5 -30	mg.
Diazepam (Valium)	2-20	mg.
Flurazepam (Dalmane)	15-30	mg.
Lorazepam (Ativan)	0.5-6	mg.
Oxazepam (Serax)	15-60	mg.
Prazepam (Centrax)	20-60	mg.
Temazepam (Restoril)	15-30	mg.
Triazolam (Halcion)	0.25-0.5	mg.

Mood Stabilizers

Lithium Carbonate	900-1200	mg.

Antidepressants

Tricyclics

Amitriptyline (Elavil)	75-300	mg.
Imipramine (Tofranil)	75-300	mg.
Doxepin (Sinequan, Adapin)	75-300	mg.
Desimipramine (Norpramin, Pertofrane)	75-300	mg.
Nortriptyline (Aventyl)	25-100	mg.

Monamine Oxidase Inhibitors

Phenelzine (Nardil)	45-60	mg.
Tranylcypromine (Parnate)	10-30	mg.

Nontricyclics

Maprotilene (Ludiomil)	75-300	mg.
Amoxapine (Asendin)	75-300	mg.
Trazadone (Deseryl)	150-600	mg.

remarkably low despite relatively high levels taken because of varying levels in absorption and differences in metabolism. The possibility that an individual is not taking a drug as prescribed must, of course, also be entertained.

All the drugs used in the management of psychiatric symptoms can, ironically, cause changes in behavior or mood or thought. The benzo-diazepines (e.g., Librium, Valium, Serax) can cause confusion, depression, and a dementiform picture even at theraputic doses.[65] Antipsychotic and antidepressant drugs can cause alterations in behavior through a number of mechanisms. Those with extra-pyramidal side-effects can cause akathisia that may be confused with an exacerbation of psychosis, The patient paces and feels he or she cannot sit still and that they are "going out of their mind." Those with strong anticholinergic effects can cause an atropine psychosis associated with confusion, agitation, hallucinations, and fear. Hypotension and cardiac arrythmias (transient or sustained) may be manifested by intense anxiety and a feeling that one is becoming worse. Constipation, urinary retention, and increased viscosity of pulmonary secretions associated with psychotropic drug use can cause confusion and increased severity of psychotic symptoms especially in older people. Finally, antidepressants can cause mania or schizophrenia[66] in patients so predisposed.[67,68,69,70,71,72] The mechanism is felt to be that of the increase in available brain amines that is considered responsible for the antidepressant effects. Finally, withdrawal from most psychotropic drugs causes a picture resembling delirium tremens.[73]

SUMMARY

Alterations in mood, thought, and behavior should be considered symptoms not diagnoses. The first step in the evaluation of depressed, anxious, schizophrenic, or violent patients is an attempt to ascertain the nature of the changes in personality seen. In some instances, these will be organically-based and possibly ameliorated by appropriate medical or surgical intervention. In other instances, they will be due to a psychiatric illness in which drugs, electroshock, or other organic psychiatric therapies may be helpful. Whether surgically, medically, or psychiatrically-based, individuals who have experienced alterations in personalities and their family broadly defined (spouse, children, lover, etc.) may benefit from psychotherapy and sociotherapy, i.e., therapeutic interventions focused on psychological issues and/or the social network/environmental context of the patient's life. History and physical and mental status examination are the cornerstones of diagnosis but a number of laboratory and clinical studies can be used to confirm a diagnosis. In some instances, alterations in personality may be due to psychotropic agents used. An integrated treatment plan is always biopsychosocial in nature and reflects the degree to which biological, psychological, and social factors influence the genesis of an individual's illness—be it medical, surgical, psychiatric, or existential—and the degree to which these same factors alter its course.

NOTES

1. R. J. Goldberg, and A. E. Slaby, *Diagnosing Disorder of Mood, Thought and Behavior* (Flushing, N.Y.: Medical Examination Publishing Co., 1981).
2. A. E. Slaby, "Emergency Psychiatry: An Update," *Hospital and Community Psychiatry:* 32 (1981): 687-98.
3. A. E. Slaby, L. R. Tancredi, and J. Lieb, *Clinical Psychiatric Medicine* (Philadelphia: J. B. Lippincott, 1981).
4. M. M. Weissman, and J. K. Myers, "Affective Disorders in an Urban Community," *Archives of General Psychiatry* 35 (1978): 1304-11.
5. Slaby, "Emergency Psychiatry."
6. A. E. Slaby, J. Lieb, and L. R. Tancredi, *Handbook of Psychiatric Emergencies* (Second Ed.) (Flushing, N.Y.: Medical Examination Publishing Co., 1981).
7. R. C. W. Hall, E. R. Gardner, M. K. Popkin, et al., "Unrecognized Physical Illness Prompting Psychiatric Admission: A Prospective Study," *American Journal of Psychiatry* 138 (1981): 636-41.
8. R. C. W. Hall, E. R. Gardner, S. K. Stickney, et al., "Physical Illness Manifesting as Psychiatric Disease. II. Analysis of a State Hospital Inpatient Population," *Archives of General Psychiatry* 37 (1980): 989-95.
9. R. C. W. Hall, M. K. Popkin, E. R. Gardner, et al., Physical Illness Presenting as Psychiatric Disease," *Archives of General Psychiatry* 35 (1978): 1315-20.
10. F. Jarvik, V. Ruth, and S. S. Matsuyama, "Organic Brain Syndrome and Aging: A Six-year Follow-up of Surviving Twins," *Archives of General Psychiatry* 37 (1980): 280-86.
11. E. K. Koranyi, "Morbidity and Rate of Undiagnosed Physical Illness in a Psychiatric Clinic Population," *Archives of General Psychiatry* 36 (1979): 414-19.
12. C. P. Maguire, and K. L. Granville-Grossman, "Physical Illness in Psychiatric Patients," *British Journal of Psychiatry* 115 (1968): 1365-69.
13. Slaby et al., *Handbook.*
14. Slaby et al., *Clinical Psychiatric Medicine.*
15. M. T. Tsuang, R. F. Woolson, and J. A. Fleming, "Premature Deaths in Schizophrenia and Affective Disorders: An Analysis of Survival Curves and Variables Affecting the Shortened Survival," *Archives of General Psychiatry* 37 (1980): 979-83.
16. L. E. Adler, L. Sadja, and G. Wilets, "Cimetidine Toxicity Manifested as Paranoia and Hallucinations," *American Journal of Psychiatry* 137 (1980): 1112-13.
17. C. C. Barnhart, and C. L. Bowden, "Toxic Psychosis with Cimetidine," *American Journal of Psychiatry* 136 (1979): 725-26.

18. M. K. Crowder, and J. K. Pate, "A Case Report of Cimetidine-induced Depressive Syndrome," *American Journal of Psychiatry* 137 (1980): 1451.
19. M. K. Shear, and M. H. Sacks, "Digitalis Delirium: Report of Two Cases," *American Journal of Psychiatry* 135 (1978): 109-10.
20. G. W. Demuth, and B. S. Rand, "Atypical Major Depression in a Patient with Severe Primary Degenerative Dementia," *American Journal of Psychiatry* 137 (1980): 1609-10.
21. J. S. Kantor, C. M. Zitrin, and S. M. Zeldis, "Mitral Valve Prolapse Syndrome in Agoraphobic Patients," *American Journal of Psychiatry* 137 (1980): 467-69.
22. S. F. Pariser, E. R. Pinta and B. A. Jones, "Mitral Valve Prolapse Syndrome and Anxiety Neurosis/Panic Disorder," *American Journal of Psychiatry* 135 (1978): 246-47.
23. T. B. MacKenzie, and M. K. Popkin, "Psychological Manifestations of Nonbacterial Thrombotic Endocarditis," *American Journal of Psychiatry* 137 (1980): 972-73.
24. J. F. Greden, "Anxiety or Caffeinism: A Diagnostic Dilemma," *American Journal of Psychiatry* 131 (1974): 1089.
25. A. J. Gelenberg, "The Catatonic Syndrome," *Lancet* 1 (1976): 1330-41.
26. A. J. Gelenberg, and M. R. Mandel, "Catatonic Reactions to High-Potency Neuroleptic Drugs," *Archives of General Psychiatry* 34 (1977): 947-50.
27. M. R. Liebowitz, E. J. Wuetzel, A. E. Bowser, et al: "Phenelzine and Delusions of Parasitosis: A Case Report," *American Journal of Psychiatry* 135 (1978): 1565-66.
28. W. W. Weddington, R. C. Marks, and P. Verghese, "Disulfiram Encephalopathy as a Cause of the Catatonia Syndrome," *American Journal of Psychiatry* 137 (1980): 1217-19.
29. S. W. Woods, "Catatonia in a Patient with Subdural Hematomas," *American Journal of Psychiatry* 137 (1980): 983-84.
30. M. S. Gold, and M. B. Bowers, "Neurobiological Vulnerability to Low-dose Amphetamine Psychosis," *American Journal of Psychiatry* 135 (1978): 1547-48.
31. A. E. Slaby, and R. J. Wyatt, *Dementia in the Presenium.* (Springfield, Ill.: Charles C. Thomas, 1974).
32. Slaby, "Emergency Psychiatry."
33. R. M. Allen, and S. J. Young, "Phencyclidine-induced Psychosis," *American Journal of Psychiatry* 135 (1978): 1081-84.
34. C. V. Showalter, and W. E. Thorton, "Clinical Pharmacology of Phencyclidine Toxicity," *American Journal of Psychiatry* 134 (1977): 1134-38.
35. Allen and Young, "Phencyclidine-induced Psychosis."
36. S. H. Block, "The Grocery Store High," *American Journal of Psychiatry* 135 (1978): 126-27.
37. R. A. Faquet, and K. F. Rowland, "Spice Cabinet Intoxication," *American Journal of Psychiatry* 135 (1978): 860-61.
38. R. C. W. Hall, M. K. Popkin, and L. E. McHenry, "Angel's Trumpet Psychosis: A Central Nervous System Anticholinergic Syndrome," *American Journal of Psychiatry* 134 (1977): 312-14.
39. Showalter and Thorton, "Clinical Pharmacology."

40. L. T. Sigell, F. T. Kapp, E. A. Fusaro, et al., "Popping and Snorting Volatile Nitrites: A Current Fact for Getting High," *American Journal of Psychiatry* 135 (1978): 1216-18.
41. M. B. Bowers, "Psychoses Precipitated by Psychotomimetic Drugs. A Follow-up Study," *Archives of General Psychiatry* 34 (1977): 832-35.
42. W. Braden, "Response to Lithium in a Case of L-Dopa-induced Psychosis," *American Journal of Psychiatry* 134 (1977): 808-09.
43. F. Brenner, "Bromism: Alive and Well," *American Journal of Psychiatry* 135 (1978): 857-58.
44. M. L. DeBard, "Diazepam Withdrawal Syndrome: A Case with Psychosis, Seizure, and Coma," *American Journal of Psychiatry* 136 (1979): 104-05.
45. L. A. Demers-Desrosiers, J. N. Nestoros, and P. Vaillancourt, "Acute Psychosis Precipitated by Withdrawal of Anticonvulsant Medication," *American Journal of Psychiatry* 135 (1978): 981-82.
46. M. W. Dusken, and C. H. Chan, "Diazepam Withdrawal Psychosis: A Case Report." *American Journal of Psychiatry* 134 (1977): 573.
47. R. S. Epstein, "Withdrawal Symptoms from Chronic Use of Low-dose Barbiturates," *American Journal of Psychiatry* 137 (1980): 107-08.
48. R. D. Franks, and A. J. Richter, "Schizophrenia-like Psychosis Associated with Anti-Convulsant Toxicity," *American Journal of Psychiatry* 136 (1979): 973-74.
49. G. Bardos, J. O. Cole, and D. Tarsy, "Withdrawal Syndromes Associated with Antipsychotic Drugs," *American Journal of Psychiatry* 135 (1978): 1321-24.
50. C. T. Gualtieri, and J. Staze, "Withdrawal Symptoms after Abrupt Cessation of Amitriptyline in an Eight-year-old Boy," *American Journal of Psychiatry* 136 (1979): 457-59.
51. R. S. Hausner, "Amantadine-associated Recurrence of Psychosis," *American Journal of Psychiatry* 137 (1980): 240-42.
52. L. L. Heston, and D. Hastings, "Psychosis with Withdrawal from Ethchlorvynol," *American Journal of Psychiatry* 137 (1980): 249-50.
53. D. J. Luchins, W. J. Freed, and R. J. Wyatt, "The Role of Cholinergic Supersensitivity in the Medical Symptoms Associated with Withdrawal of Antipsychotic Drugs," *American Journal of Psychiatry* 137 (1980): 1395-98.
54. C. Moskovitz, H. Moses, and H. L. Klawans, "Levadopa-induced Psychosis: A Kindling Phenomenon," *American Journal of Psychiatry* 135 (1978) 669-75.
55. J. S. Pevnik, D. R. Jasinski, and C. A. Haertzen, "Abrupt Withdrawal from Therapeutically Administered Diazepam. Report of a Case," *Archives of General Psychiatry* 35 (1978): 995-98.
56. S. H. Preskorn, and L. J. Denner, "Benzodiazepines and Withdrawal Psychosis: Report of Three Cases," *JAMA* 237 (1977): 36-38.
57. A. A. Rosenfeld, "Depression and Psychotic Regression Following Prolonged Methylphenidate Use and Withdrawal: Case Report," *American Journal of Psychiatry* 136 (1979): 226-28.
58. R. B. Stewart, R. B. Salem, and P. K. Springer, "A Case Report of Lorazepam Withdrawal," *American Journal of Psychiatry* 137 (1980): 1113-14.
59. A. Winokur, K. Rickels, D. J. Gruenblatt, et al., "Withdrawal Reaction from Long-term Low-dosage Administration of Diazepam. A Double-blind Placebo-controlled Case Study," *Archives of General Psychiatry* 37 (1980): 101-05.

60. J. M. Rainey, "Disulfiram Toxicity and Carbon Disulfide Poisoning," *American Journal of Psychiatry* 134 (1977): 371-73.
61. Braden, "Response to Lithium."
62. Moskovitz et al., "Levodopa-induced Psychosis."
63. D. A. W. Johnson, "Evaluation of Routine Physical Examination in Psychiatric Cases," *Practitioner* 200 (1968): 686-91.
64. L. Tsai, and M. T. Tsuang, "Computerized Tomography and Skull X-rays: Relative efficacy in Detecting Intracranial Disease," *American Journal of Psychiatry* 135 (1978): 1556-59.
65. G. E. Woody, C. P. O'Brien, and R. Greenstein, "Misuse and Abuse of Diazepam: an Increasingly Common Medical Problem," *International Journal of the Addictions* 10 (1975) 843-45.
66. F. H. Gawin, and R. A. Markoff, "Panic Anxiety after Abrupt Discontinuation of Amitriptyline," *American Journal of Psychiatry* 138 (1981): 117-18.
67. J. T. Biggs, D. G. Spiker, J. M. Petit, et al., "Tricyclic Antidepressant Overdose: Incidence of Symptoms," *JAMA* 238 (1977): 135-38.
68. G. Chouinard, and B. D. Jones, "Neuroleptic-induced Supersensitivity Psychosis: Clinical and Pharmacologic Characteristics," *American Journal of Psychiatry* 137 (1980): 16-21.
69. Gawin and Markoff, "Panic Anxiety."
70. J. C. Nelson, M. B. Bowers, and D. R. Sweeney, "Exacerbation of Psychosis by Tricyclic Antidepressants in Delusional Depression," *American Journal of Psychiatry* 136 (1979): 574-76.
71. D. Rampling, "Aggression: A Paradoxical Response to Tricyclic Antidepressants," *American Journal of Psychiatry* 135 (1978): 117-18.
72. L. M. Sheehy, and J. S. Maxmen, "Phenelzine-induced Psychosis," *American Journal of Psychiatry* 135 (1978): 1422-23.
73. G. M. Brown, H. C. Stancer, H. Moldofsky, et al. "Withdrawal from Long-term High-dose Desipramine Therapy," *Archives of General Psychiatry* 35 (1978): 1261-64.

Chapter Seven

Implications for Training, Research, and Role Definition

Each dimension of the biopsychosocial clinical model provides implications for social work curriculum content and interdisciplinary role definitions. This chapter will focus on the specific components of the clinical model and their interrelationship. A social work research study will be examined in which findings demonstrate the need for the social worker in health care to adopt a comprehensive clinical approach even when the problem being addressed initially appears to involve concrete services. The model itself requires a team approach in which each participating discipline is aware of the potential contributions of the other disciplines and knows when it is essential to seek this consultation.

THE BIOMEDICAL DIMENSION IN SOCIAL WORK TRAINING

The term "biomedical" will be used rather than simply "biological" in order to convey that clinical social work in health care requires familiarization both with a basic level of biologic information and with the diagnostic procedures and interventions of medical practice.

While the term biopsychosocial is used frequently in the social work literature in recent years, the biologic dimension is seldom specifically addressed, and when addressed, not in the manner or degree which will assume the focus of this section of the chapter. Not since the early medical social workers has the biologic dimension received the extent of attention among professional social workers that the psychological and social dimensions have been given. Regensburg, for instance, in her book on health care education and the practice of hospital-based social work frequently uses the term biopsychosocial. However, when focusing on the biologic dimension, she speaks of it more in the context of the onset of traditional illness and adjustment to it rather than illuminating the role of biologically related and potenially undiagnosed changes in the mood, thought, or behavior of the patient. "Biologic disorder does not exist in isolation; it may impair or completely interrupt the patient's pattern of carrying his or her responsibilities, that is, his or her social functioning . . . can precipitate emotional and attitudinal reactions ranging from fear and discouragement to hope and a fighting spirit . . . Biopsychosocial equilibrium is particularly labile during the course of an illness which is marked by specific threats to survival, by the need for critical decision making, by moments of great uncertainty, and the like".[1]

Similarly, the position paper of the education committee of the National Federation of Societies for Clinical Social Work used the term biopsychosocial several times[2] without really addressing the biologic dimension. (The position paper does introduce the term "health care provider" to describe the clinical social worker in the health setting.) The main definition paper of the NASW Task Force on Clinical Social Work also used the term "biopsychosocial" and in fact the term was used in almost all of the contributing papers to the task force. The definition paper did specifically address the biological component in one extended paragraph though it did so without the specificity or recognition of content which would be needed for a clinical social worker in health care. The NASW clinical social work definition did recognize that "The extent of knowledge necessary for effective clinical social work practice to some extent depends upon the special area of practice involved. Health and health related fields of practice may require more extensive knowledge of the biological component. However, in any form of clinical social work practice, inquiry into the state of health is a requirement".[3] Accordingly, the task force did recognize the varying needs of specialization as well as the importance of the biological dimensions at varying levels for all clinical social work. Similarly, the NASW report also recognized the need for social work collaboration with other disciplines and for some level of social work knowledge of biology in order to effectively work as part of a team. "Under such conditions, it is critical for the clinical social worker to be able to identify those biological signs that may require intervention by other disciplines".[4]

Social work education needs to provide academic curriculum content and field work training for the biologic component beyond normal biological growth and development and with specific attention to identifying aberrations in the mental status and understanding the relevance of standard medical tests. Bracht's *Social Work in Health Care*[5] contributes an introduction to medical terminology but is intended as a sample for orienting social workers to the wider health care setting and does not address the comprehensiveness and specificity that is being recommended here. For example, social workers must be taught to understand the importance of vital signs (temperature, blood pressure, pulse, respiration) and signals of malfunction in each of the systems of the human body. There is significant literature supporting the finding that disturbances in mood, thought, and behavior can frequently go unrecognized as attributable to undiagnosed major medical disorders.[6] Koranyi[7] reported on over 2,000 cases referred to a university psychiatric clinic in Canada during the mid-1970s. Those professionals who referred patients to the psychiatric clinic for treatment were unaware that the patients would receive a complete medical workup during the psychiatric diagnostic screening. Of the 2,090 referrals, 902 (43 percent) suffered from major medical illness. The conditions of nearly half of the 902 physically ill, that is, 417 patients (46 percent), had not been diagnosed by the referring sources. For 18 percent of the medically ill, a previously undiagnosed somatic pathologic condition *alone* was considered to be the cause of the presumed psychiatric disorder. In over half (51 percent) of the total sample of patients, some somatic illness was identified which was considered to be substantially aggravating the psychiatric condition.

A typical example in the Koranyi study was that of a middle-aged couple on the verge of separation with sexual difficulties minimized in the referral as consequential to marital problems. A glucose tolerance test led to a final diagnosis in the husband of diabetes induced impotency. In another case, a postmenopausal woman with rheumatic heart disease receiving digitalis was referred by her cardiologist for depression and diarrhea. The final diagnosis was digitalis toxicity. Similarly, a "quarreling couple" had been treated with marital therapy. Both were accustomed to having a few drinks before dinner and routinely quarreled at bedtime. A five-hour glucose tolerance test revealed that both manifested significant hypoglycemia at three hours which was a major determinant of their behavioral difficulties. The failure to recognize that major medical illness could mimic psychiatric illness was a problem for all disciplines but particularly for social work. There were a significant number of undiagnosed major medical illnesses that were diagnosed at the psychiatric clinic. Thirty-two percent of referrals from interns, 48 percent of referrals from psychiatrists, and 83 percent of referrals from social service agencies ended up in this group. While the study did not differentiate between professionally trained social workers or other social service employees, the finding is remarkable and clearly implies that biologic illness needs closer attention when aberrations of the mental status are in evidence and that social workers pointedly need more systematic training in this area in order to be aware of when to involve the help of other disciplines. The following table is provided to assist clinicians in the health setting to be alert to some of the more common somatic conditions that can masquerade as psychosocial symptomatology.

TABLE 7.1. Medical Disorders Which Masquerade as Psychosocial Symptoms

METABOLIC:	*GLUCOSE*: Low blood sugar (hypoglycemia) is a special risk for patients on insulin or oral diabetic agents.
	ELECTROLYTES: Sodium and potassium should be considered in any patient on diuretic treatment. These elements can also be abnormal in patients with many other medical disorders associated with fluid imbalances.
	KIDNEY FUNCTION: Abnormal kidney function can lead to abnormalities in blood urea nitrogen measures (BUN) or creatinine (Cr) and may lead to "psychiatric" symptoms by the accumulation of toxic substances which are normally cleared by the kidneys.
	HEPATIC (LIVER) FUNCTION: Impaired liver function due to alcoholism or other liver disease can lead to a failure of the adequate metabolism of many drugs, and enhance their toxic accumulation. The brain can also become toxic from the effects of liver failure. Typical abnormalities are reflected in high values for SGOT, SGPT, alkaline phosphate, LDH, bilirubin.
	HYPERCALCEMIA: High levels of calcium may be associated with malignancy and may lead to a variety of "psychiatric" symptoms such as anxiety or psychosis.
	THYROID: Excessive thyroid hormone (hyperthyroidism) can lead to anxiety symptoms while low thyroid function (hypothyroidism) may lead to depressive symptoms and eventually to psychosis. The former is reflected in high levels of T_4, while the latter is associated with low levels of T_4 and elevated TSH (thyroid stimulation hormone).
	ARTERIAL BLOOD GASES (ABG): Abnormally low oxygen in the blood due, for example, to lung disease does not allow the brain cells to function adequately. Similar hypoxic encephalopathy can result from problems delivering oxygen to very low bloodcounts, or reduced blood pressure. Some patients with chronic lung disease may accumulate carbon dioxide and develop confusion on that basis.
ELECTRICAL:	Patients with temporal lobe seizures may manifest a host of psychiatric symptoms including anxiety or hallucinations. After any type of seizure, that is, in the post-ictal state, patients are often confused or disinhibited. Therefore, the electroencephalogram (EEG) can play an important role in diagnosis. The EEG also is a sensitive indicator of generalized impairment of brain function (encephalopathy).
NEOPLASTIC:	Primary brain tumors, or metastatic spread to the brain can, of course, lead to a variety of "psychiatric" symptoms.
DRUG:	See Table 7.2.

182

TABLE 7.1. Medical Disorders Which Masquerade as Psychosocial Symptoms (Continued)

CIRCULATORY:	Significant drops in blood pressure can lead to strokes which are the loss (death) of brain neurons. Strokes also result from blood clots traveling from other parts of the body (embolization). When such events have results which are entirely reversed within 24 hours they are known as transient ischemic attacks (TIA's). Very small areas of neuronal damage (micro-infarcts) can result from high blood pressure eventually leading to symptoms of dementia in the older patient due to a condition known as a hypertensive lacunar state.
MECHANICAL:	Transient "psychiatric" disturbance can result from concussion (head trauma with no other obvious sequelae). Mechanical damage of the brain can also result from accumulation of pockets of blood within the skull following injury (post traumatic subdural hematomas) or from blockage of the circulation of cerebrospinal fluid (obstructive hydrocephalus).
INFECTIOUS:	Meningitis and encephalitis can present with chronic fluctuation of mental status, especially when the infection is due to a fungal agent rather than the more acute changes associated with bacteria or viral central nervous system infections. Infections in the other parts of the body can sometimes travel to the brain via the blood stream and lead to abscesses. Finally, many years after initial infection, syphilis may lead to destruction of central nervous system (CNS) tissue (tertiary syphilis).
NUTRITIONAL:	Severe dietary limitation and certain diseases of the intestines may lead to psychotic symptoms from B_{12} deficiency. More commonly, the thiamine deficiency associated with chronic alcoholism can lead to a syndrome known as Wernicke-Korsakoff which is associated with confusion and memory loss (along with trouble walking and coordinating eye movements).
DEGENERATIVE:	While there are many brain degenerative diseases, the most common is senile degeneration of the Alzheimer type which leads to neuronal loss and symptoms of dementia. Since there is currently no definitive way to make this diagnosis, it must always be one of exclusion.

Drug-induced changes in the mental status are also important for any clinician to consider in evaluating a patient's mood, thought, and behavior in the health setting. The following table is provided as a reference for clinical social workers and other health care providers as an aid in addressing the potential effects of a large number of drugs that could be significant in the evaluation of any presentation.

TABLE 7.2.   A Selection of Commonly Used Drugs That Produce Psychiatric Symptoms

---

Anti-anxiety agents
> Benzodiazepines, such as Diazepam (Valium), can produce oversedation, confusion, or impairment of cognitive and motor performance, when doses become cumulative. Depressive symptoms may also be reported. Anxiety and agitation along with insomnia may accompany abrupt discontinuation of sedative medication.

Anti-convulsants
> Patients who develop "psychiatric" symptoms while on anti-convulsants would have their plasma levels of the medication checked because such symptoms may be the result of levels which are too low or too high.

Anti-depressants
> Some anti-depressants have significant anti-cholinergic activity and can produce symptoms of confusion or agitation, in addition to the more common side-effects of sedation or lightheadedness.

Anti-hypertensives
> Some anti-hypertensives, such as propranolol (Inderal), or reserpine, can produce depressive symptoms by direct effects on brain neurotransmitters. The others which act as diuretics, such as the thiazides, can produce weakness, lethargy, or depressive feelings as a result of fluid and electrolyte imbalances which they may create.

Cimetidine (Tagamet)
> This medication deserves mention because it is one of the most widely prescribed drugs in the United States. It is associated with many "psychiatric" sequelae including anxiety, confusion, delirium, or psychosis, as well as depressive symptoms.

Central nervous system depressants
> Sedative—hypnotic medication of any sort may lead to depressive symptoms, or withdrawal agitation. ALCOHOL is the most significant culprit in this group.

Digitalis
> Toxic effects of this drug may be behavioral in nature, presenting with confusion or agitation. Such symptoms may occur even when the plasma level of the drug is within the high therapeutic range.

Narcotics
> A common problem associated with narcotic use for medical patients is the underuse of narcotics in situations where pain is severe. Patients in pain may have any sort of psychiatric consequence as a result of the pain. At other times, agitation may result from narcotic withdrawal. Narcotic abusers may develop a large number of secondary consequences such as infection, or endocarditis which can lead to delirium or brain abscesses. One narcotic, pentazocine (Talwin) is associated with a relatively high incidence of depersonalization as a side effect.

**TABLE 7.2. A Selection of Commonly Used Drugs That
Produce Psychiatric Symptoms (Continued)**

Steroids

These drugs can lead to symptoms of depression, mania, irritability, or psychosis when the dose is being increased, maintained, or tapered.

Stimulants

Drugs such as amphetamines, cocaine, or "diet pills" can lead to anxiety, insomnia, or paranoid psychosis if the dose is high enough. All stimulants have some sort of depressive withdrawal upon abrupt discontinuation.

---

*See Chapter 6 for further discussion and understanding of these drugs, their uses, and side effects.

Presumed psychological symptoms can at times be the result of a combination of an underlying biomedical condition and its treatment. For instance, a patient initially seen for depression and fatigue may eventually be diagnosed as having a collagen vascular disease such as systemic lupus erythematosus. The anti-inflammatory drugs such as steroids used to treat lupus can in their own right produce a variety of symptoms including depression, anxiety, or even psychosis.[9] Patients developing depression while on steroids may require treatment with an antidepressant medication, for example, amitriptyline (Elavil) in addition to the steroids. Social workers should be aware of the indicated and appropriate uses of medication so that they are not under the impression that the use of psychotropic medications are either contraindicated or prescribed as a substitute for "talking" or psychotherapeutic intervention.

Some of the most common drugs prescribed that can have a dysphoric effect on the mood, thought, or behavior of a patient are those which are prescribed for hypertension. Propranolol (Inderal), alphamethyldopa (Aldomet), hydrochlorathiazides (HydroDiuril)—all of these can cause depression as a side effect.[10] Chapter 6 contains an example in which the use of the drug, reserpine, by a medical resident to treat his own hypertension actually resulted in his suicide. One would have hoped that a medically trained practitioner would have foremost in mind the side effects of various medications yet the illustration demonstrates the potentially adverse effects of certain drugs despite their value in the treatment of other symptoms.

Social work training could be usefully expanded to familiarize students with the language and basic features of the medical factors that can masquerade as psychosocial symptoms. In addition, it would be helpful to direct special attention to the specific disturbances of the mental status that result from organic mental disturbances. These skills are important for clinicians working with every patient in the health setting but are especially crucial in the care of elderly patients who often have medical illness, are on several medications, and have the possibility of some degenerative form of dementia.[11]

Aside from the value of these clinical skills in their own right, a demographic shift will soon focus attention on diagnosis and the elderly. It has been said that of all the people in history who ever lived to age 65 or older, half of those people are living today.[12] It is not that the maximum age of the human race has been extended but that more people are living longer. It is expected that by the year 2,000, 31.8 million Americans will be over the age of 65. Diseases of the elderly will therefore demand increasing attention from clinical social workers and all health care providers, requiring diagnostic and treatment specialization in these areas. The ability to appropriately identify and treat the dementias (loss of mental function), for instance, is and will continue to be a needed focus in training and education. While many dementias have some identifiable and corrective elements, the majority of senile dementias are neither reversible nor medically treatable. There are several distinct forms of dementia. One form is known as primary neuronal degeneration (for example, Alzheimer's Disease) and another group is known as the multi-infarct dementias, which result from small islands of nerve death secondary to hypertensive circulation. While the actual diagnosis of such disorders requires the training of a psychiatrist, it is imperative for the training of social workers to include a level of sophistication with these disturbances because their caseloads will be filled with them and multi-infarct dementias, in particular, are not easily apparent. In order to enlist the timely consultation of a psychiatric physician, some symptoms of the illness must first be recognized.

With multi-infarct dementia, the onset is typically abrupt and the pattern of deficits is patchy, depending upon which regions of the brain have been destroyed. Certain cognitive functions may be affected early while others remain relatively unimpaired. While this dementia typically involves disturbances in memory, abstract thinking, and judgement, the presence of impulse control problems or personality changes could make the clinician mistakenly focus on psychological or social issues. With the primary neuronal, also called primary degenerative dementia (DSM-III), such as Alzheimer's, there are no motor or sensory problems but the onset is insidious and in the early stages memory impairment may be the only apparent cognitive deficit. There may also be subtle personality changes, such as the development of apathy, lack of spontaneity, and a quiet withdrawal from social interactions. With the senile onset, the average duration of symptoms, from onset to death, is about five years.[13]

For the clinical social worker effectively functioning within the context of the health care team, a basic knowledge of brain functioning is essential. The social worker should appreciate that there is more involved in mental status changes than a simple dichotomy between functional versus organic. If organic, the social worker should learn, for example, that impairments can be either diffused or localized, and if localized, a basic appreciation for brain functioning could help the social worker recognize where the deficit might be. This would make the social worker's referrals for further consultation more pointed and useful and more clinical. A minimal but systematic exposure to neurology in social work training could help the social worker as clinician identify, for instance, that patients with motor task problems secondary to a cortical brain injury may have other associated frontal lobe impairment; that patients with visual processing problems could involve impairment in the parietal and occipital lobes; and that patients with problems in personal space or distance, or emotional tone could likely have a temporal lobe deficit. (See Appendix III.) The point is not for the social worker to strive to become the ultimate diagnostician, but rather to be an effective front line clinician who could identify specific symptoms of dysfunction and require of the psychiatrist or of other specialists skillful and timely collaborative consultative input. If the social worker has the awareness at a basic level of specific brain function, high yield data can be obtained from the patient in a very short period of time. Screening tests for abnormalities in the nonverbal area of the brain typically include tasks that address spatial organization and sequential planning. For example, to get at these functions, the patient may be asked to (1) write his or her name and the date at the top of a page; (2) draw a clock at ten past eleven; or (3) construct a cube. Any interview with a patient that is limited—as it usually is—to assessment of verbal communication is incomplete, and can fail to uncover significant losses in mental functioning. Detection of deficits in any of these areas would indicate a profitable and cost-effective consultation from the psychiatrist.

An interest in brain functioning could have a positive impact on social work education. Although until recently, most social workers had prided themselves in their training on the affective rather than cognitive orientation, actually an emphasis on psychoanalytic theory over many decades in social work training seems to have reflected more the left hemisphere, that is, the rational or quantitative side of the brain. In practice interventions this was probably effective and useful with intelligent and well-organized patients, but not so helpful or appropriate with chaotic, deprived, and psychotic patients. It would appear that in engaging the latter patients, an appreciation for the metaphorical and intuitive properties of the right hemisphere would add an important dimension in training and education. The growing popularity of the communications theorists in their unorthodox engagement strategies could be evidence of a shift in theory and clinical practice toward the right hemisphere; for example, paradoxical intention.[14]

In summary, curriculum changes in social work education should incorporate in a more systematic and detailed manner content on the biomedical dimension in patient care as outlined above and as covered in Chapters 5 and 6. Some of these changes in the social work curriculum might be best effected by making a closer alliance between the practice or field work setting and the academic setting. Joint faculty positions spanning both settings as endorsed in the literature could be one solution to enhancing this process.[15]

THE PSYCHOLOGICAL DIMENSION IN SOCIAL WORK TRAINING

While the position paper of the National Federation of Societies for Clinical Social Work advocated the exclusive adoption of the psychodynamic theoretical orientation for clinical social workers, the NASW Task Force on Clinical Social Work advocated a wider array of theoretical persuasions though it did not name them specifically other than to categorize mental functions into the cognitive (perceptual or intellectual) the conative (striving, tendency to do actively or purposefully), and the emotional or affective. Beyond that, the task force did not endorse any one single theoretical approach. Similarly, Strean in his book *Clinical Social Work: Theory and Practice*[16] included a multitude of theoretical approaches under the rubric of clinical social work. The tension and urgency among some segments of the social work profession that clinical training of one theoretical persuasion or another again be emphasized may have been partly a reaction to a trend in the early and mid-1970s in which some traditional social work agencies drastically altered their policies and gave priorities to social action and social legislation, essentially doing away with many of the traditional, direct service functions. For instance, in the early 1970s, one of the oldest and most prestigious casework agencies, The Community Service Society of New York, did just that and a number of other social agencies followed their lead at least to the extent of confining direct therapeutic services to crisis intervention and short-term therapy. The emphasis on short-term therapeutic work amounted to an entirely different trend, but the perception developed that all social work after the 1960s was heading in the direction of macro-level social action and legislation. Nevertheless, this was happening at a time when economically minded administrators of social agencies were deciding to turn to baccalaureate level social work practitioners to replace master's degree graduates. Compounding this in the 1960s and 1970s were some research studies both in and out of social work that questioned whether casework and/or group work actually had any effect on improving clients' personal or social functioning.[17] In other studies, the research seemed to demonstrate that individuals and families who did not receive direct social work services appeared to function about the same as those in similar circumstances who had actually received several months to a year of social work treatment.[18] In about 50 percent of the research studies reviewed, clients receiving casework services tended to deteriorate.[19] What seemed to come out of all of this was a false dichotomy between the psychotherapeutic interests of social work and those that emphasized external forces and manipulation of the social environment. One writer commented in the mid-1970s that "The Behaviorist, organic psychiatrist and the social worker-social manipulator are in one camp; the psychoanalyst, dynamic psychiatrist, therapeutic caseworker are in the other."[20]

The fact that a false dichotomy between the psychological and social was being made (with rare allusion to the biological) appeared to be a repeat of the social work debate forged during the 1930s. In 1936, Fern Lowry attempted to bridge the gap by contributing a differential diagnostic conceptualization of social work practice.[21] Lowry pointed out that sometimes people need a concrete service exclusively, sometimes they need to express their feelings in the process, while at other times they may need to sort out their emotional conflicts without any tangible service. The dichotomy between biopsychological and concrete/social/environmental needs also has been unsupported by research which will be examined further in this chapter. While the biopsychosocial dimensions are interrelated, the essence of clinical work is that of determining which dimension or combination of dimensions or in which order should interventions be directed. Priorities are established and strategies selected through the differential diagnosis of all three. This comprehensive approach is often not present among social service practitioners who are not clinicians. The social activist, for instance, might work toward passage of certain legislation or advocate macro-level social changes. The technician or civic group official might try to fill a social need without any consideration of psychological or biological issues. The task of the clinician, however, is not to address any presentation on the surface without a differential assessment of the need across the biopsychosocial spectrum. For instance, *psychologically* a patient who presents in crisis after the loss of her family in a fire may require different intervention from a patient who threatens to abandon her children or to attempt suicide every time her welfare worker pressures her to seek employment. The clinician needs to be able to assess the personality style and coping capacities of the presenting patient as well as the dynamics of his or her family or social network. The repertoire of clinical skills would include more than an intrapsychic perspective because the patient in the health setting is often not psychologically minded but is instead focused on physical complaints in tandem with a multitude of tangible problems in daily living. The health setting population requires more focus on the development of psychological concepts designed to engage the resistant, hard to reach, nonintrospective, and somatically preoccupied patient.

The fact that an exclusive psychodynamic approach would not be advocated, particularly for a specialization in the health care field, is substantiated by extensive research and previous experimental projects in the area of health care. As long ago as the 1950s, Friedson provided a provocative analysis of the failure of the social work role in a family health maintenance demonstration project, pointedly because of the reliance of the social workers on the psychodynamic model. Friedson found that the model isolated the social workers from what the patients considered as ordinary daily living issues, thus creating a major barrier to the social workers' use in the program. Friedson[22] argued that the patients did not see emotional problems of everyday life to be distinct, and that seeing this type of clinician implied a discontinuity with normal functioning. While seeing the physician or nurse was perceived as continuous of routine care, accepting referrals to social workers who focused on the intrapsychic world required a transition in the patients' concept of their problems which they could not make. Not only did the patients resist the suggestion that the distress was attributable to emotional concerns, but the social workers also exacerbated this by their near exclusive focus on psychodynamics which seemed to alienate the patients.

More recently, another project experimented with the primary care team concept, finding among other things that the inclusion of social workers encountered considerable patient resistance because the social workers were more oriented to emotional issues and less to social context issues, more to intrapsychic insights than to environmental considerations.[23]

Mechanic, among others, has provided extensive research to support the contention that in contrast to intrapsychic attention, a focus on active coping and mastery serve to take attention away from bodily concerns and bolster confidence and self-esteem. Of particular concern to all health care practitioners, Mechanic emphasizes that in many instances of psychological distress that are not reflective of obvious psychiatric illness, it is particularly appropriate to assist patients in specifically defining external problems that are manageable to help them focus on active coping strategies that are relevant, and to encourage mastery of these problems.[24] Elsewhere, Mechanic's research has concluded that with patients in health care, therapies that focus on introspection are not necessarily helpful, particularly for people who are already introspective, including preoccupations with bodily concerns.[25]

The issue raised above is not directed at questioning whether the psychodynamic approach should be included in a social work/health curriculum but rather toward both how much emphasis it should receive and how its concepts should be translated into practice. The health setting and its need for practical interventions requires that the clinician has mastered a basic psychodynamic understanding of patients' problems. Social work curricula that exclude psychodynamic training lose a rich and vast theoretical base. Psychodynamic concepts can be drawn upon and made extremely useful if adapted to the health setting as demonstrated in Chapter 4. The psychodynamic approach, however, cannot be the exclusive training focus for social workers who aspire to practice as clinicians within a health care specialization. The curricula and practice base must be complemented by psychological strategies focused on practical problems of daily living such as those originally advocated by Perlman[26] and more recently in a very organized way by Reid, also from the University of Chicago, in his *Task Centered Casework*.[27] Above all, social workers in the context of health care need to be trained in such a way as to not see therapeutic interventions that focus on the practical problems of daily living, even concrete service issues, as low in prestige.

Of equal importance in the psychological dimension, particularly if social workers have the opportunity for collaboration with a psychiatrist on comprehensive health care teams, the social worker would need to become familiar with the language and conceptualizations of the *Diagnostic and Statistical Manual of the American Psychiatric Association*.[28] While this is a more phenomenologic approach to psychiatric illness reflective of medical psychiatry, the social worker would need to balance, for instance, a symptomatic/quantitative evaluation of depression, complementing the assessment of changes in weight, appetite, mood, and so on with a dynamic assessment of the patient's hopes and disappointments—that is, the patient's perception of his or her situation, including past and future. This would be an instance in which the basic concepts and practice strategies of psychodynamic training characteristic of the most orthodox diagnostic casework[29] could be profitably drawn upon to complement medical psychiatry.

A familiarity with the language of psychiatry and a level of sophistication with psychiatric diagnosis and treatment second only to the unique expertise of the psychiatrist cannot be overemphasized for the social worker, since social workers so often find themselves in the role of front line diagnosticians on health care teams. The social worker as a front line clinician should not continue to collude in the inadequate identification of psychiatric diagnoses that occurs so commonly in medical settings.[30] Glass[31] reported, for instance, that of 82 medical patients screened in a university affiliated hospital medical clinic, 83 percent were found to have a previously undiagnosed primary psychiatric illness. These findings, (in conjunction with those represented by Koranyi's 1979 study of undiagnosed medical illness) point to the importance of comprehensive diagnostic skills for any clinician functioning in a front line screening role in the health setting.

THE SOCIAL CONTEXT/ENVIRONMENTAL DIMENSION IN SOCIAL WORK TRAINING

To insure an effective contribution to comprehensive care, the role of the clinical social worker in the health setting needs to be distinguished from the social advocate or ombudsman role. The social advocate works to meet a social need or provide a concrete service as it is presented. The assessment of need is determined primarily by the client's self-report or the referrers' identification of a need. The only other criteria which might be considered is whether the client is technically eligible for the service as determined by an arbitrary means test, for example, level of income or ability to pay. A case example:

A hospital social worker on weekend call was phoned on Saturday afternoon by a ward nurse. The nurse reported the complaint of a 26-year-old woman hospitalized for symptoms secondary to syphilis. The patient had been denied the installation of television service by a hospital technician who remained adamant in refusing the installation, stating that the patient had been abusive and didn't have the cash for the fee anyway. The social worker phoned the technician's supervisor and learned that the patient had not paid her bill on the last two admissions in the past year, had broken one television set, and was suspected of stealing equipment on another occasion. The social worker offered to pay the fee of the television service from social service special funds but the technician's supervisor also refused to install the service. The social worker demanded a better explanation for this hospital employee accusing the patient of stealing and voiced consideration of reporting the supervisor to hospital administration. At this point, the supervisor agreed to accept the funds and start the television service. The social worker wrote up the transaction in the on-call book.

The difference between the social advocate and the clinical advocate is the breadth and depth of the assessment and intervention. Just clearing the way for the television in the above example would satisfy the function of social advocacy. Asking whether it makes sense for this patient to get a television and, if so, what is going on to cause all this trouble, would approach the role of the clinical advocate and require a biopsychosocial approach. The social worker serving in a more clinical capacity would have needed to address the patient's complaints as well as the concerns of the nurse, technician, and supervisor in the following ways:

1. The patient's infection and its possible impact on her mood, thought, and behavior would need exploration with the nurse.

2. If a fever was present or if a change in mental status had been observed, a psychiatric consult could have been recommended before resolving the television issue.

3. The systems conflicts evident among the hospital staff would have been considered as potentially diagnostic of the patient's personality style and strategies directed at easing the systems conflicts would have been in order.

4. If the clinical social worker obtained reasonable evidence that the patient tended to split staff and experience gratification from the chaos, the nurse could have been helped to initiate benevolent limits with the patient, not negotiating over demands for the television service or siding with the patient against other staff.

5. The clinical social worker would have obtained more social context data on the patient to see if the demands for the television service were stimulated by other dissatisfactions in her social network. If the family was fighting, for instance, contact could be made to see if they would visit and help hold down the chaos during the hospital stay. Such inquiries can turn up useful problem-solving data, such as the patient's worry that her mother is squandering the patient's welfare check and not providing for the patient's children properly.

While comprehensive diagnostic services are not possible over the phone, clinical attempts to go beyond the obvious often produce useful biopsychosocial data that can suggest further consultative input and recommendations for follow-up. Though seldom clearly conceptualized among parctitioners, the concept of advocacy in clinical practice is intended to take on a much different form than a prima facie social service. To be a clinical intervention, the social work practitioner must not focus on a social deficit such as employment, education, housing or income unless it is determined in the context of the clinical service itself that this is actually the area for intervention. For the clinician, social deficits should not necessarily be seen as a challenge just because they exist. It does not make clinical sense to simply take care of a social deficit. The clinician should first ask himself or herself:

- Whether the perceived social deficit is similarly perceived as a deficit by the client.

- Whether it is the primary area of intervention along the biopsychosocial diagnostic continuum.
- Whether focus on the deficit will serve to engage or alienate the client.
- Whether the client and/or time would actually allow for a rectification of the social deficit.
- Whether focus on the social deficit will enhance intervention with biomedical or psychological problem areas should these exist.
- Whether or not it would even be ethical to help alleviate the social deficit.

For instance, in the context of a medical clinic visit a patient may request that a temporary disability form be signed based on the presence of vague somatic symptoms. Further inquiry, rather than simple advocacy, may reveal that the issue with the patient actually involves not being able to obtain employment while being pressured to do so by his probation officer. On a literal level the patient needs income and the social worker could choose to "advocate" for the patient with the medical provider or, having ferreted out the latent agenda involving correctional authorities, could "advocate" for the patient to persuade the probation officer to decelerate his pressure on the patient. Both interventions might qualify the social worker to be called a social advocate but either would disqualify the social worker as a clinician. First of all, an effective clinical social worker in health care would need to be conversant with biomedical issues as described earlier. This would equip the social worker to communicate with the patient and with collaborating health providers and allow the social worker to fully participate as a team member in the assessment of the patient's physical complaints and their relevance to a disability request. Whenever a patient is not markedly and clearly disabled, medical providers commonly request consultative input from whatever members of the behavioral sciences disciplines are available in the particular setting and this is usually the social worker. Beyond these medical issues, to contribute as an effective clinician the social worker in the medical setting would also need enough psychiatric training to provide an initial evaluation of potential disorders of mood, thought, and behavior in order to recognize whether further consultative input from the psychiatrist is indicated. Most importantly, the social worker in health care would not be performing as a clinician unless the issues of the social/environmental context could be approached with clinical astuteness beyond the literal level.

Cultural, religious, and sexual issues are other potentially important aspects of the social dimension. For example, an 18-year-old, single Portuguese-American woman was referred by a physician who could find no medical cause for her vague somatic complaints of two weeks duration. After a complete biopsychosocial evaluation, including consultation with medical staff, the social worker recognized that the patient was having difficulty leaving her family for college. She had become a naturalized U.S. citizen during high school and would be not only the first college entrant in her family, but also the first daughter to separate and move away. The parents and two teenage siblings gathered into the interviewing room and the matter of leaving home was focused upon. Family members expressed their pride of the college-bound student and vowed to visit her and phone as often as possible. Their blessing to go was instrumental in alleviating the girl's symptoms since she had harbored the feeling of ambivalence that she was deserting her family as well as being deserted by them. The social context proved to be the significant area of intervention.

As another example, a 27-year-old, married, Jewish orthodox woman presented in the ER with sleep and appetite disturbance, depressed mood, and intrusive suicidal thoughts. After initial medical screening, the patient was referred to a social worker who recognized the primary issue to be a conflict between the patient's religious obligations on the one hand and family and personal expectations on the other. She had been trying to get pregnant for five years, but her religious sect restricted sexual contact to a limited number of calendar days. The social worker elected to call in her rabbi, who granted the patient a dispensation from her religious obligations in the service of her physical and mental health. The patient's mood changed abruptly and her other symptoms disappeared within a day.

PRIMARY PSYCHOSOCIAL CONCEPTS NEEDED IN THE CURRICULUM OF THE CLINICAL SOCIAL WORKER

The clinical social worker in health care needs to approach the social/environmental context with a battery of concepts and techniques worthy of this important dimension of the clinical diagnostic continuum. This section will discuss four principles of clinical work of significant importance in the health setting. These are:

1. Baseline
2. Limit setting
3. Containment
4. Appropriate use of resources

Baseline

The first important clinical principle is that of establishing the patient's baseline. The social worker needs to evaluate whether the patient's circumstances as presented are out of the ordinary or are in fact, his baseline, that is, the routine and ordinary parameters of the patient's life. In the case described earlier involving a patient's request for temporary disability in the context of the medical clinic, the social worker would need to learn the following:

- Efforts the patient made to seek employment
- The nature and consistency of his past employment history
- The reason for his involvement with his probation officer in the first place
- The nature, extent, and history of what antisocial behavior he may have exhibited
- The nature and extent of his use of the medical clinic in the past
- Whether he had kept follow-up appointments
- What other sources of financial and emotional support the patient had available to him
- Who in fact was supporting the patient at present
- When the last time he had any earned income

The list is not meant to be exhaustive but to point out that the social worker could not advocate for anything for the patient until the patient's baseline could be established. A multitude of scenarios could develop in this and similar cases when the social/environmental issues are approached along the lines of the systematic evaluation outlined above. For instance:

1. Contact with the probation officer could reveal that the patient had found a number of excuses not to accept any one of the jobs that the probation officer had gone out of his way to locate for him; that the patient is not even actively on probation; that it is the patient's wife who is pressuring the patient; that he is currently working but would rather be on disability; and so on.

2. On the other hand, the evaluation could turn out that the patient's inconsistent work history and antisocial behavior has been due to an inability to concentrate, with a low threshold of tolerance, due to adult minimal brain dysfunction and which now could be manageable through the use of an antidepressant medication obtained through consultation with the psychiatrist.

3. Another alternative outcome could have the clinician collaborating with the medical provider to sign a disability for no more than three months with the contingent agreement made with the patient to decrease his excessive though episodic abuse of alcohol.

4. Yet another outcome could take the form of the social worker collaborating with the medical provider and the probation officer to refuse to sign the disability to "advocate" for the patient to accept what employment is available. This would be advocacy in the ego-supportive sense: appealing to the patient's healthier side, as will be described in the following section.

Limit Setting and Containment

In the later instance, "advocacy" would embody the clinical technique of limit setting, essentially avoiding the regressive side of the patient and allying with the more adult side, while closing off avenues of manipulation.

Another concept that has clinical relevance and usefulness within the domain of the social/environmental context is containment. This is a practice concept that is fundamental to comprehensive clinical work and provides a distinct boundary with the role of the social advocate. Containment refers to sealing over or managing the crises of individuals and social networks whose baseline is one of perpetual chaos. The professional literature both within and without social work has provided more conceptual development to reconstructive or insight-oriented intervention than to containment. Insight, in brief, implies a therapeutic relationship in which a patient would be allowed to depend on the therapist over time, experience some regression to childlike emotional expectations of the therapist, relive these unmet earlier needs, and then recognize the difference between past hurts and present unintended reminders as stimulated by the person of the therapist or other current relationships in the patient's life. This recognition or "insight" reputedly allows the patient to begin anew. Containment, on the other hand, views personality change as unlikely or at least uneconomical in terms of time and manpower, and suggests a therapeutic approach in which dependency and regression are avoided, responsibility for decisions remains emphatically with the patient, and the expectations of the therapist and their attendant anxiety are clearly limited and structured by the therapist. Management or "containment" of conflicts, not insight, is viewed as the more productive and humane course. Containment is therefore seen as more benevolent because it does not get the patient's hopes up for the fulfillment of primitive needs that the therapist could likely never fulfill.

The above discussion is essentially the debate found amidst mental health professionals' conceptualizations for treating the "borderline" personality.[32,33,34,35] Notwithstanding the contribution of the *Diagnostic and Statistical Manual of the American Psychiatric Association*, to avoid further impasse over what constitutes a "borderline," the concept of the *chaotic character* has been used throughout this volume. (The chaotic character, as defined in Chapter 3, is that individual and/or social network whose baseline behavior is one of perpetual chaos. The clinician is always soon aware that he or she is face-to-face with great turmoil and a challenging management/disposition problem.) The concepts of baseline, containment, and the chaotic character are included here within the discussion of the social/environmental context because most patients for whom these concepts are particularly useful and helpful typically are not effectively evaluated, treated, or triaged without accompanying assessment and/or contact with the social network and environmental issues with which they are enmeshed and intertwined. For chaotic characters, the social/environmental context often takes precedence over the biological or psychological because these patients can rarely be understood, managed, or engaged without an examination of this dimension. When chaotic characters present as suicidal, for instance, it is more likely a network conflict (that the clinician must assess but not be drawn into) that is the actual precipitant, though it is not often identified by the patient nor immediately apparent. Frequently, the clinician needs to decide whether to directly intervene or to purposely back off from the presentation. The patient is often not an appropriate candidate for a psychopharmacologic agent, hospitalization, or a traditionally ventilative psychotherapeutic strategy. It is in these situations that the social worker with clinical skill is most useful to the health care team in ferreting out the social context issues in the diagnostic process. The team itself reaches its peak of efficiency and comprehensiveness when sorting out the elements of a workable treatment plan for the chaotic character. Social advocacy in the place of clinical social work skill manifests its visible limitations in these cases and restricts the diagnostic effectiveness of the health care team.

Following is an illustration of a chaotic character for whom a clinical advocate employing the principles of determining baseline, setting limits, and containing turmoil, might have been more helpful.

A 31-year-old man repeatedly presented in the emergency room requesting help for different concrete needs ranging from money for transportation, job referrals, temporary shelter, and food. The case was always referred directly to a social service aide and bypassed the clinical team. The social service worker did his best to attend to every need, often having to leave the ER interviewing office to arrange for vouchers or make collateral contacts. When medical staff eventually learned that the patient had been stealing and selling prescription pads from the area offices, the social service aide could provide no information on the patient's past criminal record as reported in the newspaper. The patient hanged himself after his subsequent arrest and was found to have extensive psychiatric history unknown to the social service aide.

Appropriate Use of Resources

When the social worker as clinician can recognize the interrelatedness of biopsychosocial dimensions, he or she will need to know what community resources are available and which ones, if any, would actually be useful in the disposition. This is the principle of appropriate use of resources. Many community resources are not useful with difficult to manage patients because the resources cannot handle them, are not equipped to make clinical interventions, and the patient has usually worn out his or her welcome there already. Inappropriate referrals often make the situation worse and, moreover, ruin the reputation of the clinician in the community where credibility in urgent situations and emergencies is crucial. Community resource manuals are also often not helpful with chaotic characters because they have been formulated by social advocates and community planners who, though well-meaning, usually have little understanding of clinical emergencies. The social worker as clinician must also be an active teacher and consultant with the other team collaborators who may be expert in biomedical and psychologic diagnosis but may not be as clinically skilled with the community resource dimension of the assessment and intervention. An illustration follows.

A chaotic, married 37-year-old woman presented with a suicide gesturing drug overdose and had bruises from being battered. After hospital admission, the joint consultation by the team psychiatric nurse and psychiatrist skillfully produced a diagnosis of borderline personality and placidyl abuse, yet recommended a discharge for temporary residence at the local women's center for battered victims and referral to an outpatient drug treatment program. (The principles of base line and appropriate use of community resources were overlooked.) The social worker was able to point out that the patient's own record included evidence that she had caused turmoil at the women's center in the past by providing her husband with the center's address and that she did not meet the strict criteria for acceptance into the drug program. A referral to the local community mental health center was advised as a more effective disposition because it would provide consistency, limits, emergency availability, skillful staff with chaotic clients, and would test the patient's motivation for later referral to the drug program when she would be more likely to utilize it and be accepted by the program. The social worker also recommended use of the shelter facilities at the Salvation Army if the patient really feared returning home. That way she could reconcile with her husband as carefully or as impulsively as she needed without jeopardizing her option at the women's center for a time when she may more desperately need it. The team incorporated the social work consultation and both the patient and the team was spared undue community conflict.

Contemporary.social work textbooks have not specifically focused on conceptualizing assessment and intervention strategies with diffucult clients or emphasized a clinical approach to the social/environmental context. Both Pincus and Minahan[36] and Compton and Galoway,[37] used widely in social work education in recent years are systems-oriented but more for community organizers than clinicians, especially not for clinical social workers in the health setting. Examples such as organizing neighborhood block clubs or setting up programs for minority groups are more common than illustrations drawn from clinical work.

THE CORE ISSUE FOR CLINICAL SOCIAL WORK

When social deficits are determined, the challenge for the social worker who is a clinician is that of knowing when to do something and what, and when to do nothing, and why. This clinical skill could be rightfully embraced as a primary contribution of the social work profession, and approached uniformly and systematically in social work education. Practice methods workbooks in classroom teaching could benefit from more emphasis on cases that underscore a clinical approach to the social environment. For example, the patient who is brought by the police to the emergency room because he is homeless does not receive service that could be considered "clinical" if accommodations are arranged in a nearby boarding house, and paid for by the general hospital, only later to find out that the patient has been sleeping in the bus station for years. No matter how skilled some social workers are with psychotherapy, or others with social advocacy, they are unlikely to be effective clinicians in health or community mental health settings unless systematic skills are also brought to bear on social/environmental issues. Most importantly, social advocates or pure psychotherapists would be particularly unhelpful and of only limited use in general hospitals in the years ahead, in which a wide spectrum of patients with social problems are presenting increasingly with only initially somatic and/or psychiatric complaints.[38,39,40] Social deficits require evaluation, treatment, and/or triage by professionals who have the differential diagnostic skills required to sort out this dimension as well.

Considering the preponderance of social problem presentations mushrooming in the medical setting, the training and education of professional social workers will need to equip them with the skills to both differentially treat the social problems within that dimension and to look beyond the social deficits into the possible psychological and biological dimensions to determine the times when those areas need to be addressed. A basic mastery across the biopsychosocial continuum will also enhance the use of timely and appropriate collaborative input from the other health care team professionals. In the following section, research needs of social work will be evaluated including the analysis of a clinical social work research project at Rhode Island Hospital in 1981 which helps to substantiate the importance of the social worker being trained to both handle social referrals and to approach them with a biopsychosocial differential diagnostic process.

SOCIAL WORK RESEARCH

While progress is being made in social work research, particularly with early case finding in the medical setting,[41] with discharge planning and with the development of high risk screening tools,[42] more research needs to focus on the clinical process itself. As was mentioned earlier, what social work research has been done on the clinical process has been consistent with research outside of the social work profession on psychotherapy, most of which is not optimistic and has not provided much direction for improvement.[43,44,45] One social work researcher recently concluded that the moral to be drawn is not that controlled studies should be abandoned but that research should be designed to serve the profession better.[46] Some encouraging social work research has begun on facilitating patient compliance with medical programs[47] and with the specific contribution of the social worker enhancing the relationship between the physician and patient.[48] However, considering that social workers are the largest provider group of mental health services in the nation and the largest professional segment of the helping professions in medical care, research has to become more commonplace in social work training and education than has been realized to date. The following description of a research study at Rhode Island Hospital is provided as a contribution to this effort.

THE RHODE ISLAND HOSPITAL STUDY

The 1981 Rhode Island Hospital study "Medical Referrals to Social Work: A Review of 100 Cases"[49] examined 100 consecutive patient referrals from the general medical outpatient clinic to a clinical social work team. It was felt that such a systematic investigation was called for in order to begin to address a number of important and as yet unresolved issues of health care delivery. Some of the questions prompting the study included: What are the reasons medical clinic practitioners refer patients to social work? What are the problems actually encountered with such referrals and what kinds of skills are required to deal appropriately with them? Are there unique roles for a psychiatrist and a social worker in the medical clinic setting, and if so, how should they relate to referrals, each other, and the medical staff?

There is widespread agreement that psychosocial problems and psychological disorders are highly prevalent among patients in an ambulatory medical setting[50,51] and that the appropriate management of such problems within the context of medical care is a formidable clinical challenge.[52] It has been estimated that from 10 to 40 percent of all primary practice contacts are for nonmedical reasons, and that the time physicians allot to nonmedical problems is as high as 50 percent.[53] In addition to the pervasiveness of psychosocial problems, psychiatric disorders per se are also common. Koranyi's study was mentioned earlier in the chapter. In Regier's review of this area,[54] he estimated that about 15 percent of the U.S. population (based on community epidemiologic surveys) would qualify as having a psychiatric disorder, and that about 60 percent of these receive their care in the general medical sector and not in a specialized mental health sector. Given this significant amount of psychiatric care which is called for in the medical sector, it is somewhat alarming to review numerous reports of the problems that general medical practitioners have in recognizing and appropriately managing such disorders.[55,56] Many patients who express social dysfunction and/or psychological distress through organic symptoms are, in fact, often subjected to unnecessary medical and surgical interventions.[57] As will be detailed further on, the results of the Rhode Island Hospital study seem to indicate that treatable psychiatric disorders also masquerade as social problems and are apparently perceived by medical providers as capable of resolution exclusively on the level of social management.

While much has been written from a theoretical or anecdotal perspective on the contribution of social work to medical care, there have been relatively few attempts to look in detail at actual practices.[58,59] The "Caversham" project[60] represents one of the most systematic attempts so far to study in action the contribution of social work to the identification and treatment of psychosocial problems in general practice. While this study addressed the contribution of the social worker in great detail, it overlooked two of the main issues chosen for examination in the Rhode Island Hospital study: (1) what is the incidence of social work referrals that require an intervention other than that for which the referral was made? and (2) how many, for example, would require the social workers to involve collaboration and consultation with psychiatrists? Other studies of social work in general medical practice[61,62,63] fail to address what we see as central issues: What cases were referred in the first place? How is it decided when to refer to social work and when directly to psychiatry? What assessment is performed by the social worker? and What attempt was made to assess whether the intervention was correct? Even if the medical staff were to accept the social worker on the level of a social problem solver, one contention in performing the study was that such a role would not be adequate clinical work and that the social worker would need skills including but beyond the social problem dimension. Nevertheless, since it was thought that medical staff might conceive of social interventions in isolation as possible and ordinary, specific data would need to be gathered in order to test the study's hypothesis and thereby promote comprehensive clinical work.

The Clinic Setting

Rhode Island Hospital is a 719-bed, nonprofit general medical hospital affiliated with Brown University's program in medicine. The Medical Primary Care Unit in which the study took place is an ambulatory clinic with approximately 13,000 visits per year. The clinic is staffed by three nurse practitioners, 46 medical residents who each spend one-half day per week there, and seven full-time attending staff physicians. Social work services are provided predominantly by a single master's level clinical social worker who has an office within the clinic and is available for consultation and evaluation, usually by appointment because of the preponderance of referrals, but who is very visible there. Other social work services are provided to a lesser degree by the Director of the Division of Psychiatric Social Work who spends approximately one-half day per week in the clinic and by at least two second-year, clinical social work interns who spend about two full days per week in the clinic over the course of two academic semesters. The main clinic social worker attends weekly staff conferences including journal club, case conferences, and a variety of other clinic meetings, being fully integrated into the clinic setting as is recommended by the extensive British social work literature on medical clinic "attachment schemes."[64,65] Medical staff also have the option to refer patients directly to a separate psychiatric outpatient service by filling out a clinic referral form should they feel the specific need for what they might perceive to be more exclusively psychiatric services. The outpatient psychiatric services are actually provided by several mental health disciplines including psychiatrists, psychologists, psychiatric nurses, as well as clinical social workers, though this was most likely not fully apparent to the medical staff. (These are the most commonly represented disciplines within psychiatric services: social workers are currently the largest provider group of mental health services in the nation comprising 42 percent of the staff of all mental health facilities, with psychiatrists representing 30.7 percent, psychologists 22.4 percent and psychiatric nurses 4.9 percent.[66]

While the social work staff in the medical clinic may have been known by some members of the medical staff to be integrated disciplinary members of the department of psychiatry, there actually was no formal policy providing criteria for medical staff to use as guidelines in deciding to which disciplines they might refer different patients for varying problems.

Sample and Results

The study sample consists of 100 consecutive referrals from medical clinic staff to the clinical social work staff, covering a time period of January 27, 1981 to November 3, 1981. Thirty-nine patients were seen on the same day of referral, 19 within one week, 19 within two weeks, and 19 within one month. For the remaining patients, contact took place more than four weeks after the time of referral. Forty-three patients were male and 57 female. Ages ranged from 18 to 87 with a mean of 48 years. In our study sample, 28 percent were 65 years of age or older. Educational level was obtained on 67 patients, of whom 26 had eight or fewer years of schooling and only six had education beyond high school. Fifty were unemployed, 13 retired, 4 disabled, 15 were housewives, and 18 were working at the time of the evaluation. Of the 18 working, 14 had been at their current job for less than one year. Of those not working, 15 had never worked and 40 had been unemployed for greater than one year. The majority of patients, 87, lived in the greater Providence area. Forty-three lived alone, an additional 19 lived only with young children at home, and 37 lived with spouse or extended family. Sex, age, and employment level did not differ from the general clinic population.

In evaluating the referrals, the social work staff relied on the content of the biopsychosocial data base as described in Chapter 5 but used a research structured data collection instrument to organize the information collected from the clinical interviews for the purposes of the study (see Appendix IV). Evaluation of DSM-III Axis IV (severity of psychosocial stressors) found only nine patients were listed as having minimal or no psychosocial stressors, 38 were found to have mild or moderate, and the remaining 55 were considered to have severe (or worse) psychosocial stressors. On evaluation of DSM-III Axis V (highest level of adequate functioning in the past year) 22 were judged to be on at least good, 43 fair and 34 were considered to be functioning poor or worse.

Thirty-nine patients reported a history of previous psychiatric treatment (data was unavailable on eight). Thirty-five were currently involved with other social agencies (data was unavailable on four). Of the 100 referrals, 23 were made from attending medical physicians, 45 from medical residents, 19 from other staff nurses or nurse practitioners, 6 from medical students, 3 were self-referred, and 4 came from outside the clinic.

Written and Verbal Reasons for Referral

Data regarding referral and assessment were categorized into clusters as follows:

Concrete Services (52 referrals) This cluster consists of a direct request for concrete services such as nursing home placement, housing, food stamps, transportation, medical supplies, or home health care assistance. Also included in this cluster are requests to assist patients with means of financial support including requests for vocational rehabilitation, placement in community facilities, assessment for referral to financial resources, or assistance in getting disability. Fifty-two patients were referred for this cluster.

Psychiatric Assessment (30 referrals) This cluster consists of request for psychotropic medication, or for evaluation of symptoms including depression, anxiety, or somatoform disorder. Such verbal or written requests were present for 30 referrals.

Social Work Counseling (20 referrals) The term "counseling" is chosen arbitrarily and with some reservations because it is also used by nonclinicians (for example, the auto club, AAA, now refers to its dispatchers as counselors). The term is used here simply in order to distinguish this category from others that will follow. The term "casework" has been used in previous studies[67,68] to characterize the talking therapy dimension of social work practice but that term appears to have virtually dropped out of existence, especially in its use by medical providers. No referral asked for "casework" as a needed service. The "social work counseling" cluster in the Rhode Island Hospital study consists of a request for assessment and/or counseling for a variety of reasons including medical noncompliance or adjustment to a medical disorder, vocational, marital, family, interpersonal, social system, or personality problems which were difficult for the consultee. Twenty patients had a written or verbal referral for this cluster.

Substance Abuse (11 referrals) This cluster consists of requests to assist the patient with a drug or alcohol problem. Such requests accounted for 11 verbal or written referrals.

Four patients were self-referred, in 13 cases there was no written reason for referral and in five cases no verbal reason.

Patients' Understanding of Reasons for Referral

Information regarding the patients' understanding of the reasons for referral was obtained in 68 cases and was compared to the clinician's written or verbal reason (see Appendix V). In these cases, 18 felt they were referred for counseling, 13 for concrete services, 12 for assistance with finances or in locating appropriate social agencies, 8 understood the referral was about substance abuse, and one reported thinking that the referral had to do with a personality conflict with the referring physician. Two patients felt that they were being seen to get another medical opinion, and 11 felt they were to be seen in a psychiatric evaluation.

Reliability and Validity

While one goal of this study was to obtain a complete DSM-III diagnosis on each referral, such data could not be collected on every patient. In a number of cases, the clinical needs of the situation made it impossible or impractical to do so. For instance, in two cases, the social worker was currently interviewing another patient when interrupted by medical staff, requesting that the social worker just call the appropriate staff person within social service to authorize a taxi voucher to return the patients to their homes. The social worker was able to ask a few questions to make sure the authorization at face value would be valid and reasonable, but was not able to gather any other sociodemographic or clinical information useful for the research study. Fortunately, this happened few enough times that potentially obtainable data would not have apparently biased the study results. Whenever possible, it was the policy of the psychiatric social work division covering the medical clinic to thoroughly evaluate each patient referral with the biopsychosocial data base regardless of how trivial the request might initally appear. (The clinical wisdom of pursuing such a course seems, as will be further detailed, to have been substantiated by the results of this research study.) Because of the existence of the few cases described, we could not, therefore, state with certainty the DSM-III diagnosis of every patient in the sample. However, this is balanced by the coded information that was gathered through the assessment of two well-trained and experienced clinical social workers and two clinical social work interns under their close supervision, all of whom were involved in ongoing medical/psychiatric supervision and case discussion. Therefore, we believe that there is reliability and validity in the clusters to which assessment was assigned.

What Did the Social Worker Conclude Was the Actual Issue Underlying the Referral

The most frequent request was for concrete services (see Appendix VI) which were asked for with 52 of the patients. Concrete services as the sole issue involved with the patient was confirmed by the social worker in 26 of these 52 referrals. In three additional cases, concrete services were needed but also other issues were involved in the case. Of the remaining cases, seven involved a need for psychiatric services, and in three of the 52 cases a substance abuse problem which needed to be addressed was overlooked by the referring person. In five cases counseling was needed. Accordingly, ten of the 52 cases or 19.2 percent involved problems that required consultation and further biomedical diagnostic input from the psychiatrist. This issue will be addressed later in the discussion section.

Need for a psychiatric evaluation was the verbal or written reason for referrals in 30 cases. Depression was identified as requiring evaluation in 11 of these. A somatoform disorder (a physical symptom without an apparent medical explanation) was identified in seven of the cases, anxiety in three, and other psychiatric problems in eight. In ten of these 30 cases, psychiatric evaluation was found to be the sole issue involved, and a psychiatric issue was involved in 14 of the additional cases that required some other intervention. The need for psychiatric intervention turned out actually to be an overlooked substance abuse problem by the consultee, in four patients; two patients actually required concrete services and two others counseling.

The need for counseling was asked for in 12 cases. In six of these cases, this was found to be the sole issue involved in the referral. However, in five cases an overlooked psychiatric problem was found; in one case a substance abuse problem requiring intervention had been overlooked by the consultee.

The need for attention to a substance abuse problem was the referral requested for 11 patients. This was found to be the sole issue in nine cases; however, in the other two, a psychiatric problem had been overlooked in one and the need for counseling in another.

Discussion of the Research Study

While the need for some psychiatric services in medical care is generally accepted, the extent of such needs is not well appreciated, nor is the mechanism to deal with such needs agreed upon. Every study which has looked at the prevalence of psychiatric disorder in an ambulatory medical setting has found a significant number of medical clinic patients to have psychiatric problems. The study mentioned earlier in this chapter by Glass et al.[69] found that only 17 percent of patients in a university hospital general medical clinic could be considered to be psychiatrically well, even though rather strict diagnostic criteria were used. Neilson and Williams[70] reported a prevalence of 18.3 percent for depression in ambulatory medical patients using the Beck Depression Self-Report Inventory. A review of medical charts in those cases showed that the primary physician failed to diagnose about 50 percent of such patients. It is, therefore, no surprise that psychiatric problems were *not* recognized in about 17 of 100 patients in the Rhode Island Hospital's clinical social work study described above. One must, therefore, conclude that the social worker on the health care team must be trained to recognize the presence of psychiatric disorders as opposed to merely functioning as a "technician" who might simply process requests for services on a literal level without applying clinical evaluative skills. In that over 50 percent of the cases referred to the social worker were for concrete services, and that nearly one-fifth of these turned out to have a a psychiatric disorder as the primary area in need of intervention, social workers in the medical setting require training to approach these social referrals with a clinical expertise spanning the biopsychosocial diagnostic continuum. A unique role for the professionally trained social worker in health care can be that of specializing in the assessment of social/environmental issues by applying comprehensive clinical skills. These skills would include recognition of needed interdisciplinary consultation, such as from the psychiatrist, whose complementary unique role will be described in the next section. This study attempted in part to look at the perception of the social work role by medical and nursing staff from the vantage point of the services they requested.

Of course, any particular clinic setting may have a different availability of psychiatrists and social workers for the staff to choose from in making referral decisions. In the Rhode Island Hospital Medical Clinic, at least, the social worker is more available and visible than the psychiatrist; nevertheless, direct consultation from the psychiatrist was always a clear option. Thirty of the 100 referrals to the social worker in this study were for problems that were considered by the authors to require the involvement of a psychiatrist in the evaluation process at least as a consultant and/or medical supervisor to the social worker.

This is not to imply that a psychiatrist would want to evaluate social referrals nor would the psychiatrist necessarily be the most effective clinician for the majority of social referrals in which psychiatric disorder is not present. The clinical social worker can be trained to be effective in screening all cases and providing a part of the treatment for many as long as psychiatric consultation is available and appropriately utilized. Inherent in this is a definition of psychiatric illness potentially involving a biologic component that would require a medical intervention. This conception goes beyond the idea of emotional problems or recognition of transitional adjustment to physical illness. Social workers and other nonmedical helping professions can be effective in treating a spectrum of social and psychological problems, but intervention is not comprehensive and can be unsafe if medical illness is not ruled out or if changes in mental status are not recognized and treated. The social worker in health care is most useful when he or she can be entrusted as a clinician to diagnose the sequelae of what on the surface appear to be even trivial concrete service issues. In doing so, the clinical social worker can be counted on to obtain interdisciplinary consultation at the appropriate time and with the appropriate cases. Comprehensive diagnostic skills insure a balanced interreliance among health team professionals. Specifically, the social worker would need to know when to seek consultation for safety and when to avoid overuse and duplication.

Social work research that focuses on identifying the clinical dimensions of the population served, diagnostic issues, and intervention strategies will enhance the role definition and visible contribution of the clinical social worker. When social workers can recognize and document diagnostic considerations beyond the obvious elements of a patient presentation, they demonstrate clinical skill and an awareness of the essential complementary contributions of the other members of the comprehensive health care team.

THE ROLE OF THE PSYCHIATRIST

Comprehensive care is not the only by-product of the team approach. Another benefit is that each discipline can become aware of the specialized and essential roles of the others.

As can be seen from the research reviewed in the previous section, clinical social workers on an interdisciplinary health care team can uncover even with social problem referrals, complaints such as depression, anxiety, and somatoform disorders that require a differential diagnosis that must include assessment of a variety of potential medical causes. While biopsychosocial training as outlined would enhance the clinical ability of the social worker to effectively identify symptom clusters and conditions suggestive of psychiatric or medical disorder, the actual differential diagnosis must be made by a specialist whose sole expertise is the area of disorders of mood, thought, and behavior. That specialist is the psychiatrist. Several studies, including Koranyi's which was described earlier in the chapter, have suggested that there is a significant percentage of unrecognized medical disorders which underlies presumed psychiatric complaints and that such medical disorders are missed about one-third of the time by internists and almost always (83 percent) by social workers. While it is essential to the social work contribution to health care that this percentage be immensely lowered, it would not be the intention of improved training to make the clinical social worker a medical diagnostician.

The social worker as clinician can be trained to include a listing of active medical problems and a basic medical history in the evaluative process, but it is the psychiatrist who must be called upon to decide the actual diagnostic relevance of medical factors in the perception of the patient's psychological or social dysfunction. Though the social worker can be trained, for instance, to realize the importance of thyroid disturbance in inquiring of the patient's medical history, it is the psychiatrist who must be asked to carefully review the patient's lab tests, medical record, initiate a review of the patient's medical status with the primary physician, and serve as primary psychiatric consultant to the social worker, medical provider, and other members of the health care team. Because of the psychistrist's specialized expertise in the role of physician in diagnosing the biomedical dimensions of potential disorders of mood, thought, and/or behavior, the psychiatrist's role must be reserved for appropriate consultation. The psychiatrist's potential contribution would not be time- or cost-effective in the role of initial evaluator for every referral of suspected psychological or social dysfunction. Notwithstanding the fact that the Rhode Island Hospital research study reported on in this chapter demonstrated that even concrete social service referrals can camouflage primary psychiatric disorders, the psychiatrist would not be properly utilized nor necessarily proficient in fielding every human service problem. The unique role of the psychiatrist can be test appreciated in team work with other helping professionals, such as clinical social workers, whose biopsychosocial training would facilitate complementary collaboration without role confusion.

Continuing the illustration of potential thyroid disturbance, for instance, the social worker can most effectively involve the specialized consultation of the psychiatrist by being trained to realize that a symptom presentation of agitated depression, coupled with a past history of thyroid problems, could mean treatable hyperthyroidism. Identifying both the depresssive symptoms and the thyroid history, presented in turn to the psychiatrist in the context of an organized evaluative data base, can optimally engage the expertise of the psychiatrist in a timely and effective manner, while both restricting expansion of health dollars and promoting safe and comprehensive patient care. Similary, social work training can be expanded to produce clinical thinking that could formulate: (1) symptoms of retarded depression, (2) history of thyroid disturbance, (3) possible hypothyroidism, and (4) initiate consultation from the psychiatrist. Such a formulation would attest to the presence of a social work/health provider whose valuable contribution becomes essential, in part, for the very fact that the social worker sees the essential contribution of the psychiatrist and knows how and when to seek that contribution. Without the social worker's combined psychotherapeutic and social/environmental clinical skills, the health care process would be lacking. Equally, without the psychiatrist's uniquely combined psychobiological diagnostic and treatment expertise, patient care would be incompletely served and even jeopardized.

HEALTH CURRICULA IN SOCIAL WORK EDUCATION

It has been estimated that in the last 15 years the number of social workers employed in health care has increased to 40,000.[71] Considering the needs of the patient population and the nature of patient presentations that have been described throughout this book, there is a need for emphasis on the biopsychosocial clinical model in social work education. Recognizing the shortage of educational funding in this era of economic contraction, perhaps some social work schools could specialize in health curricula while others could focus in the fields of child welfare, corrections, or public welfare service. Perretz[72] surveyed 85 members of the Council on Social Work Education in 1972 and 1973 in almost all regions of the United States and Canada. Of the 62 schools that responded (73 percent), 37 offered courses in health care while 25 did not. None offered specialized curricula exclusively devoted to the mushrooming needs of health care, even though the majority of professional social workers already practiced in this area. While field placements included community mental health centers, general hospitals, and psychiatric hospitals, none specifically reported psychiatric programs within general hospitals.

Most of the social work literature during the mid to late 1970s argues for a focus on health care in social work education because of the then expected adoption of a national health insurance plan.[73,74,75] However, at this point the adoption of national health insurance by the U.S. Congress does not appear likely at least for the rest of this century. This change of direction carries implications for social work in health care as well as for the other mental health and psychiatric services in health care in the forseeable future. Community mental health services are being cut back to a level of chronic care services. General welfare and entitlement programs are being cut back. It is likely that the non-chronic care psychiatric patients who will no longer be served by the community mental health centers will join those clients with wide-ranging social and economic deficits in turning to the general hospitals and other health care settings to have their needs addressed in the context of somatic presentations.[76] Hospitals have already seen this influx of patient presentations throughout the late 1970s when several states (for example, Massachusetts and Rhode Island in 1976), redefined their general public welfare eligibility so that all indigent individuals between the ages of 18 and 65 would not be eligible for financial assistance, regardless of lack of income, unless they could show proof of a temporary medical or psychiatric disability. Accordingly, medical providers, in turn calling for consultation from social workers and psychiatrists, have had to increasingly field questionable requests for medical and psychiatric disabilities because their patients were lacking for adequate income, housing, health insurance, and other mechanisms of survival. With the economic programs of the early 1980s, this trend is likely to increase in the general direction of medical care.[77,78] During a period of scarce resources social workers will need to develop their clinical skills and research instruments in the direction of effectively determining which clients are in need and not squandering what is available on those who need it least.[79] Clinically, the biopsychosocial model provides the framework necessary for effective current practice, conceptual development, and future research.

The challenge to clinical social work in the health setting, in teamwork with its other primary collaborators such as psychiatry and medicine, will be to provide service to patients that will be as humane as possible while at the same time achieving a level of clinical assessment perhaps unprecedented in its requirements for biopsychosocial comprehensiveness. The scope of this clinical model can equip the social worker with the skills needed to identify each dimension of the problems presented and with the capacity to match these problems with the solutions available, including those systematically elicited from the patient.

NOTES

1. Jeanette Regensburg, *Toward Education for Health Professions* (New York: Harper & Row, 1978).
2. Helen Pinkus, Jean Haring, Florence Lieberman, Judith Mishane and Jeanne Pollock, "Education for the Practice of Clinical Social Work at the Master's Level: A Position Paper," *Clinical Social Work Journal* 5, 4 (1977).
3. Jerome Cohen, "Nature of Clinical Social Work," in *Toward a Definition of Clinical Social Work*, ed. Patricia L. Ewalt (Washington, D.C., NASW, 1979).
4. Ibid.
5. Neil Bracht, ed. *Social Work in Health Care: A Guide to Professional Practice* (New York: Haworth Press, 1978).
6. Robert S. Hoffman, "Diagnostic Errors in the Evaluations of Behavioral Disorders," *Journal of the American Medical Association* 248, 8 (August 1982): 964-67.
7. Edwin K. Koranyi, "Mobidity and Rate of Undiagnosed Physical Illness in a Psychiatric Clinic Population," *Archives of General Psychiatry* 36 (1979): 414-19.
8. Richard Goldberg and Andrew Slaby, *Diagnosing Disorders of Mood, Thought and Behavior: 50 Clinical Case Studies* (New York: Medical Examination Publishing Co., 1981).
9. Michael Ling, Paul Perry and Ming Tsuang, "Side Effects of Corticosteroid Therapy: Psychiatric Aspects," *Archives of General Psychiatry* 38 (April 1981): 471-77.
10. Eugene S. Paykel, Ruth Fleminger, and James P. Watson, "Psychiatric Side Effects of Antihypertensive Drugs Other Than Reserpine," *Journal of Clinical Psychopharmacology*, Williams & Wilkins Company, 1982.

11. John Beck, Frank Benson, Arnold Scheibel, James Spar, and Lawrence Rubenstein, "Dementia in the Elderly: The Silent Epidemic (UCLA Conference)," *Annals of Internal Medicine* 97, 2, (August 1982): 231-41.
12. John W. Rowe, "Aging and Dementia - An Overview," paper presented at Butler Hospital, Providence, R. I., April 1982.
13. DSM-III, *Diagnostic and Statistical Manual of the American Psychiatric Association*, 1980.
14. Paul Watzlawick, John Weakland, and Richard Fisch, *Change: Principles of Problem Formation and Problem Resolution* (New York: W. W. Norton, 1974).
15. Lawrence Shulman, "Social Work Education for Health Care Practice: Response to Professor Raymond," *Social Work in Health Care* 2, 4 (1977): 439-44.
16. Herbert S. Strean, *Clinical Social Work: Theory and Practice* (New York: Free Press, 1978).
17. M. Siporin, *Introduction to Social Work Practice* (New York: Macmillan, 1975).
18. E. Mullen and J. Dumpson, *Evaluation of Social Intervention* (San Francisco: Jossey-Bass, 1972).
19. Joel Fischer, "Is Casework Effective? A Review," *Social Work* 18 (January 1973): 5-20.
20. R. Fine, "The Bankruptcy of Behaviorism," *Psychoanalytic Review* 62, 3 (1975).
21. Fern Lowry, "The Client's Needs as the Basis for Differential Approach and Treatment," *Differential Approach in Casework Treatment* (New York: Family Welfare Association of America, 1936).
22. Eliot Friedson, "Specialties Without Roots: The Utilization of New Services," *Human Organization* 18 (1959): 112-16.
23. G. Silver, *Family Medical Care: A Design for Health Maintenance* (Cambridge, Mass.: Ballinger, 1974).
24. David Mechanic, *Students Under Stress: A Study in the Social Psychology of Adaptation* (Madison: University of Wisconsin Press, 1978).
25. David Mechanic, "The Management of Psychosocial Problems in Primary Care: A Potential Role for Social Work," *Journal of Human Stress* 6 (1980): 16-21.
26. Helen Harris Perlman, "The Problem-Solving Model in Social Casework," in *Theories of Social Casework*, ed. R. Roberts and R. Nee, (Chicago: University of Chicago Press, 1970).
27. William J. Reid and Laura Epstein, *Task Centered Casework* (New York: Columbia University Press, 1972).
28. DSM-III *Diagnostic and Statistical Manual of the American Psychiatric Association*, 1980.
29. Florence Hollis, *Casework: A Psychosocial Therapy* (New York: Random House, 1972).
30. C. P. Leeman, "Diagnostic Errors in Emergency Room Medicine: Physical Illness in Patients Labelled Psychiatric and Vice Versa," *International Journal of Psychiatry in Medicine* 6, (1975): 533-40.
31. Richard Glass, Andrew Allen, E. Uhlenhuth, Chase Kimball and Dennis Borenstein, "Psychiatric Screening in a Medical Clinic," *Archives of General Psychiatry* 35 (October 1978): 1189-95.
32. Otto F. Kernberg, "The Treatment of Patients with Borderline Personality Organization," *International Journal of Psychoanalysis* 49 (1968): 600-19.

33. Otto F. Kernberg, *Borderline Conditions and Pathological Narcissism* (New York: Jason Aronson, 1975).
34. John Frosch, "Techniques in Regard to Some Specific Ego Defects in the Treatment of Borderline Patients," *Psychiatric Quarterly* 45 (1971): 216-20.
35. Henry J. Friedman, "The Psychotherapy of Borderline Patients: The Influence of Theory on Technique," *American Journal of Psychiatry* 132 (1975): 1042-52.
36. Allen Pincus and Anne Minahan, *Social Work Practice: Model and Method* (Itasca, Ill.: F. E. Peacock, 1973).
37. Beulah Compton and Burt Galoway, *Social Work Processes*, Rev. ed. (Homewood, Ill.: Dorsey Press, 1979).
38. Florence W. Slepian, "Medical Social Work in Primary Care," *Primary Care* 6, 3 (September, 1979).
39. Ellen Bassuk and Stephen Schoonover, "The Private General Hospital's Emergency Service in a Decade of Transition," *Journal of Hospital and Community Psychiatry* 32, 3 (March 1981).
40. Mechanic, op. cit., (1980): 16-21.
41. Barbara G. Berkman and Helen Rehr, "Early Social Service Case Finding for Hospitalized Patients: An Experiment," *Social Service Review* 47 (June 1973): 256-65.
42. Eleanor Nishiura, Charles F. Whitten and Dorothy Jenkins "Screening for Psychosocial Problems in Health Settings," *Health and Social Work* (1980).
43. Siporin, op. cit.
44. Mullen and Dumpson, op. cit.
45. Fischer, op. cit.
46. Rosalie A. Kane, "Lessons for Social Work from the Medical Model: A Viewpoint for Practice," *Social Work* 27, 4 (July 1982).
47. Rona Levy "Facilitating Patient Compliance with Medical Programs: An Area for Social Work Research and Intervention," in Bracht, op. cit.
48. Sandra Blatterbauer, Marg Jo Kupst, and Jerome L. Schulman, "Enhancing the Relationship Between Physician and Patient," *Health and Social Work* 1 (February 1976): 45-57.
49. Richard Goldberg, Stephen Wallace, Joan Rothney, and Steven Wartman, "Medical Referrals to Social Work: A Review of 100 Cases," *General Hospital Psychiatry*, in press.
50. Beatrice Rosen, Ben Locke, Irving Goldberg and Haroutun Babigian, "Identification of Emotional Disturbance in Patients Seen in General Medical Clinics," *Hospital and Community Psychiatry* 23, 12 (December 1972).
51. J. Hankin and J. Oktay, "Mental Disorder and Primary Medical Care: An Analytical Review of the Literature," National Institute of Mental Health, Series D., no. 5, Rockville, Maryland 1979.
52. David Mechanic, "Social Psychologic Factors Affecting Presentation of Bodily Complaints," *New England Journal of Medicine* 286 (May 1972).
53. Slepian, op. cit.
54. D. Regier, "The Nature and Scope of Mental Health Problems in Primary Care: Variability and Methodology," Mental Health Services in General Health Care, A Conference Report, Vol. 1, Institute of Medicine, National Academy of Sciences, Washington, D.C.: 1979.

55. G. Murphy, "The Physician's Responsibility for Suicide: I, An Error of Commission II, An Error of Omission," *Annals of Internal Medicine* 82 (March 1975).
56. Shirley Cooper, "Reflections on Clinical Social Work,' *Clinical Social Work Journal* 5, 4 (1977).
57. T. B. Bart, "Social Structure and Vocabularies of Discomfort: What Happened to Female Hysteria?" *Journal of Health and Social Behavior* 9 (1968): 188-93.
58. J. Stoeckle, R. Sittler, and G. Davidson, "Social Work in a Medical Clinic: The Nature and Course of Referrals to the Social Worker, *American Journal of Public Health* 56 (1966): 1570-79.
59. Alice Ullman, "The Role of the Social Worker in Teaching Four Year Medical Students," *Journal of Medical Education* 34 (March 1959): 239-46.
60. E. Matilda Goldberg and June E. Neil, *Social Work in General Practice*, (London: George Allen and Unwin, 1972).
61. R. Corney and B. Bowen, "Referrals to Social work: A Comparative Study of a Local Intake Team with a General Practice Attachment Scheme," *Journal of the Royal College of General Practitioners* 30 (1980): 139-47.
62. James Forman and E. M. Fairbairn, *Social Casework in General Practice: A Report on an Experiment Carried Out in a General Practice*, (London: Oxford University Press, 1968).
63. G. Smith and J. Ames, "Area Teams and Social Work Practice: A Program for Research," *British Journal of Social Work* 6 (1976): 43-70.
64. R. H. Corney and M. E. Briscoe, "Investigation into Two Different Types of Attachment Schemes," *Social Work Today* 9, 15 (1977): 10-14.
65. Roslyn H. Corney, "Factors Affecting Operation and Success of Social Work Attachment Scheme to General Practice," *Journal of the Royal College of General Practitioners* 30 (March 1980): 149-58.
66. Marianne Quaranta, *NASW News* 27, (May 1982).
67. Stoeckle, op. cit., 1570-79.
68. Ullman, op. cit., 239-46.
69. Glass, op. cit., 1189-95.
70. A. C. Neilson, and T. A. Williams, "Depression in Ambulatory Medical Patients: Prevalence by Self-Report Questionnaire and Recognition by Non-Psychiatric Physicians," *Archives of General Psychiatry* 37 (1980): 999-1004.
71. Barbara G. Berkman, "Knowledge Base and Program Needs for Effective Social Work Practice in Health: A Review of the Literature," Society for Hospital Social Work Directors, American Hospital Association, 1978.
72. Edgar Perretz, "Social Work Education for the Field of Health," *Social Work in Health Care* 1, 3 (Spring 1976): 357-75.
73. Peter Hookey, "Education for Social Work in Health Care Organizations," *Social Work in Health Care* 1, 3 (Spring 1976): 337-45.
74. Helen Rehr and Gary Rosenberg, "Today's Education for Today's Health Care Social Work Practice," *Clinical Social Work Journal* 5, 4 (1977).
75. Perretz, op. cit., 357-75.
76. Bassuk, op. cit.

77. Harvey Bluestone and Menochem Melinek, "Effects of the Urban Crisis on the Community General Hospital," *Hospital and Community Psychiatry* 33, 6 (June 1982): 477-80.
78. Jack R. Anderson, "Social Security and SSI Benefits for the Mentally Disabled," *Hospital and Community Psychiatry* 33, 4 (April 1982): 295-298.
79. Kane, op. cit.

Afterword

PSYCHIATRY/SOCIAL WORK RELATIONSHIP

The issues of role definition, interdependence, and teamwork raise the question as to when and to what degree the health professions can function autonomously. Certainly the matters of role overlap and preeminence have repeatedly become focused on the professions of social work and psychiatry.

The unique and overlapping roles of social work and psychiatry were described in Chapters 2, and 7. It is ironic that some argument persists at times as to which group produces the better psychotherapists since psychiatrists commonly teach in the graduate schools of social work and nearly 600 social workers serve as faculty in the 116 medical schools and psychiatric training programs throughout the country.[1] Many psychiatrists and social workers have had the same supervisors in their training.

While productive collaboration, harmony, and mutual respect between psychiatry and social work are being enjoyed in some sectors of the country, the relationship between the professions has not always been smooth. Natural complementarity was exerienced in the early decades of the twentieth century when both professions contributed to the expansion of the mental hygiene movement and the development of dynamic psychiatry. The famous psychiatrist, Adolph Meyer, credited social work with the single greatest contribution to the advancement of psychiatry up until 1920.[2] Social work's professional friendship with men like Meyer is best understood through the philosophy of dynamic psychiatry which pictured man as a biological organism constantly adapting to his environment. Like the early social workers, the dynamic psychiatrists were interested in all the facts—physical, mental, and social—in order to complete the clinical picture.

The next developmental stage of the mental health field also provided for a near identical mission among psychiatrists and social workers. Major segments of both groups pursued the intrapsychic dimension under the influence of the Freudian psychoanalytic movement. Particularly in the child guidance movement of the 1920s and early 1930s, a common philosophy and a convenient division of labor (with the psychiatrist analyzing the child, and the social worker treating the parents or family), to a great extent avoided territorial conflict and generated the mutual impression of productive, professional collaboration.

The good feelings of close association between psychiatry and social work probably reached their historical pinnacle in a symposium on the treatment of behavior and personality problems in children sponsored by the *American Journal of Orthopsychiatry* in 1930. Among others, the Buffalo psychiatrist, Samuel W. Hartwell, and the renowned social worker Charlotte Towle, joined arm in arm in singing the lyrics together of the following chorus:

> Thus we pool each contribution
> Synthesize a true solution,
> Engineer a revolution of
> personality.[3]

However, either for lack of conceptualization or for lack of emphasis, the unique contributions of each of the disciplines were not distinguished. Hartwell himself, in commenting on the lack of distinguishable space between the disciplines said that they "are so closely associated in their attempt to alter undesirable behavior in social traits . . . that it is not easy even for discussion to separate the function of each."[4]

Beyond the problem of blurring of disciplinary lines, the onset of the Great Depression of the 1930s generated the first significant break between psychiatry and social work. While the president of the American Psychiatric Association in 1923, H. W. Mitchell, had devoted a significant part of his presidential address to endorsing the team approach, "in 1932 and 1933 the successive presidents of the American Psychiatric Association explicitly attacked the incursions of nonmedical and nonpsychiatric personnel into psychiatric practice."[5] Two years later, another conservative medical statesman, Edward A. Strecker of Philadelphia, used a striking depression metaphor in attacking the movement toward which both psychiatry and social work had for more than a decade devoted mutual efforts. Strecker said that the mental hygiene movement "has been overpropagandized, overdramatized and oversold, so that it is in the unfortunate position of being obliged to default on some of the dividends that it had so lavishly promised."[6]

Not surprisingly, the Great Depression and its attendant economic fears had the same impact on the relationship between psychiatry and social work that it had on the rest of the country. In commenting on the role of economics, the noted medical historian, John C. Burnham of Ohio State University, commented that:

> Anyone familiar with medical history or medical sociology might predict that before long the physician would attack these lay interlopers into the province of mental medicine. So it happened in the 1930's. American physicians suffered severe economic setbacks during the Great Depression, and even relatively liberal physicians were not inclined to encourage competition; although , of course, in many individual circumstances professional considerations predominated over the economic.[7]

With the great demand for mental health services following World War II, psychiatry and social work were back in business together. Unfortunately, unique disciplinary contributions were again not distinguished, though with enough work for everyone, this did not lead to the conflict of the 1930s. One noted social worker of the period, Annette Garrett, conceptualized that the psychiatrist would work with the unconscious and the social worker with the conscious.[8] Since this delineation applied only to the analytically trained psychiatrist, the differentiation did not widely take hold. The predominant focus of both psychiatry and social work with the psychotherapeutic dimension reached its culmination in 1969 when the Group for the Advancement of Psychiatry undertook a study of the psychotherapy of psychiatrists and the social casework of social workers, concluding that they could not be distinguished.[9]

The psychiatrist abandoning the unique biomedical role of the physician seemed to reach its outer extreme in the late 1960s when the American Psychiatric Associaton allowed the one-year internship in general internal medicine for psychiatrists to be dropped from the training residency programs. The requirement for the medical internship was readopted in the early 1970s and going into the 1980s, a mutual collaboration between psychiatry and social work based on unique disciplinary contributions again seems promising.

The areas of conflict between psychiatry and social work that remain can be summarized as follows:

- The degree to which segments of both disciplines will recognize the competency of the other with psychotherapeutic interventions;
- The degree to which social workers and psychiatrists will recognize the mutual teaching capacities of each to the other, for example, for social

workers to learn biomedicine from psychiatrists, and for psychiatrists to learn the clinical aspects of the social environmental dimension from social workers.

- The degree to which social workers will recognize the necessity for medical supervision from psychiatrists for the biomedical dimensions of diagnosis and treatment; and the similar degree to which psychiatrists will recognize the parameters of medical supervision, that is, that it cannot dictate interventions in the psychotherapeutic and social environmental dimensions after the differential diagnosis has been established. Medical supervision is specific and restricted, not global.

There are arguments on both sides of these issues even within the field of medicine itself. For instance, three physicians writing in the *Lancet* contended that:

To call for "medical supervision" of all social work in mental health is both destructive of interprofessional relationships and totally unrealistic. Any supervision of social workers should be by other social workers who are more experienced or specialized. There should obviously be close integration with psychiatrists on the basis of mutual respect, rather than a dominance-submission hierarchy.[10]

In the above criticism, the term "medical supervision" appears to have been conceptualized in the more global sense to cover psychosocial issues as well as the more specific biomedical issues. The need for clarification arises in part from the fact that some segments of psychiatry itself have at times departed from identification with the medical model[11] and by episodic trends among some psychiatrists away from the role of physician.[12]

On the other side of the spectrum is the "Position Statement on Psychiatrists' Relationships with the Non-Medical Mental Health Professionals," which concedes that while

No profession should attempt to define the functions and responsibilities of any other profession . . . in medical settings . . . the physician-psychiatrist retains the primary medical responsibility, established by law and custom, for the admission, diagnosis, treatment, rehabilitation, and discharge of patients.[13]

The 1973 position paper of the American Psychiatric Association goes on to say that the psychiatrist working in a nonmedical setting

220

as a consultant, supervisor, therapist, or administrative staff member . . . has essentially the same relationship to the organization as other professionals have in the medical setting. However, he must retain ultimate responsibility for the psychiatric and medical care of the patients or clients whom he serves.[14]

The current resistance among clinical social workers to any model of service delivery that incorporates a supervisory role for psychiatrists originates in part from their concern that psychiatrists will not restrict their domain of expertise to biomedical issues and the specific role of physician. Seasoned social work practitioners know that expert psychotherapeutic and sociotherapeutic strategies develop through both training and experience and that these skills are not particular to psychiatry as a subdiscipline of medicine. As pointed out in Chapter 1, social workers have at times witnessed the weaknesses of a clinical model that appoints the psychiatrist as team leader even when he or she is the least experienced among the interdisciplinary group. In such instances, perhaps due to a lack of thorough clinical experience or because of the nature of medical training itself, the psychiatrist has been known to assume an authoritative level of case review beyond the biomedical role of physician, often failing to identify character styles or social context issues essential to an accurate diagnosis and effective treatment plan. The absence of clinical maturity with psychosocial data is common to all beginning practitioners regardless of discipline. Nevertheless, the scenario is troubling to the clinical social workers who are experienced, both because the model has determined the responsibility for leadership by the unquestioned preeminence of one discipline over others, and because the psychiatrist attempted to assume clinical authority beyond the biomedical dimension recognized by other disciplinary team members.

The authors recognize that the ideal arrangement would be one in which the leader possesses the seasoned clinical skill and the wisdom to recognize and draw upon what expertise may be available within the health care team. We have suggested elsewhere[15] that a team "captain" should be determined by leadership ability, not by discipline, and that when the physician is not the leader, the physician's supervisory authority would be restricted to biomedical expertise only. The true ideal as well would be the team in which all members respected and even liked each other. In practical terms, however, what is being suggested is a comprehensive service model in which clinical social workers would expand their psychosocial skills to at least a basic level of biomedical skills as well. To do this, the cornerstone of

221

this model is the need for supervision from psychiatrists for this biomedical component whether the psychiatrist is the leader of the team or not. All other territorial issues are beyond the scope of this clinical model and will no doubt continue to be debated for years to come.

The authors do recognize that it is often difficult to separate clinical issues from political ones. Even when the role of supervision is restricted to the biomedical dimension, the very use of the word supervision suggests enough of a hierarchical connotation to clinical social workers that it is viewed by many as an intrusion upon the autonomy of their profession. Knoll has pointed out that in recent years the need for medically oriented supervision has become reemphasized more often to coincide with health insurance reimbursement than in response to clinical conceptualizations. When funding has been limited, social workers have been both allowed and expected to provide mental health services with little or no psychiatric physician involvement.[16] With clinical social work practice having been autonomous and often exclusive in many health and mental health settings, the notion of supervision directed even solely at biomedical issues is controversial to promote, despite its merits on a clinical basis. It would be inviting to use the term "consultation" instead of supervision because the former connotes more of a relationship among equals. At this point in history, however, it would not be accurate to portray clinical social workers and psychiatric physicians as on equal terms with biomedical issues. One primary objective of this book, in fact, has been to expand social work skills in identifying biomedical issues pertinent to patient presentations to assure timely and cost-effective psychiatrist involvement. As this clinical model becomes more integrated within social work education and training, the term "medical consultation" would be more appropriate than "medical supervision."

There may be need to reemphasize that we are talking about clinical settings, such as health and mental health facilities, in which biomedical as well as psychosocial assessment and intervention would be the expected standard of patient care. In community agencies or in group or solo private practice, clinical social workers have for many years provided psychotherapeutic and sociotherapeutic assessments and interventions without the benefit of systematic biomedical consultation or supervision. Though research has demonstrated the limitations of this approach in terms of accurate diagnosis,[17] these services have been very responsive to community needs. Drawing upon the comprehensive clinical framework for social work practice provided in this book, community practitioners can enhance those valuable services and assure systematic interdisciplinary referral to appropriate health and mental health resources as needed.

The model we have described is designed to increase the domain of social work practice in the health setting on a clinical level, both to meet current needs and to pick up on the early historical skills of medical social workers who at that time often had medical training. The choice of the psychiatrist for medical supervision as opposed to nonpsychiatric physicians is based on the greater potential skill among psychiatrists for addressing the interface of medical illness and disorders of mood, thought, and behavior. A theme of the book has been to emphasize the potential impact of medical illness on the mental status, for psychiatrists to become integrated within the health care team for this area of expertise, and for clinical social workers in health care to adopt this comprehensive clinical approach using psychiatrists for medical backup.

NOTES

1. Richard Grinnell, Nancy Kyte, S. K. Hunter, and Thomas Larson, "The Status of Graduate Level Social Workers Teaching in Medical Schools," *Social Work in Health Care* 1 (Spring 1976): 317-24.
2. Alfred Lief, (ed.), *The Common Sense Psychiatry of Dr. Adolph Meyer* (New York, 1948).
3. R. L. Jenkins, "Symposium: The Treatment of Behavior and Personality Problems in Children," *American Journal of Orthopsychiatry* 5 (1935).
4. Ibid.
5. John C. Burnham, "The Struggle Between Physicians and Paramedical Personnel in American Psychiatry, 1917-1941," *Journal of History of Medical and Allied Sciences* 21 (1974): 93-106.
6. Edward A. Strecker, "The Practice of Psychiatry," *Archives of Neurology and Psychiatry* 31 (1934): 415-17.
7. Burnham, op. cit., 93-106.
8. Annette Garrett, "The Worker-Client Relationship," *American Journal of Orthopsychiatry* 19, 2 (1949).
9. Group for the Advancement of Psychiatry, *On Psychotherapy and Casework* (New York: Committee on Psychiatry and Social Work, 1969).
10. Hugh Freeman, Michael Tarsh and V. J. T. Scerri, "Social Workers in Mental Health Services," *The Lancet* August 19, 1972.
11. George Engel, "Sudden Death and the 'Medical Model' in Psychiatry," *Canadian Psychiatric Association Journal* 15 (1970): 527-37.
12. Thomas P. Hackett, "The Psychiatrist: In the Mainstream or on the Banks of Medicine?" *American Journal of Psychiatry* 134, 4 (April 1977): 432-34.
13. W. W. Zeller, R. S. McKnight, R. H. Thrasher, A. N. Franzblau, A. Levine, E. E. Williams and D. F. Moore, "Position Statement on Psychiatrists'

Relationships with Nonmedical Mental Health Professionals," *American Journal of Psychiatry* 130, 3 (March 1973): 386-90.

14. Ibid., 386-90.
15. Andrew E. Slaby, Richard J. Goldberg and Stephen R. Wallace, "Interdisciplinary Team Approach to Emergency Psychiatric Care," *Psychosomatics* 24, 7 (July 1983): 627-37.
16. Donald Knoll, "Psychiatric Supervision for Social Work?" *Clinical Social Work Journal* 7 (1979): 214-17.
17. Edwin K. Koranyi, "Morbidity and Rate of Undiagnosed Physical Illness in a Psychiatric Clinic Population," *Archives of General Psychiatry* 36 (1979): 414-19.

ADDITIONAL REFERENCES

Bergman, Ann S. and Gregory K. Fritz, "Psychiatric and Social Work Collaboration in a Pediatric Chronic Illness Hospital," *Social Work in Health Care* 7, 1 (Fall 1981): 45-55.

Berlin, Richard, Joyce Kales, Frederick Humphrey II and Anthony Kales, "The Patient Care Crisis in Community Mental Health Centers: A Need for More Psychiatric Involvement," *American Journal of Psychiatry* 138, 4 (April 1981): 450-54.

Engel, George, "The Biopsychosocial Model and Medical Education: Who Are to Be the Teachers?" *The New England Journal of Medicine* April 1, 1982): 802-05.

Starr, Sonya, "Social Work and Liaison Psychiatry: A Psychosocial Team Approach to Patient and Staff Needs in a Hemodialysis Unit," *Social Work in Health Care* 7, 3 (April 1982): 77-82.

Stine, Bradley A., "Social Work and Liaison Psychiatry, *Social Work in Health Care* 1, 4 (Summer 1976): 483-87.

Wilder, Jack F. and Aaron Rosenblatt, "An Assessment of Accountability Areas by Psychiatrists, Psychologists and Social Workers," *American Journal of Orthopsychiatry* 47, 2 (April 1977): 336-40.

Appendix I

The following is a statistical summary from the survey conducted by the Henry Ford Hospital. A review of the survey data revealed three distinct groupings based on bed capacity:

Institution	Beds	No. of Social Workers	Admissions
GROUP A			
(900 beds or greater)			
Cook County	1,384	63	46,000
Baylor	1,275	5	41,000
Barnes	1,204	24	40,000
Johns Hopkins	1,097	80	32;000
Massachusetts General	1,084	99	30,000
Henry Ford	1,052	16.6	27,000
Houston Memorial	1;000	4	36,000
University of Michigan	967	68	Not reported
William Beaumont	940	10	27,084
Harper	917	25	24,000
GROUP B			
(600-899)			
Abbott Northwestern	825	13	24,000
Yale New Haven	818	45	30,000
Dallas County	800	11	30,000
University of Minnesota	788	34	22,000
Rhode Island	719	29	22,000
University of Chicago	691	50	22,000
U.C.L.A.	689	32	23,000
GROUP C			
(Fewer than 600 beds)			
St. Joseph Mercy	558	8	20,000
Bethesda (NIH)	541	21	6,658
Sinai of Baltimore	507	9	18,000
Vanderbilt	509	19	18,000

Appendix II

Biopsychosocial Data Base

(Patient's ID card to be run off in this space)

NAME _____ UNIT # _____

ADDRESS _____ PHONE: _____

BIRTH DATE _____ S.S.# _____ # YEARS SCHOOL: _____

REFERRED BY _____ REFERRAL PROBLEM: _____

PRIMARY CLINICIAN _____ OCCUPATION: _____ RACE: B   W   H   ORIENTAL   AMER. INDIAN   OTHER

INSURANCE STATUS _____ SEX: F   M | RELIGION: J   P   RC   OTHER: _____

MARITAL STATUS: _____ S   M   D   W   SEP. | NO. OF CHILDREN: _____ OCCUPATION OF PARENT IF SINGLE OR SPOUSE IF MARRIED: _____

RESPONSIBLE PERSON: _____ RELATIONSHIP TO PATIENT: _____

ADDRESS: _____ PHONE: _____

VITAL SIGNS: BP _____ | PULSE _____ | TEMPERATURE _____ | RR _____

PATIENT'S CHIEF COMPLAINT: _____

HISTORY OF PRESENT ILLNESS: _____ INFORMANT: _____

_____

_____

_____

_____

_____

_____

_____

_____

_____

_____

_____

_____

SIGNIFICANT RECENT LIFE EVENTS: _____

_____

M-309 CAT. #2984771 REV. 6/81   **1**

CHART COPY

PAST PSYCHIATRIC HISTORY:

_____

_____

_____

_____

DEVELOPMENTAL AND SOCIAL HISTORY:
Perinatal Complications: _____ Infancy: _____
Problems Starting School: _____ MBD: _____
Anti-Social Behavior: _____
Other: _____

Living Arrangements: _____
Social Support: _____
Daily Activity: _____
Self-Care: _____
School, Work, Military History: _____

_____

HABITS (Alcohol, Drugs, Tobacco, Caffeine): _____

_____

FAMILY HISTORY (Psychiatric and Medical Disorders: Note Special or Stressful Relationships):

CURRENT MEDICATIONS (Dose, Duration, Recently Discontinued): _____

_____

_____

MEDICAL HISTORY:

Allergies:	Surgery:
Head Injuries:	When Next Period is Expected:
Chronic Medical Problems:	Active Medical Problems:

M-309 CAT. #2984771 REV. 6/81   2 __

PERTINENT NEUROLOGIC AND MEDICAL FINDINGS: _____

_____

_____

MENTAL STATUS EXAMINATION: Appearance: _____   Participation: _____

Organic Mental Disorder:		Psychotic Disorder:
Judgement:		Hallucinations:
Orientation:		Delusions:
Intellect:		Paranoia:
Memory:		Incoherence:
Affect:		Phobias:
Aphasia Screen:		Anxiety/Panic:
Affective Disorder:		
Mood:		Suicidal:
Sleep Change:		
Appetite:	Fatigue:	Homicidal:
Guilt:	Anhedonia:	
Psychomotor Change:		Personality:

DIFFERENTIAL DIAGNOSTIC IMPRESSIONS: Circle and Provide DSM III code if Confirmed:

_____

_____

_____

_____

DISPOSITION AND TREATMENT PLAN: _____

☐ Social Work   ☐ Behavioral Medicine

☐ Psychology Testing   ☐ Psychiatry

☐ Medical-Neurology-Surgery   ☐ Outside Referral

☐ Other Records

_____

_____

_____

_____

SIGNATURE: _____   DATE: _____

Appendix III
Higher Functions of the Brain

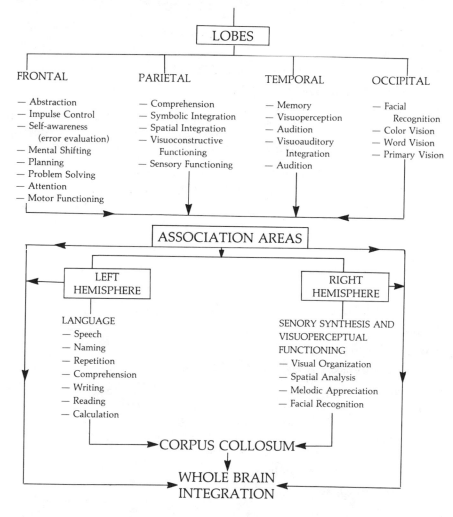

LOBES

FRONTAL

— Abstraction
— Impulse Control
— Self-awareness
    (error evaluation)
— Mental Shifting
— Planning
— Problem Solving
— Attention
— Motor Functioning

PARIETAL

— Comprehension
— Symbolic Integration
— Spatial Integration
— Visuoconstructive
    Functioning
— Sensory Functioning

TEMPORAL

— Memory
— Visuoperception
— Audition
— Visuoauditory
    Integration
— Audition

OCCIPITAL

— Facial
    Recognition
— Color Vision
— Word Vision
— Primary Vision

ASSOCIATION AREAS

LEFT HEMISPHERE

LANGUAGE
— Speech
— Naming
— Repetition
— Comprehension
— Writing
— Reading
— Calculation

RIGHT HEMISPHERE

SENORY SYNTHESIS AND VISUOPERCEPTUAL FUNCTIONING
— Visual Organization
— Spatial Analysis
— Melodic Appreciation
— Facial Recognition

CORPUS COLLOSUM

WHOLE BRAIN INTEGRATION

Note: Although it is true that certain functions can be isolated to specific sites within the brain, it is more accurate to understand the brain as a complex system of connections, interconnections, and feedback loops. Lesions (or disruptions) in a given system (anywhere) may yield behavior simplistically viewed as specific to a certain area but in fact may be located outside that area but within the interconnecting system. The best example of this is limb apraxia, which may be attributed to a lesion anywhere along the arcuate fasciculus of the left hemisphere. (Diagram constructed in collaboration with Frank Sparadeo, Ph.D., Neuropsychologist, Department of Psychiatry, Rhode Island Hospital.)

Appendix IV

DATABASE   Date of Contract

1981 PSYCHIATRIC SOCIAL WORK RESEARCH
PRIMARY CARE MEDICAL CLINIC
__Name of patient and ID number
__Date of referral
__Written reason for referral
__Verbal reason for referral
__What was the patient's understanding of the reason for the referral?
__Demographies:
Sex
Age
Source of Income
Level of Income
Years of education
Occupation
How long at present job?
How long since last worked?
Where does patient live?
How long there?
Who does patient live with?
Any family or friends in contact with patient?
Any family or network conflicts?
__Is there a psychiatric diagnosis?

        Axis - I
        Axis - II
        Axis - III
        Axis - IV
        Axis - V

__Previous psychiatric treatment?
__Currently involved in other social service agencies?
     How many?   which?

__First medical clinic consult?
__Referral was from:

Nurse	Other psychiatric clinician
Primary care physician	Nurse practitioner
Medical resident - 1st year	2nd year 3rd year
Medical student	Outside agency
Self	Other (identify)

__What did the social worker conclude was the primary need for
intervention?

__Disposition

__What did patient understand of the disposition?

__How did referring person react to disposition?

Appendix V

	Written and/or Verbal Reasons for Referral (n = 100)	Patient's Understanding of Reason for Referral (n = 68)
Counseling	20 (14 alone + 6 mixed)	16 (14 alone + 2 mixed)
Concrete Services	52 (42 alone + 10 mixed)	28 (27 alone + 1 mixed)
Substance Abuse	11 (9 alone + 2 mixed)	7
Psychiatry	30 (23 alone + 7 mixed)	8
Unclear	29*	10

While there were 100 cases referred, the number of reasons for referral exceeds 100 because more than one reason for referral was often expressed. Sometimes one reason for referral was specific while another reason on the same case was unclear.

Appendix VI

Comparison of Reasons for Referral with Evaluation Findings

	Consultation Request	Confirmed as the Sole Issue	Found to Be Needed, but Not the Only Issue	Referral Reasons Inaccurate; Other Issue Overlooked by Medical Staff
Need for concrete services	52	26	11	Psych: 7 Substance: 3 Counsel: 5
Need for psychiatry evaluation, treatment	30	10	14	Counsel: 2 Substance: 4 Concrete: 2
Need for counseling	12	6	0	Psych: 5 Substance: 1
Need for evaluation, treatment, substance abuse	11	9	2	Psych: 1 Counsel: 1

Index

acceptability of services, 30
accessibility of services, 29–30
accountability, 32–33, 35–36
ACTA scans, 168
active crisis, 74, 81, 85
advocacy: clinical, 192–97; clinical vs. social, 192–95; full-time community, 44; legislation, purpose of, 82; social. *See* social advocacy
affect, patient, 60, 123–24
alcohol hallucinosis, 164
alcohol paranoia, 164
alcohol use, 138
Alexander, Franz, 103–4
Allen, Woody, 105
alliance, therapeutic, 97–98, 105–8
almshouses, 3
ambivalence: attention getting and, 100–1; in patient engagement, 113–19; strategies for, 115
American Association of Hospital Social Workers (AAHSW), 8, 12
American Association of Schools of Social Work, 8, 11
American Hospital Association (AHA), 7, 18
American Journal of Orthopsychiatry, 218
American Psychiatric Association, 218, 219, 220–21
anxiety, medical and surgical illnesses presenting with, 159–61; brain diseases and, 161; drug abuse and, 159–61; hyperthyroidism and, 161; hyperventilation syndrome and, 161; hypoglycemia and, 161;

hypokalemia and, 161; withdrawal from chemical substances and, 159
Athey, Helen, 7
attainability of services, 30
attention of patient. *See* engagement, patient
attributional theory, 155
availability of services, 30

baseline, establishing patients', 195–96
Bebring, G. L., 33
Beck Depression Self-Report Inventory, 207
behavioral sciences perceptor, 57, 58
Bellvue Hospital (New York City), 3, 4
benevolent parameters, establishing, 119–20
biomedical education, 179–88, 211; importance of, 179–81; need for, 41–42
biopsychological vs. concrete/social/environmental needs, 189
biopsychosocial data base, 131–49; allergies, 141; developmental history, 144–45; family history, 137–38; habits, 138–39; head injuries, 141–42; medical conditions, acute and chronic, 142–43; medical findings, 144; medications, 139–41; mental status examination, 145–47; multi-axial diagnosis, 147–48; neurologic findings, 144; past psychiatric history, 136–37;

patient identification, 133–34; perinatal complications, 144–45; pregnancy, 141; purpose of, 131–33; and social workers, use of, 147–48; sociodemographics, 133–34; surgery, 144; vital signs, 134–36

biopsychosocial model, 13–14; dimensions of, 12–13; horizontal diagnosis in, 13–14; social work contribution to, 14–15; vertical diagnosis in, 13–14

blood pressure, and personality changes, 135–36

blood studies, 168–72

borderline personality, 197

Boston Psychopathic Hospital, 9

Boston University School of Social Work, 11

Bracht, Neil, 180

Brackett, Jeffery, 7

brain functioning, 186–87

Brown University, 203

burn out, 86

Cabot, Richard, 5–6, 7, 12, 14, 20

caffeine use, 138

Cannon, Ida, 6, 7, 8, 10, 11, 16, 17, 20

Caplan, Gerald, 74

Cassel, J. C., 33

CAT (computerized axial tomography) scans, 168

Catholic hospitals, 4

Caversham Project, 38, 39, 49; limits of, 202

chaotic character. See crisis-ridden character

Charity Organization Society (COS), 5, 7

Children's Aid Society (Boston), 5

clinical advocacy principles, 195–200; baseline, establishing patients', 195–96; containment, 197–98; limit setting, 197–98; resources, appropriate use of, 198–200

clinical advocacy vs. social advocacy, 192–95

Clinical Social Work: Theory and Practice, 188

clinical social worker. (See also medical social work) clinical skills of, and primary care team development 41; core issue for, 200–1; diagnostic approach of, 189–90. (See also biopsychosocial model); on primary care team, 36–38; and psychiatrist, relationship between, 15, 36–38, 63–64, 208–10, 217–23; training of (See social work training); unique function of, 208; value of, 188–89

Cobb, S., 33

community mental health services (CMHCs), 44, 46, 47

community resources. See resources, appropriate use of

concrete services, clinical dimension of providing, 59–60

Community Service Society of New York, 188

comprehensiveness of services, 30–31, 43–44; components, 48; information gathering and, 53–54

Compton, Beulah, 200
conflict, containment of, 197
conflict resolution, ambivalence and, 114–15
confusion technique, the, 104–5
containment, 197–98
continuity of services, 31–32, 43–44
coordination of services, 31, 34–35
coordinator, patient care, 31
coping skills of patient, mobilizing, 59, 61, 98, 108–9, 110–12
corrective emotional experience, 103–4
Coulton, Claudia, 19
Council on Social Work Education, 211
counter-projective statement, 104
crisis: active, 74, 81, 85; characteristics of, 73; ego-syntonic, 77–80, 83; expanding concepts of, 77–80; grief, 72; medical illness as, 74; preventive plans, 74; stages of, 74
crisis intervention, 71–91; crisis-ridden character and, 76–77; history taking for, importance of, 73; hospitalization, 82–85; legal vs. clinical conflict in, 82–85; medical illness and, 74; origins of, 72–74; short-term treatment, 52; social environment and, 74–75; social network assessment and, 75; social workers' contribution to, 74–75
crisis intervention techniques, 80–82
crisis-ridden character, 76–77, 197–98; assessment of, 85–87; community agencies and, 87, 198–99; limited resources

available to, 87; presenting pattern of, 76; treatment expectations, 77–79, 80–82; treatment of, 76–77, 80–82
crisis teams, 52
curriculum. *See* social work training

Decker, J. B., 82
defenses: confronting, 115–19; in patient engagement, 112–13; siding with, 115–19
dementias, diagnosis of, 186
depression, 142–43, 146–47; alcohol and, 158; diseases associated with, 158–59; drug abuse and, 158; endogenous, 156; infections and, 158; medical causes of, 156–59; medical and surgical illnesses presenting with, 156–59; medications as causes of, 154, 156, 158; pancreatic cancer and, 158; tumors and, 158
Diagnostic and Statistical Manual of the American Psychiatric Association, 191, 197
displacement, 114
doing and undoing, 116
drugs: and depression, as causes of, 154; normal therapeutic toxic levels of, 168–72; and patient assessment, 139–41; producing psychiatric symptoms, 184–85; psychotropic, doses of, 172–74
drug use and abuse, 138, 159–61, 162
Dunbar, Flander, 33

education. *See* biomedical education; psychological education; social work training

ego regressive interventions, 59

ego supplementing, 111–12

ego support, 59, 196; in patient engagement, 108–12

ego-syntonic crises, 77–80, 83

elderly, diagnosis of, 186

electroencephalography, 167–68

Emerson, Charles P., 5

engagement, patient, 93–130; by ambivalence, recognition of, 100; concept of, 95; defenses in, role of, 112–13; fundamental principle of, 99–100; and mental status exam, 122–24; origins of focus on, 102–5; by paradoxical intention, 99–100; social workers as consultant for, 98–99; strategies, usefulness of, 98–99; termination and, 124–26

engagement techniques, 95–98; affect, identify patients', 123–24; alliance, therapeutic, 97–98, 105–8; for ambivalence, 113–19; coping skills of patient, mobilizing, 98, 108–9, 110; for dealing with defenses, 112–13; ego supplementing, 111–12; ego support, 108–12; elucidation of perception of previous treatment, 96; establishing benevolent parameters, 119–20; humor, 105; paradox, 105; presenting style, tolerance of, 121; professional ethics and, 101–3; recognition of situation and feelings, 95; responsibility for treatment, 97; social environment, use of, 120–22; treatment sample, providing, 120; validation of uniqueness and attributes of patient, 95–96; ventilation of feelings about previous providers of care, 96–97, 109

environmental baseline, 195–96

Erickson, Milton, 104–5

Franklin, Benjamin, 102

Franz, Alexander, 33

Freidson, Eliot, 190

French, Thomas, 33

Freud, Sigmund, 11, 102–3

functional disturbances, 134

funding problems, 19–21

Galoway, Burt, 200

Garrett, Annette, 219

Glass, Richard, 191, 207

Glasser, 103

Great Britain. *See* Caversham Project

Great Depression, 218–19

grief, role of, in crisis, 72

Group for the Advancement of Psychiatry, 219

Hartwell, Samuel W., 218

Health and Social Work, 12

health care. (*See also* crisis intervention; medical social work; primary care) biopsychosocial model of 13–14; in colonial

America to 1900, 3–4; interdisciplinary, 38–40, 46–48. *See also* primary care team
health curricula, 211–12
health maintenance organizations (HMOs), 17
Health Planning and Public Health Service Amendments, 20
Henry Ford Hospital, 19
history, patient, 59, 62–63. (*See also* biopsychosocial data base; information gathering) in crisis intervention, 73; developmental, 144–45; family, 137–38; past psychiatric, 136–37
home visitor, 5
hospital(s): in colonial America, 3–4; mortality rate in early, 4
Hospital Social Service, 10
Hospital Social Service, Committee on, 9
Hospital Social Service Association of New York City, 10
hospital social workers. *See* medical social workers
hospital social work standards, 18
Houston Consortium Program, 55
Houston Memorial Hospital, 19
humor, as engagement technique, 105

information gathering (*See* also biopsychosocial data base; history, patient) comprehensiveness of services and, 53–54; problem areas, 53–54; risk/benefit ratios in, 53–54
insight, 197
institutions, manifest vs. latent functions of, 75

insurance reimbursements, 19
intention, paradoxical, 100
interdisciplinary health care, 38–40, 46. (*See also* primary care team); role blurring, 47–48
interdisciplinary training, 55

Johns Hopkins Hospital, 5
Johns Hopkins Training School for Nurses, 7
Johns Hopkins University, 5
Joint Commission for Accreditation of Hospitals (JCAH), 18
journals, professional, 12

Kahnan, R. J., 33
Kasl, S., 33
Kimbal, Chace P., 33
Koranyi, Edwin K., 181, 191–92, 202, 209

labeling, 155
laboratory studies, use of, 167–72
Lancet, 220
Leigh, Hoyle, 33
licensing, 10, 18–19
limit setting, 119, 197–98
Lindemann, Eric, 72, 73
Locke, Ben A., 34
Lowry, Fern, 189

Marx Brothers, 105
Massachusetts General Hospital [MGH (Boston)], 5, 6, 8, 19
Master of Social Work (MSW) degree, 10, 11, 18

Mechanic, David, 33, 37, 49, 190

medical consultation vs. medical supervision, 222. *See also* supervision

medical disorder(s): as crisis, 74; presenting psychosocial symptoms, 182–83. *See also* biopsychosocial data base

medical model, 33–34

medical profession: collaboration with, 18–19; and psychiatry, attitude towards, 17; and social work, history of, 3–22; and social workers, attitudes toward, 17; transition to primary care, difficulties facing, 33–36

medical records, 32

"Medical Referrals to Social Work: A Review of 100 Cases." *See* Rhode Island Hospital study

medical social work. (*See also* clinical social worker) autonomy, struggle for professional, 18–19; challenge of, 12–13; Dr. Richard Cabot, contributions of, 5–6; early principles of, return to, 15–17; early struggle of, 6–7; funding problems, 19–21; hospital for, 18; interdisciplinary nature of, 15–16; licensing requirement for, 10; and medical profession, conflict with, 10; nurses in, 6–7; origins of, 5; professionalization of, 7–8; and social work profession, conflict with, 10–12; staffing problems, 19–21; territorial issues, unresolved, 17; World War I and, 9

medical supervision, 220. *See also* supervision

medications. *See* drugs

mental disorders. (See also anxiety; depression; schizophrenia) incidence of, 202; organic, 145–46

mental status examination, 145–47; depression, 146–47; engagement and, 122–24; importance of, 145; organic mental disorders, 145–46

Merton, Robert K., 75

Meyer, Adolf, 11, 12, 16, 217

Minahan, Anne, 200

Mitchell, H. W., 218

Mount Sinai Hospital (New York City), 18

multidisciplinary teams. *See* primary care team

National Academy of Sciences report on primary care (1976), 29, 33, 35

National Association of Social Workers (NASW), 12, 18; Task Force on Clinical Social Work, 180, 188

National Federation of Societies for Clinical Social Work, 180, 188

National Organization for Public Health Nursing, 9

Neilson, A. C., 207

neurology, and social work training, 186–87

New England Hospital for Women and Children (Boston), 4

New Haven Hospital, 4

New York Hospital, 4

New York Infirmary for Western Women and Children, 5

New York School of Social Work, 8
New York State Charities Association, 4
nicotine use, 139
nonintrapsychic approach, nurses, as medical social workers, 6–7
nursing schools, 4

organic mental disorders, 145–46
organic vs. psychogenic illness, 151–55
organizations, professional, 12

paradox, as engagement technique, 105
paradoxical intention, 100
Parsons, Talcott, 34
patient advocacy legislation, 82
patient care coordinator, 31
patient identification, 133–34
Penn, William, 3
Perlman, Helen Harris, 191
Perretz, Edgar, 211
Philadelphia School of Social Work, 8
physicians. *See* medical profession
Pincus, Allen, 200
P. L. 89–749, 20
"Position Statement of Psychiatrists' Relationships with the Non-Medical Mental Health Professionals," 220
preferences, patient, 32
primary care, 27–66; background of, 27–29; clinical social worker's role in, 39; clinical interventions, 48–51; definition of, 29–33; information

gathering, risk/benefit ratios in, 53–54; and medical profession, difficulties facing transition to, 33–36; short-term treatment, 51–53; social network treatment, 51–53;and social work, role of, 36–38; treatment plans, 43–45
primary care attributes: accessibility, 29–30; accountability, 32–33; comprehensiveness, 30–31; continuity, 31–32; coordination, 31
primary care residents, 57–58
primary care team: case illustration, 55–64; clinical social worker, potential role of, 36–38; development, clinical social worker's skills and, 40–48; enhancing, 55; interdisciplinary roles in, 38–40, 47–48; psychiatrist's role, 39–40
problem, identifying, 49–51
professional organizations, 12
psychiatrist: acceptance of, in hospitals, 17; conflict areas of, with social worker, 219–20; primary care team, role of, 39–40; role of, 209–10; and social worker, relationship between, 15–16, 36–38, 63–64, 208–10, 217–23
psychodynamic approach, limitations of, 190–91
psychodynamic training, importance of, 190
psychogenic vs. organic illness, 151–55
psychological education, 188–92

psychotropic drugs, doses commonly used, 172–74
pulse rate, and psychiatric symptoms, 136

Rapaport, Lydia, 72
reaction formation, 114
referrals, nature of, 36, 39, 51–53. *See also* Rhode Island Hospital study
Regenburg, Jeanette, 179
Regier, D., 202
Reid, William J., 191
resistance, patient, 103
resources, appropriate use of, 61–63, 198–200
respiratory rate, and psychiatric symptoms, 136
Rhode Island Hospital, Primary Care Medical Unit, interdisciplinary team approach of, 55–64
Rhode Island Hospital study, 131, 201–9; findings, 206–9; patient's understanding for referral, 205–6; referral and assessment data, 205; reliability of, 206; sample and results, 204; setting, 203–4; validity of, 206
Richmond, Mary, 10

scapegoating, 114
schizophrenia: brain infections and, 165–66; drug abuse and, 162; medical disorders presenting with, 162–64; medications causing, 164–65; misdiagnosis of, 154–55; symptoms, 161–62; vitamin deficiency and, 164; withdrawal from chemical substances and, 164–65
Schneiderian First Rank symptoms of schizophrenia, 162
schools of social work, 8–9. *See also specific school*
self-blame, 60–61
self-esteem, enhancing, 58–59
Sheppard-Towner Act of 1921, 27
short-term treatment, 51–53
sibling rivalry, 114
Simmons School of Social Work (Boston), 7–8, 11
Slaby, Andrew E., 34
Smith College, 9
social advocacy, 192–95; vs. clinical advocacy, 200–1
social baseline, 195–96
social/environmental context: crisis intervention and, 74–75; in patient engagement, 120–22; psychiatry and awareness of, 16; psychosocial concepts needed for, 195–200; social work training in, 192–95
social/environmental advocacy principles, 195–200
social network, 51–53; crisis intervention and, 75; and primary care treatment, 51–53
social work, conflict within, profession, 10–12. *See also* clinical social worker; medical social work
Social Work: Essays on the Meeting Ground of Doctor and Social Worker, 6
Social Work in Health Care, 12, 180

Social Work Oncology Group (SWOG), 12
social work research, 200
social work training: biomedical dimension, 179–88; biopsychosocial differential diagnostic skills, 200–1; environmental dimension in, 192–95; health curricula in, 211; psychological dimension in, 188–92; social context in, 192–95; social/environmental advocacy principles, 195–200
Society of Hospital Social Work Directors, 12
sociodemographics, use of, 133–34
staffing problems, 19–21
Strategies in Psychiatry for the Primary Physician, 146
Strean, Herbert, S., 188
Strecker, Edward A., 218
Stubblebine, J. M., 82
suicide prevention, hospitalization for, 82–84
Sullivan, Harry Stack, 104
supervision, 19, 220–22
symptom formation, 114

Task Centered Casework, 191
temperature, elevated, and behavioral/personality changes, 134–35
therapeutic alliance. *See* alliance, therapeutic
thought disorders, medical and surgical disorders presenting with, 161–66
Towle, Charlotte, 218
training. *See* social work training
treatment plans, 43–45, 58

ventilation, 96–97; inappropriate, 109–11
violent behavior, medical disorders presenting with, 166–67
vital signs, 134–36; blood pressure, 135–36; pulse rate, 136; respiratory rate, 136; temperature, 134–35

Wernicke Korsakoff Syndrome, 146
Williams, T. A., 207
World War I, 9